TOUGH ON CRIME

PITT LATIN AMERICAN SERIES

Catherine M. Conaghan, Editor

TOUGH ON CRIME

THE RISE OF PUNITIVE POPULISM IN LATIN AMERICA

MICHELLE D. BONNER

University *of* Pittsburgh Press

Published by the University of Pittsburgh Press, Pittsburgh, Pa., 15260

Manufactured in the United States of America
Printed on acid-free paper
10 9 8 7 6 5 4 3 2 1

Cataloging-in-Publication data is available from the Library of Congress

ISBN 13: 978-0-8229-4582-6
ISBN 10: 0-8229-4582-7

Cover photograph: *Police Special Forces* by Davidlohr Bueso, licensed under CC BY 2.0
Cover design: Melissa Dias-Mandoly

CONTENTS

ACKNOWLEDGMENTS

Many people have contributed to this book. First and foremost, I want to thank all my interviewees, from Argentina, Chile, and elsewhere, who generously gave me their time, knowledge, and perspectives. I also thank Marcelo Saín, Graciela di Marco, Lucía Dammert, Hugo Frühling, and Claudia Lagos who graciously put me in contact with many of the people I spoke to in the two countries, along with my tenacious research assistants Florencia Franco (Argentina), Nicole Villagra (Chile), and Enrique Castro (Chile) for organizing my interview schedules. I also thank my research assistants María Paz Lundin, Pablo Ouziel, and Teboho Makalima who took on the momentous task of transcribing my interviews. My research assistants, Ariel Taylor, João Sterrett, and Marta Kleiman also helped with various aspects of the book.

I have presented versions of these chapters at conferences and workshops where I received valuable feedback from discussants, audience members, and others. Thanks in particular to Sallie Hughes, Winifred Tate, Pablo Policzer, Greg Weeks, and Guillermina Seri. Thanks also to Mary Rose Kubal, Manuel Antonio Guerrero, Patrice McSherry, and Marlea Clarke, who very kindly read and provided feedback on some or all of the chapters. Thanks also to the anonymous reviewers. Finally, thanks to Josh Shanholtzer at the University of Pittsburgh Press for his support and excellent editorial advice. Finally, thanks to my family, Germán Ebert Correa, Simona Ebert, Máximo Ebert, Margot Bonner, Ken Bonner, Marta Correa, and Rubén Ebert, for their constant support.

Funding for this project was provided by a Social Science and Humanities Research Council (SSHRC) Insight Grant, and by additional support from the University of Victoria. The project benefited from the time given to me through a fellowship at the Centre for Global Studies at the University of Victoria, whose fellows also commented on an early version of one of the chapters.

ACRONYMS AND ABBREVIATIONS

AMIA — Asociación Mutual Israelita Argentina/Argentine Israelite Mutual Association

Andha — Asociación Nacional de Deudores Habitacionales/National Association of Housing Debtors (Andha Chile a Luchar)

APDH — Asamblea Permanente por los Derechos Humanos/Permanent Assembly for Human Rights

BAPP — Buenos Aires Provincial Police

CADeP — Coordinadora Antirrepresiva por los Derechos del Pueblo/Antirepressive Coordinator for People's Rights

CECT — Comisión Ética contra la Tortura/Ethical Commission against Torture

CED — Centro de Estudios del Desarrollo/Center for Development Studies

CELS — Centro de Estudios Legales y Sociales/Center for Legal and Social Studies

CEP — Centro de Estudios Públicos/Public Research Center

CeProDH — Centro de Profesionales por los Derechos Humanos/Professionals' Center for Human Rights

CIPER — Centro de Investigación e Información Periodística/Center of Journalistic Research and Information (CIPER Chile)

CODEPU — Corporación de Promoción y Defensa de los Derechos del Pueblo/Corporation for the Promotion and Defense of People's Rights

COFAVI — Comisión de familiares de vícimas indefensas de la violencia social-policial-judicial-institucional/Commission of Family Members of Defenseless Victims of Social, Police, Judicial, and Institutional Violence

CONADEP — Comisión Nacional Sobre la Desaparición de Personas/National Commission on the Disappearance of People

COPESA — Consorcio Periodístico de Chile/Chilean Newspaper Consortium

CORREPI	Coordinadora Contra la Represión Policial e Institucional/ Coordinator against Police and Institutional Repression
CPM	Comisión Provincial por la Memoria/Provincial Commission for Memory
DINA	Dirección de Inteligencia Nacional/National Intelligence Directorate
EMOL	El Mercurio On-Line
ENUSC	Encuesta nacional urbana de seguridad ciudadana/National Urban Survey of Citizen Security
FASIC	Fundación de Ayuda Social de la Iglesias Cristianas/Social Assistance Foundation of the Christian Churches
FATPREN	Federación Argentina de Trabajadores de Prensa/Argentine Federation of Press Workers
FECH	Federación de Estudiantes de Chile/Chilean Student Federation
FOPEA	Foro de Periodismo Argentino/Argentine Press Forum
FTV	Frente Tierra y Vivienda/Land and Housing Front
HRW	Human Rights Watch
ICPC	International Centre for the Prevention of Crime
IDRC	International Development Research Centre
IMF	International Monetary Fund
INDH	Instituto Nacional de Derechos Humanos/National Institute of Human Rights
ISI	Import substitution industrialization
La Liga	La Liga Argentina por los Derechos del Hombre/Argentine League for the Rights of Man
LAPOP	Latin American Public Opinion Poll
NGO	Nongovernmental organization
MEDH	Movimiento Ecuménico por los Derechos Humanos/Ecumenical Movement for Human Rights
PDI	Policía de Investigaciones de Chile/Investigative Police of Chile
PFA	Policía Federal Argentina/Argentine Federal Police
PR	Public relations
RN	Renovación Nacional/National Renovation Party of Chile
RNTS	Registro Nacional de Casos de Tortura y/o Malos Tratos/ National Register of Cases of Torture and/or Mistreatment
RTU	Red de Television de Universidad de Chile/University of Chile Television Network

TN	Todo Noticias
TVN	Televisión Nacional de Chile/Chilean National Television
UNDP	United Nations Development Programme
UNODC	United Nations Office on Drugs and Crime
UP	Unidad Popular/Popular Unity
USAID	United States Agency for International Development
WOLA	Washington Office on Latin America

TOUGH ON CRIME

Introduction

MEDIA AND THE RISE OF PUNITIVE POPULISM

In March 2004, twenty-three-year-old Axel Blumberg was kidnapped and murdered on his way to his girlfriend's house in Greater Buenos Aires. His father, Juan Carlos Blumberg, took his grief public and mobilized hundreds of thousands of people, including members of human rights organizations, in protest against insecurity. He then set out his demands, which reflected tough-on-crime measures, including lowering the age of criminal responsibility, increasing punishments for various crimes, and decreasing possibilities for parole. At this point, members of human rights organizations distanced themselves from Blumberg and his demands. Yet Juan Carlos Blumberg and the protests he led had established themselves as symbols of public opinion in the mass media. The national newspaper *La Nación* described the first protest as "the true voice of the silent majority."[1] Despite having framed his campaign and government in terms of human rights, the newly elected president Néstor Kirchner responded to this construction of public opinion by initiating the first of three tough-on-crime "Blumberg" laws, passed by the Senate on April 14, 2004.[2]

In many countries, crime and insecurity are pressing and sensitive issues. They are political landmines where popular tough-on-crime solutions exist in tension with concerns for human rights. Tough-on-crime rhetoric is sometimes articulated in a manner that very explicitly undermines human rights. For example, in 1999, during an electoral campaign to become governor of the province of Buenos Aires, Carlos Ruckauf infamously stated: "Criminals should be shot" (*Hay que meterle bala a los ladrones*). He won that election. More often tough-on-crime positions are articulated with less colorful language. Instead, they simply but emphatically advocate for more police, greater police powers, and severer punishments. Whether articulated in colorful or less colorful language, the solutions emphasize an institutional and retributive response that sacrifices the rights of some in the name of security for others. Such solutions sit in opposition to both criminological research on crime control and international human rights agreements.

Tough-on-crime rhetoric and policies are now common throughout Latin America, Europe, North America, the Antipodes, and parts of Asia and Africa (sometimes slurred with anti-immigration rhetoric[3]), and are receiving an increasing amount of public support (e.g., Clarke 2018; Fenwick 2013; Schneider 2014). Recent examples of "tough-on-crime" presidents include Donald Trump in the United States (2016–present), Rodrigo Dutuerte in the Philippines (2016–present), and Nicolas Sarkozy in France (2007–2012). In Latin America, Otto Pérez Molina, used "tough on crime" (*mano dura*) as his campaign slogan and won the 2010 presidential elections in Guatemala. Presidential candidates Felipe Calderón in Mexico (2006), Tony Saca in El Salvador (2004), and Jair Bolsonaro in Brazil (2018) also won victories using similar rhetoric.

Certainly political leaders can win elections without using tough-on-crime rhetoric: examples include Néstor Kirchner (2003) and Cristina Fernández de Kirchner in Argentina (2007 and 2011), Mauricio Funes in El Salvador (2009), and Álvaro Colom in Guatemala (2008). Yet, as the opening example illustrates, many of these leaders have pursued tough-on-crime policies (or combined them with preventive programs) once in office. Their change in strategy often follows a shift in perceived public opinion following a highly mediatized crime incident.

For example, in June 2010 Dieciocho gang members burned a bus in El Salvador, killing seventeen passengers. In response to the significant media coverage and public outcry, President Funes introduced a new anti-gang law and deployed 2,800 military personnel to assist the National Civil Police in crime control (Lineberger 2011, 197; Wolf 2012, 203). He justified this action using language that mirrored former British prime minister Tony Blair's slogan, "Tough on Crime. Tough on the Causes of Crime." Funes explained: "We know that in the long term the policies of social inclusion and prevention will deliver results, but in the short term the violence is being fought with repression. And this is what the government has been doing and will continue to do" (quoted in Lineberger 2011, 195–196).

As these examples illustrate, the mass media play an important role in the dominance of "tough-on-crime" rhetoric and policies. This role is recognized in the large body of literature on the phenomenon (e.g., Garland 2001; Green 2008; Hall et al. 1978; Pratt 2007; Roberts et al. 2003). Yet ideally, this is not the role of the mass media in a democracy. Rather, the mass media should be an actor of democratic accountability (Curran 1991, 2005; McNair 2003; Peruzzotti and Smulovitz 2006). In this ideal, mass media are expected to challenge the tough-on-crime rhetoric and policies made by political leaders and state officials, require them to answer for their choices and omissions, or at least to provide an open forum for debate that includes those state and society actors who oppose tough-on-crime measures. Similarly, journalists will ideally expose police violence and, drawing on a plurality of voices from state and civil society, challenge state actors to respond with sanctions and reforms that ensure nonrepetition.

Given the failure of the mass media in many countries to play this democratic role adequately, it becomes important to ask: Why do the mass media privilege tough-on-crime rhetoric and policies? What broader communicational dynamics shape whether mass media play their ideal role in democratic accountability and how they do so? I argue that the ways in which media are organized (media systems) matter. This argument makes an important contribution to the growing literature on democracy's ability to produce undemocratic outcomes (Achen and Bartels 2016; Agamben 2005; González n.d.; Levitsky and Ziblatt 2018) and the large literature on democracy and democratization.

CONTRIBUTION TO THE LITERATURE ON DEMOCRACY

Studies of regime types consistently identify the mass media as an important feature that distinguishes authoritarian, semiauthoritarian, and democratic regimes. In authoritarian regimes, the state is said to heavily censor and repress the media and there is little freedom of expression or plurality of views or information (Levitsky and Way 2002). The mass media are a platform for the state to communicate to society. If the authoritarian state wishes to prioritize crime fighting as a policy issue and ignore or legitimize police violence, then media will reinforce this position. Civil society is limited in its ability to challenge these ideas.

However, the mass media can play a role in a transition to democracy by resisting state censorship, exposing state wrongdoing, and providing citizens alternative sources of information. Indeed, a feature of the liberalization of an authoritarian regime is "less censorship of the media" (Linz and Stepan 1996, 3). This may spur or support a resurgence of civil society activity that challenges the state and may push the regime to hold democratic elections (O'Donnell and Schmitter 1986, 55–58; Oxhorn 1995; Schneider 1995).

In semiauthoritarian or competitive authoritarian regimes, the challenges, such as state censorship and repression, are similar to authoritarian regimes, but tend to be subtler and less open (Levitsky and Way 2002, 53). Media may be controlled through state ownership, proxy ownership, patronage, or other "illicit means" (Levitsky and Way 2010, 11). Yet the opportunities for the media to contribute to the improvement or deepening of democracy are greater in that, while democratic institutions—such as the media—are badly flawed, they can still provide avenues to challenge the government. Indeed, Levitsky and Way argue that in competitive authoritarian regimes media are one of four key "arenas of democratic contention" (2010, 54, 57–58). Thus it is possible, albeit difficult, for tough-on-crime rhetoric and policies to be challenged under such regimes.

In democratic regimes media are ideally pluralistic, unencumbered by state censorship, and thus able to provide citizens and civil society a platform to exercise their freedom of expression, access alternative sources of information, and attempt to hold state actors accountable (Diamond 1999, 11; O'Donnell 1999,

29–30). Indeed the literature on social movements recognizes the mass media as playing an important, although ambiguous, role in the ability of these organizations to have their diverse perspectives heard and legitimized (Tarrow 1994).[4] This, in turn, facilitates the democratic role of civil society to provide accountability and enrich a democratic political culture (see chapter 6). Yet as Philip Oxhorn notes, when civil society attempts to establish a new moral consensus (such as less repressive crime control) "it matters which groups participate in the social construction of that consensus" (2011, 13). The voices of human rights organizations that expose police violence, demand accountability for this wrongdoing, and challenge tough-on-crime rhetoric and policies are not always heard in the mass media debates on the issue.

Placing less importance on civil society's access to the mass media, the literature on democracy and democratization generally equates a democratic media with the establishment of a "free" or "independent" media—assuming, but not always explicitly stating, that this is freedom and independence from state control (Diamond 1999, 11, 240–241; Levitsky and Way 2002, 57; O'Donnell 1999, 29, 44). For example, Larry Diamond specifies that "mass media can only perform their democracy-building roles if they have autonomy in their financing, operations, and legal standing" (Diamond 1999, 250). Following this logic, if the dominant voices found in a pluralistic media, uncensored by the state, support tough-on-crime policies, then this is consistent with democracy and presumably representative of public opinion. Thus, like elections (Achen and Bartels 2016) or states of emergency (Agamben 2005), democratic media can strengthen and disseminate undemocratic ideas.

Yet even in countries where tough-on-crime rhetoric is dominant, there are always state, media, and civil society actors who disagree with it and are concerned about its consequences for human rights and democracy. So how do some voices come to dominate public debate? The literature on democracy and democratization leads us to conclude that these opposing voices must represent the views of a minority that have competed unsuccessfully in a free and uncensored public debate.

However, missing from these studies of democracy and democratization is a discussion of the influence of the market on the democratic role of the media. This is despite the existence of a large literature in media studies, particularly focused on the United States, that has exposed the significant limits market-based media systems place on the democratic role of the media (Curran 2002; Entman 1989; Gans 2003).

Moreover, by focusing on the macro level, the literature on democracy and democratization neglects the many different ways of organizing media in democracy, each of which has very specific and varied influences on communicational practices and the resulting news we receive (see chapter 2). Not all media systems that are uncensored by the state and relatively pluralistic (compared to authoritarian or semiauthoritarian regimes) contribute equally to the democratic goals of holding power to account, providing alternative sources of information, and offering an open platform for freedom of expression. Nor do they all cover civil society organizations in the same manner or to the same extent. That is, when we move from the macro level of regime types to the everyday practices of journalists and those state and society actors attempting to have their voices heard in the mass media, we find that media systems matter to the mass media's ability to play the roles deemed important to democracy identified by scholars of regime types.

THE ARGUMENT

Drawing on a comparative analysis of Argentina and Chile, this book argues that the neoliberal reform of media policies (most notably privatization and especially deregulation) and the resulting everyday communicational practices used by journalists, in interaction with state and civil society actors, are central to explaining the rise of punitive populism. Together, these changes reduce the ability of the media to hold punitive rhetoric and policies to account, homogenize public opinion as punitive, and increase the saliency of crime and punitive ideas in policymaking. In this manner punitive voices come to dominate public and media discourse thus encouraging political leaders to use punitive populist strategies to win elections and popular support. Rather than a simple, two-variable, causal relationship, this argument reflects constructivist understandings of relational causes, similar to a narrative (Kratochwill 2008, 94–97). The causal chain functions as illustrated in figure I.1. Recognizing these communicational dynamics and their relationship with democracy is a first step toward identifying the types of changes that could potentially challenge mass media's receptiveness to punitive populism.

While based on an in-depth analysis of the cases of Argentina and Chile, the findings aim to be relevant to all democratic countries whose media systems have undergone neoliberal restructuring, regardless of the extent or type of crime experienced in the country. This is because punitive populism (discussed next) is about politics not crime control. The study is based on interviews conducted in the capital city of each country, but the influence of mass media practices is not limited to those cities. Most mass media based in Buenos Aires and Santiago have a national reach. This is seen through: the dissemination of print, broadcast, or internet news nationally; the cross-ownership of national and regional news outlets (increased through neoliberal media policies); and the use of events in the capital cities as proxies for the nation (Gans 2003, 54). I use the term "mass

FIGURE I.1. Media and the rise of punitive populism.

media" to refer to the most widely circulated print, digital, and broadcast news sources. I do not privilege the internet as a utopian or dystopian news source, but rather one among many, with distinctive characteristics, but equally affected by minimal regulation. Although TV has much larger audiences, newspapers remain the agenda-setting news sources in both Argentina and Chile, so the book pays particular attention to their practices.

Neoliberal economic policies refer to a specific set of economic policies that aim to reduce the role of the state in the market and in the provision of social services, and generally include fiscal austerity, privatization, deregulation, trade liberalization, and policies aimed at reducing the welfare state. As will be shown, neoliberal restructuring of the media resulted in the reduction or elimination of public broadcasting (which was never strong in Latin America), media privatization (mostly relevant for television in Latin America), and media deregulation (a pillar of media neoliberalization in all countries pursuing the model). Privatization requires media companies to make profit their primary purpose. Competition then becomes based on attracting the largest audiences at the lowest cost in order to increase profits. Crime, as revealed with increasing detail throughout this book, provides an excellent formula for low-cost stories that attract large audiences. Cost-cutting also encourages journalists to use fewer sources to the benefit of more punitive voices (particularly, the police, victims, and those able to provide professional public relations material). In turn media deregulation facilitates ownership concentration across media formats (which may or may not be important for punitive populism, depending on the type of media concentration) and, more important, limits (or even eliminates) the ability of the state to regulate news content in ways that might ensure a greater diversity of perspectives (see chapter 2).

Rather than the presence or absence of neoliberal economic and media policies, most countries exist on a sometimes fluctuating spectrum of degrees of implementation of neoliberal economic and media policies. That is, as David Harvey notes, there is no one "neoliberalism" in practice, but there are threads (noted above) that persist between countries and over time (2005, 70). Thus the term "neoliberalization" is used in this book to refer to a transition from less to more neoliberal economic and media policies. The extent of privatization and deregulation of the media needed to favor punitive populism likely depends on how these new policies combine with previous and persistent mass media practices (discussed in more detail throughout the book).

WHAT IS PUNITIVE POPULISM?

Punitive populism, also known as "populist punitiveness" (Bottoms 1995) or more commonly penal populism (Green 2008; Pratt 2007; Roberts et al. 2003), refers to political leaders' use of tough on-crime rhetoric and policies in order to gain popular support and win elections. Punitive populism is "populist" if we understand the term to refer to a particular political strategy or logic used by all political leaders to varying degrees (Laclau 2007; Weyland 2003). Indeed, for Ernesto Laclau, populism *is* politics, not a deviation from it. As he notes, populism has minimalist and maximalist forms depending on how existing institutions absorb diverse demands and the extent to which those demands challenge the institutional order (Laclau 2007, 154). All political discourse produces "the people." However, the range of demands included as the will of "the people" will be narrower in institutionalist types of discourse and more expansive in "rupturist discourse" (Laclau 2007, 154).

Drawing on Laclau, the populist strategy can be seen in punitive populism in two key ways. First, the strategy involves the leader creating "the people" through rhetorically and symbolically representing their heterogeneous demands, which have emerged from some sort of rupture (such as the implementation of neoliberal economic policies). The leader connects these disparate demands through rhetoric, creating an "equivalential chain" (Laclau 2007). The leader then uses what Laclau calls an "empty signifier" (a word or person that symbolizes the demands of "the people") to evoke this chain of demands as the will of "the people." As shown in chapter 1, heterogeneous demands might include many concerns with security such as precarious employment, decreased social services, and real or perceived increased crime. Empty signifiers that unite these demands in favor of punitive populism might include the specific leader; victims of crime; or language, such as "security", "tough on crime," or even "human rights" (e.g., human right to security), depending on the local context. The empty signifier is confirmed as the will of the people not only through rhetoric, it is also reinforced through references to public opinion polls and election results as evidence (Weyland 2003, 1105). It is rupturist when, as is often the case, the will of the people is framed along the lines of "the old institutional order is ineffective; the new order will resolve insecurity."

Second, the leader uses rhetoric to divide society into two irreconcilable groups, usually "citizens" and "criminals." This unites "the people" or "citizens" against a common enemy. Certainly, political leaders on the left and the right may disagree as to whether or not criminals are born "bad people" or can be prevented from becoming so through socioeconomic structural changes. However, in both cases, when punitive populist rhetoric is used those deemed "criminal" are the enemy of "the people/citizens" and are to be combated with a strong state response.

To be sure, not all political leaders who draw on the populist logic (regardless of the extent of their use) will use punitivism to unite support behind them. However, an increasing number of political leaders do, on both the left and the right. When they do, different punitive populist leaders within and between countries may advocate different degrees of punishment and vary in the extent to which they emphasize laws or policing or both in their rhetoric. That is, while I often equate punitive populism with the more extreme *mano dura* (iron fist), punitiveness can be measured on a spectrum from more to less.

At its core, the punitive element of punitive populism is composed of calls for the state to provide greater security and control measures in the form of more and tougher laws and punishments, as well as more police with greater powers and discretion. In this manner, it advocates for an expanded role of the criminal justice system, securitizing issues that could be or may once have been deemed issues of social welfare, development, or simply ignored as minor offenses. Specifically, it shifts the public conversation from how to address the causes of crime to how to punish a broader range of people deemed to be criminals. For example, the "broken windows" theory of criminal justice, introduced by George L. Kelling and James Q. Wilson (1982) in the *Atlantic Monthly*, and used in the punitive populist discourses disseminated to Europe and Latin America, advocates for the expansion of the definition and enforcement of crime to include a crackdown on petty acts of vandalism and drug possession.

Certainly, many studies of punitive populism limit their attention to the judiciary and prisons (Campbell 2008; Lacey 2008; Tonry 2007)—likely accounting for their preference for the term "penal populism"—and use prison population statistics to measure rises in punitiveness. Like Europe and the United States, Latin America has experienced a significant increase in its prison populations (Iturralde 2016, 140). Yet, while the punitive impact of the police is more difficult to measure (see chapter 1), the police are in fact the central actors in most countries. In all countries, police have considerable decision-making autonomy (González n.d.; Marenin 1996; Seri 2012). It is the police who decide whether or not to arrest someone (enforcing all laws all the time is a logistical impossibility). Police often decide which neighborhoods or types of people to police more than others, based on geography, class, race, sexual orientation, gender, and so forth (Hall et al. 1978; Schneider 2014; Seri 2012). That is, the criminal cases the judiciary receives depends on choices made by the police. Moreover, police also choose the level of force they deem appropriate for the situation and that they assume state and society will accept (Bonner 2014a; della Porta 1998; Geary 1985).

Tough-on-crime policies often advocate for an expansion of police powers (such as when and who police can arrest and the level of force they can use) and a reduction of oversight in order to "free the hands of police." For example, in 2018, Argentine president Mauricio Macri's government pursued penal code modifications that would expand police officers' right to shoot—only in cases of "legitimate defense" or in the defense of others to now include when a suspected criminal is running away.[5] In this manner, police discretion and thus the scope of acceptable police violence widens.

Of course, tough-on-crime policies can also expand other forms of violence caused, for example, by clientelism, vigilantism, criminal activity, private security, military, and paramilitary forces (Abrahamsen and Williams 2011; Goldstein 2012; Moncada 2016; Müller 2016). Yet, unlike these other actors, the police represent the state's legitimate use of domestic coercive force. Their use of this coercion is intended to enforce the rule of law and thus minimize violence by these nonstate actors (the military in a democracy is expected to be used only for external threats). Police actions and omissions thus shape citizens' experience with violence and the boundaries of their rights in democracy. For this reason, most liberal democracies have state institutional oversights on police actions and omissions: police violence is ideally kept in check by the judiciary (where charges can be brought and the rule of law maintained) and government (through ministerial sanctions such as dismissals). Yet in most countries these checks are weak (Bonner et al. 2018) and punitive populism can weaken them further (Hall et al. 1978; Lacey 2010, 110; Schneider 2014).

In addition to policies, punitive populist *rhetoric* also encourages police violence by influencing the choices police make as to how to use their increased discretion. Police are the only state institution in a democracy with the legitimate right to use (even lethal) violence against citizens. The difference between legal and illegal police violence depends on police justifications and the willingness of dominant state and society actors to accept the justifications. For example, in most countries a police officer can legally kill someone as long as it is done in self-defense or to protect others. The justification is central and is what the judge, police and political superiors, oversight bodies, and even the media will evaluate in order to determine wrongdoing. To reinforce police legitimacy and ensure legal predictability for officers, the scope of acceptable justifications in most countries is wide (Bonner 2018; Squillacote and Feldman 2018).

The centrality of justifications and their acceptance increases the importance of the mass media in police accountability. That is, police violence is not simply an outcome or measure of punitive populism. From a constructivist perspective, dominant discourses in the mass media shape the scope of actions and omissions for which police justifications are likely to be accepted (Bonner 2014a; Chan 1996; della Porta 1998; Geary 1985; Waddington 1998). Alternatively, these discourses can provide accountability by framing actions or omissions, formerly deemed acceptable, as wrongdoing, as well as demanding answers and potentially punishment (Bonner 2014a, ch. 2). The way ideas are constructed and reinforced in the mass media is important to the boundaries of policing in democracy and the resonance (or not) of punitive populist rhetoric and policies.

Of course the assertive state desired in punitive populism is not new in the broad history of the state or democracy, nor is it new to Latin America in particular. Targeted state coercion exists in all democracies (Bonner et al. 2018; González n.d.; Seri and Lokaneeta 2018). Instead, what has drawn the attention of criminal justice scholars in many countries is the particular way current punitive rhetoric and policies in democracy undermine the contributions of criminal justice experts and limit the scope of human rights enforcement. The implications of this for democracy are significant. It is thus imperative that we better understand the causes of the rise of punitive populism and the role of the mass media in it.

EXPLAINING THE RISE OF PUNITIVE POPULISM

A significant amount of the scholarship on punitive populism centers on its rise since the early 1970s in the United States and Great Britain, with other studies that follow its later spread to France, Australia, New Zealand, Ireland, the Netherlands, and Japan (Bottoms 1995; Campbell 2008; Fenwick 2013; Green 2008; Hall et al. 1978; Pratt 2007; Roberts et al. 2003; Wacquant 2009). As early as 1972, Stuart Hall and his coauthors (1978) traced the importation of the concept of "muggings" and its associated racialized crime "crisis" to Great Britain from the United States through the mass media. The crime "crisis," whether real or not, contributed to the increased use of law-and-order rhetoric and policies by political leaders and state officials. It provided a justification for preexisting police efforts to target and increase policing of working-class black neighborhoods. It also expanded the number of arrests and lengths of sentences. Britain, Hall argued, was "drifting into a law and order society" (1980).

In Latin America, punitive populism is a more recent concern. This is largely due to the authoritarian regimes and civil wars that preoccupied most of the region throughout the 1970s and 1980s. Following these regimes, most scholarly, activist, and practitioner work focused its attention on avoiding a return to the violence of the past with measures such as asserting civilian control over the military, publishing truth commission reports, and, seeking justice in the courts for past human rights abuses. Whereas some political leaders on the right continued to use punitive authoritarian rhetoric after the return of democracy, it was not a primary concern of scholars and practitioners. However, this changed as human rights organizations revealed the implications of these leaders' electoral successes and, in many countries, the political left began to incorporate punitive populist rhetoric and policies to compete (e.g., Holland 2013 on El Salvador; Müller 2016 on Mexico; and Seri and Kubal 2018 on Argentina). Scholars and practitioners of police reform and citizens' security now consistently identify punitive populism as a significant obstacle to deepening democracy, achieving police reforms, and resolving insecurity (Eaton 2008; UNDP 2013b; Ungar 2011).

Whether in the Global North or South, it is thus important to ask: What explains the rise in punitive populism? In what follows I examine five possible answers from the extant literature in order to situate the relative importance of the mass media and the gap this book fills.

CRIME RATES (A NONANSWER)

Almost all authors agree that the crime rate is a nonfactor in punitive populism (e.g., Holland 2013, 49; Müller 2016, 18; Tonry 2007, 6).[6] I highlight this because the use of the literature on punitive populism to understand Latin America is sometimes dismissed because the crime rate in Latin America is high. Part of the conundrum in North America and Europe has involved explaining why punitive populism has risen as crime rates declined. In contrast, it is often assumed that Latin Americans are rightfully fearful of crime and are responding accordingly. Latin America, as a region, has the highest homicide rates in the world and fourteen of twenty of the world's most dangerous cities (UNODC 2013; see chapter 1 and table 1.1 in this volume).[7]

Yet the region's high crime rate does not justify or explain the rise of punitive populism. Punitive populism offers a crime *solution* that can be popular whether the crime rate is factually high or merely perceived to be high. In either case, it is a solution that most criminologists agree does not reduce crime (e.g., Darley 2005; Doob and Webster 2003; Waller 2008) and may increase it (UNDP 2013a, 2013b; Wolf 2017). For example, while punitive populists advocate for longer prison sentences for a wider range of crimes, one study in El Salvador found that 10 percent of prisoners who were not members of gangs when they entered prison joined a gang while in jail (UNDP 2013b, 82).

Moreover, there is considerable debate in criminology regarding the measurement of crime (see chapter 1). As will be discussed, mass media choices regarding how to present these measurements have important implications for the way in which the public understands the problem, its relative importance, and the solutions. Thus while crime rates do not cause punitive populism, the way they are portrayed in the mass media can amplify (or minimize) the policy relevance of crime.

INTERNATIONAL POLICY DIFFUSION

Another answer to explain the rise in punitive populism is that it has been a successful policy transfer from the United States to elsewhere in the world. For example, the New York-based Manhattan Institute for Policy Research (established in 1977 and a self-described "leading voice of free-market ideas") has promoted tough-on-crime policy solutions to social issues in both the United States and abroad (Davis and Lunes Reyes 2007; Kubal 2012; Wacquant 2009). It has provided a vocabulary (e.g., "zero tolerance," "broken windows"), pseudo-academic evidence,[8] and has actively sought to connect globally with potential supporters of their ideas. For example, it hosted Juan Carlos Blumberg, the Argentine father discussed at the beginning of this chapter, for a visit to New York in June 2004.[9] Former New York mayor Rudolph Giuliani has also drawn on the institute's work and participated in its conferences (Wacquant 2009, 252–265). In turn, Giuliani's security consultancy firm, Giuliani Partners, has worked with governments around the world to assist with the implementation of zero-tolerance policies (Müller 2016, 13–16).

Some scholars have studied the effect of attempts to transfer tough-on-crime policy to Latin America (Davis and Lunes Reyes 2007; Kubal 2012) and others have focused on the cross-national sharing of this electoral strategy. For example, Tim Newburn and Trevor Jones examined the tough-on-crime electoral strategy transfer from Bill Clinton to Tony Blair in the 1990s, which contributed to Blair's reinvention of the New Labour Party, its 1997 electoral victory, and Labour's 1998 Law on Crime and Disorder (2005, 82–85), a law Wacquant describes as "widely recognized as the most repressive penal legislation of the postwar period" (2004, 170). In turn, Rita Abrahamsen and Michael C. Williams (2011) trace the contribution of changes in security governance in the Global North to the flourishing of private security firms that now participate with local state and nonstate actors around the world in what they call "global security assemblages" that transcend nation-state borders. These assemblages, they argue, have reconfigured power in ways that retain, but reshape, state power as well as where (and for whom) security is provided (Abrahamsen and Williams 2011, 4). Similarly, Markus-Michael Müller (2018) traces Brazilian leaders' adoption of tough-on-crime policies learned from their participation in the UN peacekeeping mission in Haiti.

Yet all these studies acknowledge that each country's political actors make choices as to if and how they will adopt such policies, practices, and rhetoric and how different domestic factors will affect the relative success of policy transfer attempts (Davis and Lunes Reyes 2007; Kubal 2012; Lacey 2010; Roché 2007). While the international media can play a (frequently overlooked) role in international policy diffusion, it is the domestic media that help connect these ideas to citizens' local lived reality. As a consequence, most research on punitive populism aims to assess the domestic risk factors.

NEOLIBERALISM

Almost all authors refer to the socioeconomic and cultural changes that occurred in Western European countries and the United States (beginning in the 1970s) and in Latin America (beginning in the 1980s) as being among the most important explanations for the rise of punitive populism. Marking the field, David Garland (2001) identified this change to be the result of "late modernity" or, more specifically, a combination of social, economic and cultural changes (e.g., the democratization of social and cultural life, shifts in the structure of the family and household, and changes in technology) with the embracing of "free-market 'neoliberalism' and social conservatism" (Garland 2001, 75, 78). While some authors argue that domestic institutional factors have protected some countries, such as those in Scandinavia, from the full impact of neoliberal economic reform and punitive populism (Campbell 2008; Lacey 2008, 2010; Tonry 2007), almost all authors identify the relative implementation of neoliberal economic policies as a key reason for the rise of punitive populism (Green 2008; Lacey 2008; Pratt 2007; Reiner 2012; Wacquant 2009). For example, Michael Cavadino and James Dignan (2006) compared twelve countries with four different capitalist economies (in Europe, North America, Africa, Asia, and the Antipodes) and found a correlation between neoliberal economies and punitive penal policies. They found that the factor most correlated with penal severity is economic inequality produced by neoliberal economies (Cavadino and Dignan 2006, 451).

More commonly, the contribution of neoliberal economic policies to punitive populism emphasized in these studies is the shift in thinking about crime control they produce. Most criminologists argue that the best way to reduce crime is to address the socioeconomic challenges that favor criminality and to invest in rehabilitation (e.g., Garland 2001; Reiner 2012; Waller 2008). Indeed, this "penal welfare" approach to crime control was dominant in most countries in Western Europe, North America, and the Antipodes from the Second World War until the 1970s/1980s (Garland 2001). The influence of neoliberal economic policies and practices, according to Garland (2001) and in reference to the United States and the United Kingdom, caused a fundamental transformation of the criminal justice field from "penal-welfare" (led by criminal justice experts) to punitive populism (emphasizing punishment and control and led by public opinion).[10]

Since neoliberal economic policies include a reduction or cut in the provision of social services, political leaders cannot respond to public demands for social programs or secure employment, nor are "penal welfare" policies viable. Yet, due to a contradiction between neoliberal theory and practice, political leaders can advocate for strong (even repressive) policing in order to maintain or create a good business climate (Brown 2006; Harvey 2005; McSherry 1997). This encourages political leaders supportive of neoliberalism to stoke and respond to citizens' fear of crime (Chevigny 2003, 78).

Rather than "late modernity" and the rupture of "penal welfare," studies of Latin America instead analyze the transition from import substitution industrialization (ISI) or state-led development to neoliberal economic policies that were imposed on most Latin American countries as part of structural adjustment programs from the International Monetary Fund and World Bank in the 1980s and 1990s. These programs included significant cuts to social spending (most notably to health and education), increased already high inequality of wealth (see chapter 1), increased the size of the informal sector (Müller 2016), expanded clientelism into security provision (Müller 2016), and increased crime. Thus crime is one of many insecurities produced by neoliberal economic reforms, but it is not necessarily the most salient issue for all people (see chapter 1). As this book reveals, neoliberal media practices favor the public and political interpretation of insecurity as caused by common crime.

Studies have found that political leaders also pursue punitive populist policies in response to pressures from the neoliberal global market to establish global cities that are attractive to international business investment and tourism. Assessing Colombia, Eduardo Moncada (2016) argues that political and criminal violence (defined as homicide) impedes such aspirations, and thus neoliberalism can help put pressure on political leaders to reduce urban violence. However, Müller (2016) counters that the processes involved in creating a global city increases violence and insecurity (beyond homicide) for the most marginalized people. He provides examples from Mexico City of punitive policies aimed to rid the streets of informal workers such as street merchants, squeegees, street kids, and prostitutes, in historical centers and areas of prime real estate investment. These informal workers are removed with violence and often sent to increasingly populated prisons. Indeed, the prison population in Mexico increased 47 percent between 1992 and 2013 (Iturralde 2016, 140).

Daniel M. Goldstein (2012) provides a similar analysis of marginalized urban indigenous communities in Bolivia, and finds they are controlled and criminalized by neoliberal security policies. He argues that neoliberalism defines security as security for global capital, its investment interests, and its protection from public opposition (Goldstein 2012, 17). This has included an expansion of domestic and international private security companies, which have further exacerbated violence in marginalized communities (Abrahamsen and Williams 2011; Goldstein 2012; Müller 2016). In this manner, as Enrique Desmond Arias and Goldstein (2010b) argue, neoliberalism has produced "violent pluralism" in the region, rather than peaceful and more robust democratic processes.

While not discussed in any detail in the literature on neoliberalism and punitive populism, the mass media, as we will see throughout this book, have also been reshaped by neoliberal economic policies. The resulting everyday communicational practices, in turn, favor some state and civil society conceptions of insecurity and its solutions over others to the advantage of punitive voices. This helps build public support for policies that may benefit global capital at the expense of marginalized citizens.

THE OUTCOME OF DEMOCRACY

Certainly neoliberalism is central in most studies of the rise of punitive populism. Yet some studies contend that democratic institutions matter, not only in the degree to which neoliberal economic policies have been implemented but also in the degree to which punitive populism has come to dominate public discussions on crime.

According to many studies of punitive populism in Europe, North America, and the Antipodes, democratic structures that limit public input in crime policy decision making are the best protection from punitive populism. In particular, they find that proportional representation electoral systems that result in coalition governments (Tonry 2007), as well as countries with coordinated economic markets or corporatism (Lacey 2010), and unelected judges and prosecutors (Tonry 2007) have built-in protections for political leaders against the punitive pressures of public opinion. As Joseph Schumpeter argued in his classic work, crime is one policy area that should be protected from democracy because of the emotions involved (2003 [1943], 292).

Other scholars disagree, arguing that criminal justice policies can be both open to democratic public debate and nonpunitive, depending on how political institutions are organized. For Lisa Miller (2016), comparing the United States, United Kingdom, and the Netherlands, multiparty parliamentary systems are more likely to both reduce violent crime and address social conditions in high crime areas precisely because there is more public participation than in two-party or presidential systems. Similarly, but on a smaller scale, Albert W. Dzur (2010) argues that restorative justice programs allow for public participation in a manner that discourages punitive populism. From this perspective, public participation in criminal justice policymaking is important for democracy, and is not necessarily punitive.

While Latin American countries generally have multiparty proportional representation electoral systems that, in some countries, produce coalition governments, and often have unelected judges and prosecutors, these institutional structures do not necessarily reduce opportunities for punitive populism. In part this is due to the weakness of state institutions in the region (Chalmers 1977; O'Donnell 1996). Instead, studies of democratic processes in Latin America emphasize the role of powerful nonstate actors and informal practices.

Certainly political parties matter. Assessing El Salvador, Alisha Holland (2013) argues that right-wing political parties choose to use punitive populism to win elections when opposition left-wing political parties reject militarized solutions to crime and promote human rights, and there are divisions within the Right on economic policies. Crime is a policy issue that cuts across classes and political ideology, and the Right benefits from its traditional concern with social order. Electoral competition encourages left-wing political parties to then adopt similar policies.

Other scholars argue that the shift to punitive populism is not an inevitable outcome of electoral politics, but rather depends on the types of coalitions between political parties and social movements (Bermeo and Yashar 2016) or whether citizen claim-makers (or social movements) are fragmented or cohesive in their opposition to punitive policies (Fuentes 2005; González n.d.). The more fragmented, the more likely the police (whose coercive power makes them persuasive in policymaking) will influence political leaders toward authoritarian policing practices (González n.d.).

Of course, punitive populism does not emerge at the national level alone. Kent Eaton (2008) found that federalism creates paradoxes in police reform policies. One level of government may be elected based on a policy of reducing police powers, but then at another level a political leader, using punitive populism, sabotages those efforts.

Cities also matter. Both Müller (2016) and Moncada (2016) argue that pervasive decentralization in Latin America has increased the importance of mayors in policymaking on crime. Müller (2016) contends that decentralization has promoted punitive populism for a number of reasons, including the limited funds available at the municipal level to address the socioeconomic roots of crime. Comparing three cities in Colombia, Moncada (2016) more optimistically views punitive populism to be the outcome of particular combinations of mayors and business communities. Punitive populism, he holds, is more likely if the mayor has an affinity to clientelism and supports punitive policy options, and the business community is fragmented on crime policy or disengaged from it. These conditions open up space for civil society, international, and criminal actors to influence policymaking, often toward more punitive options.

Finally, studies of countries in both the Global North and Global South have noted that weak citizen trust in democratic state institutions contributes to a rise in punitive populism (e.g., Garland 2001; Tonry 2007, 6; Ungar 2011). For this reason, there has been considerable academic and practitioner attention on how to build trust, particularly, in the police (e.g., Ellison 2000; Frühling 2007; Tankebe 2010; Tyler 2007). Yet trust can be built as much through perception as practice and can thus sit uncomfortably with punitive populism. Notably, it is possible to trust a state institution that uses high levels of violence if that violence is unknown to most people or is deemed acceptable (see chapter 1; Bonner 2013). The mass media play a significant role in this perception.

Certainly democratic institutions matter and some institutions may be more likely to produce authoritarian policies than others. It is imperative that we understand these dynamics. However, consistently glossed over in most of these studies is the role of the mass media in these interactions. As the literature on policymaking recognizes, the mass media are important in creating opportunities for new policies, facilitating communication between policy actors, providing advantages and support for some ideas or policy actors over others, and influencing and constructing public opinion in particular ways (Bennett 1996; Cook 2005; Kingdon 2003). For example, Sonja Wolf (2017) argues that the ability of nongovernmental organizations to engage the mass media was key to their relative participation in crime policy debates in El Salvador. Thus while some of the studies noted above assume either that civil society is punitive or that nonpunitive civil society/citizens voices can reduce punitive populism, the mass media play an important role in deciding which civil society and policy actors' voices are heard and how.

THE MASS MEDIA

The final domestic risk factor for punitive populism is the mass media (Green 2008; Pratt 2007; Roberts et al. 2003). Indeed, some scholars argue that it is a central factor when combined with many of the issues discussed above (Sparks 2001, 196; Stenson 2001, 16; Tonry 2007). Focusing primarily on mass media discourses, the literature contends that the mass media amplify and distort the threat of crime, glorify victims of crime over the voices of criminal justice experts, stoke citizens fear of crime, thus creating moral panic, and exclude nonpunitive voices—especially those from civil society (Calzado 2015; Chevigny 2003, 79; Dammert 2012, 25–26; Hall et al. 1978; Müller 2016, 33; Reiner, Livingstone, and Allen 2001; Seri 2012, 25–26; Stanley 2010, 158; Ungar 2011, 22–28; Wolf 2017). The studies attribute these discourses to increased media tabloidization and changes in media technology, mainly within the assumed context of market-based media systems (Garland 2001; Roberts et al. 2003).

Yet such analyses usually portray these changes as unrelated to political economy. Only a few studies have examined or mentioned the different role of mass media in criminal justice debates in nonmarket-based media systems (Green 2008; Pratt 2007). With a limited analysis of the reasons, these studies find that nonmarket-based media systems favor less punitive discourses. Few studies, if any, have fully examined the broad range of mass media, state, and civil society communicational practices that together contribute to punitive populist outcomes and their links to neoliberal media policies, which is the focus of this book.

METHODOLOGY

At its core, this is a study of politics but not in the sense of formal state institutions or procedures. It is an analysis premised on the importance of everyday practices of governance and the formation of discourse (Foucault 1991; Migdal 2001). That is, governing involves not only state institutions and laws but also multiple relations of power. Small everyday practices contribute to the construction of particular dominant discourses that ultimately frame state and society's understanding of the most important problems facing their country and the most desirable solutions. They also shape and constrain the possibilities for counterframes to challenge these dominant diagnoses and solutions. More specifically, and in interaction with the influences of neoliberal economic reforms and media policies, I reveal how the definitions of crime and insecurity and their solutions, as well as the presence or absence of police violence in these debates, are shaped by: (1) journalists' practices; (2) state actors' communicational practices; and (3) civil society's communicational practices (see figure I.1). Identifying the intersection of the practices used by key state and society actors and journalists illuminates how dominant communicational frames are constructed and challenged.

Several caveats should be highlighted. First, this is a study of the practices that contribute to frame formation, not a discourse analysis. In other studies I have used discourse analysis (e.g., Bonner 2009a, 2009b, 2014a, 2016) and I will draw on the findings of such research, but in this book I concentrate on the *practices* that contribute to the production of discourses. Second, there are some excellent studies on the practices that shape discourse and communication that center on the mass media (e.g., Chibnall 1977; Entman 1989; Gans 2003), the police (e.g., Chermak and Weiss 2005; Ericson 1989; Mawby 2002), or civil society (e.g., Fenton 2010; Koopmans 2004; Waisbord 2011). By focusing on a single actor, these studies are able to provide significant depth, often from a neoinstitutional perspective, on the communicational practices used by these particular actors and thus are of important value and will be engaged with in this book. However, what I am most interested in here is how the practices of journalists, the state, and civil society *interact*. Thus I have sacrificed depth for breadth in order to capture these interactions and changes over time. The aim then is not to simply understand, for example, how the police manage their communications, but to understand, using the same example, how police practices contribute to a wider context of competing communicational practices that together produce dominant and counterdiscourses.[11]

In this manner, the study uses an interpretative method (Sikkink 1991; Yanow and Schwartz-Shea 2014), which involves developing theory from a careful analysis of data, especially interviews, with an eye to understanding actors' practices and choices from their perspective. The chapters that analyze the interview data focus on the issues deemed most important to each set of actors. Thus, while not a complete overview of all communicational practices, which an ethnographic or process tracing study might produce, the interpretative method allows us to better understand the choices and priorities made by key actors.

The study is based on 194 in-depth semistructured interviews with media, state, and civil society actors engaged in communications on issues of crime, security, or police violence, or all three. Most interviews took place in Argentina and Chile from 2006 to 2015. In some cases the same people or organizations were interviewed more than once, enabling the identification of changes over time (see appendix 1) This book also draws on many academic studies as well as documents and reports collected through these interviews.

Applying the comparative method (Mill 1906), the book analyzes two countries in Latin America, Argentina and Chile, which serve two interconnected purposes. First, the cases, both drawn from Latin America, offer a fresh perspective on punitive populism that challenges some of the endogeneity in the literature that assesses Europe, the United States, Canada, and the Antipodes. By situating the cases in conversation with the EuroAmerican literature, the most different comparison reveals that punitive populism is not the result of "late modernity" and thus specific to Western industrialized countries (Garland 2001; Green 2008), and that it is also not merely a legacy of authoritarianism or persistent violence in the region. Instead I show punitive populism to be much more significantly tied to neoliberal media reform and the communicational practices it produces, which in turn structure public debate.

Second, the cases of postauthoritarian Argentina and Chile allow us to assess the relative influence of neoliberal economic and media policies on communicational structures favorable to punitive populism compared to the pressures of liberal democracy. As discussed, some scholars argue that particular liberal democratic institutions protect some countries from punitive populism. Others counter that these institutions are not sufficient (as in the case of Latin America) or that neoliberal polices (such as decentralization) have altered these structures in ways that encourage punitive populism (e.g., Müller 2016). More broadly, some scholars contend that neoliberal economic policies have contributed to the erosion of liberal democracy (notably the cornerstones of civic liberties, accountability, the rule of law, and freedom of the press) in countries such as the United States (e.g., Brown 2006; Harvey 2005; Wacquant 2009). Rather than eroding democracy, the cases of Argentina and Chile allow us to see how neoliberal economic and media policies affect the (re)establishment of liberal democracy after authoritarianism. In both case studies there is a clear before and after authoritarian rule, yet the timing of the adoption of neoliberal media policies is different, allowing for another most-different case study comparison.

Milton Friedman's test case for neoliberal theory was Chile. It was one of the first countries to broadly adopt the economic policies and it did so under the military authoritarian regime of General Augusto Pinochet (1973–1990) (Valdéa 1995). Thus, in Chile, the extensive implementation of neoliberal economic and media policies predated electoral democracy and shaped the media system and communicational practices going into democracy. Tough-on-crime rhetoric and policies have been relatively consistent in Chilean political discourse since the return of electoral democracy.

In contrast, in Argentina (1976–1983), military leaders and the dominant media at this time were more divided on whether or not to implement neoliberal economic policies, some preferring state-led development (Sivak 2013; Teichman 2001). Thus, in this case, while some neoliberal economic reforms were implemented during the military regime, mass media democratization (the expansion of the number of sources used by journalists and increased possibilities for watchdog journalism [see chapter 2; Hughes 2003; Waisbord 2000]) predated the extensive implementation of neoliberal economic and media policies.[12] Only in 1989 did civilian president Carlos Menem introduce neoliberal policies to mass media ownership regulation, and throughout the 1990s he continued to dramatically implement a wide range of neoliberal economic and media policies (see chapter 3).

Consequently, in Argentina media democratization and media neoliberalization intertwined in distinct ways to shape the media system and communicational practices within which journalists, state, and civil society actors work. In this case, tough-on-crime rhetoric competed with human rights rhetoric to define dominant public discourse, with the former gaining strength as the influence of neoliberal media reforms was felt by journalists and media outlets. Thus the case of Argentina allows for an additional comparison, a within-case most similar comparison of before and after neoliberal media reforms in democracy.

Due to the different timing of the implementation of neoliberal media policies, the two-country comparison highlights a number of important issues. First, tough-on-crime rhetoric and policies are not necessarily uniquely an outcome of an authoritarian legacy, "late modernity," democratic institutions, or international pressures. Second, a tradition of a classic populist movement, such as Peronism (discussed in detail in later chapters), is not necessary for a rise in the use of a punitive populist strategy. Third, and most important, when implemented, (neo)liberal media policies favor communicational practices that elevate and reinforce tough-on-crime rhetoric and policies. These practices decrease the ability of media to hold punitive rhetoric and policies to account, favor the homogenization of public opinion as punitive, and, increase the role of media in policymaking.

CHAPTER OUTLINE

Chapter 1 reassesses the available statistics on crime, insecurity, and police violence generally, and in Latin America and Argentina and Chile specifically. It aims to put mediatized debates into context by highlighting the diversity and malleability of existing measures. In so doing the chapter argues that, while crime is a very real issue in many countries, the subjectivity of what we know lends itself to media and political interpretation. As a consequence, the ways in which dominant media construct these facts into stories become very important to the rise of punitive populism.

Chapter 2 begins the analysis of mass media constructions of insecurity. The chapter recognizes that a key challenge posed by punitive populism is that it offers a place for emotions in politics that sits in direct tension with Enlightenment ideas of rational legal authority. The chapter argues that rethinking the media system and its resulting communicational dynamics may facilitate the inclusion of emotions into politics in a manner that better represents a diversity of emotions and rational legal solutions. Given the importance of public opinion to punitive populism, media representation of public opinion is particularly important. The chapter examines the types of journalistic practices found in different media systems that produce contrasting constructions of public opinion.

Chapter 3 goes further to compare the history and contemporary media environments of Argentina and Chile and their relationship to the coverage of crime, security, and police violence. It argues that despite the different timing of neoliberal media reforms, their implementation favored a greater receptivity to punitive populism in both countries. This factor is highlighted as more important than the authoritarian legacy or the tradition of a classic populist movement (in the case of Argentina).

Chapters 4 to 6 explore the details of the communicational practices of journalists, state actors, and civil society, respectively, including the ways in which together they shape the production of discourse on crime, security, and police violence in Argentina and Chile as well as what we learn from this comparison that is relevant to other countries. Chapter 4 explores the importance of journalists' choices of the sources they use to construct crime stories and the implications of these choices for punitive populism. It argues that the relatively late implementation of neoliberal media policies in Argentina initially contributed to a divergence in the array of sources used by journalists in the two countries after their respective returns to democracy. However, once implemented, the policies have led to a convergence in which both media systems favor journalists' use of sources that are more likely to voice punitive populist perspectives.

Chapter 5 examines how state actors engage the media, and argues that state actors' choices, while not always strategic or necessarily effective, have had an important effect on the salience of punitive voices. In particular, the comparison of Argentina and Chile shows how neoliberal media policies have favored an expanded use of state public relations to the benefit of some (more punitive) state institutions over others, increased the importance of media in policymaking, and finally, encouraged the state to negotiate with the media through reality-TV police programs.

Chapter 6 explores the ways in which civil society actors working on issues of police violence, crime, and/or security attempt to access the media. Comparing the cases of Argentina and Chile, I find that neoliberal media policies and the resulting journalistic practices affect how civil society organizations engage the media and which organizations are more likely to gain coverage, to the advantage of more punitive voices. The concluding chapter returns to the case of Juan Carlos Blumberg that began this introduction, summarizes the findings of the book, and points to areas in need of further research.

Chapter 1

INTERPRETING STATISTICS ON CRIME, INSECURITY, AND POLICE VIOLENCE

To say that media practices construct dominant discourses on crime, insecurity, and police violence is not to deny that these are real and important issues in many countries. They certainly can be, and a wide range of evidence supports this claim. Yet the statistics used as evidence have different strengths and weaknesses as well as areas of attention and inattention, which can be used to formulate particular and different articulations of the problem and appropriate solutions.

This chapter presents some criticisms of those statistics. From a constructivist perspective, I argue that while we can know some aspects of crime, insecurity, and police violence as "facts," a great deal is unknown or subjective. Dominant public narratives offer an interpretation of available statistics that shape the articulation of the problem of crime (that is, what types of crime are the problem), the saliency of crime as an issue relative to other potential causes of insecurity, and whether police violence is presented as part of the problem, part of the solution, or simply as irrelevant. In this manner, the available statistics can be used in the mass media to support punitive populism or facilitate discursive accountability. The latter would involve initiating a public conversation that could redefine an act once considered "normal," "legitimate," or "acceptable," such as punitiveness or police violence, as unacceptable and in need of an answer and remedy (Bonner 2014a, ch. 2).

CRIME

Crime is the central focus of punitive populist rhetoric and policies. Of course, crime exists in all countries and in all historical time periods. It is neither new nor specific to countries in which punitive populists are found. It is not a phenomenon unique to Latin America. However, most people in countries where punitive populism is commonly used argue that levels of crime are high in their country and that crime is increasing. In some countries evidence shows that this is true (see tables 2.1 and 2.2) and many scholars contend that crime has increased with the spread of neoliberal economic policies—as an outcome of the higher socioeconomic inequalities and the retraction of social welfare programs known to reduce crime (Fajnzylber, Lederman, and Loayza 1998, 2002; Harvey

2005; Ostry, Loungani, and Furceri 2016; Seri 2012). Yet in this section I am less concerned with what *causes* crime, and more interested in assessing the dominant tools used to measure it and their implications for the way in which crime can be constructed. Three sources of crime statistics are commonly used: reported crimes, homicide rates, and victimization surveys (see table 1.1).

REPORTED CRIMES

As many scholars have pointed out, all available statistics have methodological weaknesses and are, at best, an approximation of levels and changes in crime. At first glance, the number and types of crimes reported to the police can appear to be the most reliable. Yet reported crimes may not measure what is intended. In some countries, people may not report crimes because they do not trust the police or may even fear that the police are involved in the crime that affected them. However, more commonly, many crimes are not reported (and this is true in all countries) because people do not see some crimes as important enough to bother going to the police or because there is little the police can or would do (ENUSC 2014; Sinha 2015, 7). In other cases, crime statistics can appear to be either high or increasing because police have improved their techniques or expanded the categories for which they collect crime statistics (Hall et al. 1978; Reiner 2012).

Unreported crimes commonly include petty theft, nonviolent crimes, and sexual violence. The characteristics of the victim (e.g., gender), the victim's relationship to the perpetrator, and severity of the crime can also affect whether or not a victim reports a crime (Sinha 2015, 4). One study showed that only 5 percent of victims of sexual violence in Latin America and the Caribbean report the incident to police (UNDP 2013a, 9). Similarly, in Canada, unwanted sexual touching by a nonspousal perpetrator was the least reported crime with only 7 percent of victims reporting the crime (Sinha 2015, 6).

Consequently, a crime rate, based on reported crimes, might fluctuate due to changes in levels of reporting not changes in numbers of crimes. For example, in Chile, the crime-reporting rate was 37.2 percent in 2014 but 40.3 percent in 2015 (ENUSC 2015, 31). In comparison, in Canada in 2009, approximately one-third of crimes were reported, which reflects a drop in the reporting of some crimes from 1999 (Sinha 2015, 3). Thus, although both countries have relatively strong and stable confidence in the police (see table 1.4), the vast majority of crimes are not reported.

HOMICIDE RATES

For these reasons, criminologists often use homicide rates as a better indicator of crime because homicides are more likely to be reported. As noted in the introduction, Latin America as a region has the highest homicide rate in the world. However, homicide rates are often given for a country as a whole and not disaggregated by region or cause of homicide (Daudelin 2017). Taking a closer look, parts of some countries in Latin America have homicide rates equivalent to or lower than those in the United States or some European countries, whereas others are much higher. For example, the homicide rate for Argentina in 2012 was 5.2/100,000 people. Yet the rate in the province of Cordoba was 1.3 and in Chubut it was 13.7 (in the United States, 4.7 and in the United Kingdom, 1).[1] Moreover, even statistics on homicide can vary significantly. For example, Seri notes that in 2005, the World Health Organization recorded 2,028 homicides, and the Argentine government recorded 2,731 (2012, 32)

Moreover, homicide statistics are rarely disaggregated based on cause. Thus, homicide rates can vary dramatically based on the rise and fall of organized crime and, particularly, disputes between organized crime groups. In contrast, femicide (the killing of women based on gender) or domestic murder may in fact be stable over time (Daudelin 2017). Killings by police may or may not be counted as homicide and are almost never disaggregated from homicide statistics. Furthermore, one study of Brazil showed that sometimes organized crime groups strategically choose whether homicides become officially known or not (Willis 2017). Finally, even if disaggregated by region and cause, there is no necessary correlation between homicide rates and those of other crimes, as found in victimization surveys (see tables 1.1 and 1.2).

VICTIMIZATION SURVEYS

Victimization surveys are widely used in the United States and Europe as one of the more accurate measures of crime (e.g., Green 2008). These surveys ask members of the general public whether they have been a victim of crime in the past X number of months and, if so, what type of crime (from a selection of choices). These have the advantage of capturing unreported crimes and crimes that include but are not limited to homicide. Yet they still suffer from a number of weaknesses. In Britain, they have been criticized for not reaching those most affected by crime, particularly young men living in cities (Green 2008, 17). However, even when surveyed, the questions require respondents to accurately remember incidents that they may or may not have reported to the police. Thus, ideally surveys would ask about incidents over the past three months to enhance memory, but many polls, such as the World Values Survey and the Latin American Public Opinion Poll (LAPOP)/AmericasBarometer, ask about the previous year. It is also important that the survey questions ask about specific crimes so there is less interpretation by the respondent of what counts as a crime. Some surveys fail to do this. For example, the World Values Survey simply asks: "Have you been a victim of crime during the past year?"[2]

TABLE I.1: Crime and Insecurity in Latin America

Country	Average perception of insecurity 2014[1]	Crime victimization 2014[2]	Homicide rate 2012/2013 (per 100,000 people)[3]
Argentina	46.2	24.4	7/–
Belize	42.3	13.8	45/–
Bolivia	55.1	22.2	12/–
Brazil	49.6	16.4	27/27
Canada	22.0	11.6	2/1
Chile	42.2	11.9	3/–
Colombia	45.3	19.6	31/32
Costa Rica	48.7	12.5	8/8
Dominican Republic	55.9	23.4	22/–
Ecuador	40.4	27.5	12/–
El Salvador	46.9	18.6	41/40
Guatemala	44.6	17.0	35/–
Guyana	36.8	7.4	18/19
Haiti	42.3	15.7	10/–
Honduras	38.6	18.3	91/84
Jamaica	27.2	6.7	39/43
Mexico	51.0	23.4	22/19
Nicaragua	41.3	17.2	11/–
Panama	41.5	8.2	17/17
Paraguay	41.3	12.8	10/9
Peru	56.6	30.6	10/7
Trinidad & Tobago	28.6	9.6	28/30
United States	27.4	16.7	5/4
Uruguay	45.8	22.8	8/8
Venezuela	63.2	24.4	54/–

Source: LAPOP/AmericasBarometer and World Bank.

1. Arturo Maldonado and Mariana Rodríguez, "Safety and Security as Influences on Everyday Life," in *The Political Culture of Democracy in the Americas, 2014: Democratic Governance across 10 Years of the AmericasBarometer*, ed. Elizabeth J. Zechmeister, 29–71. Report Funded by USAID, LAPOP/AmericasBarometer, and Vanderbilt University, 2014, www. LapopSurveys.org from p. 63.

2. Nicole Hinton, Daniel Montalvo, Arturo Maldonado, Mason Moseley, and Daniel Zizumbo-Colunga, 2014. "Crime and Violence across the Americas," in Zechmeister, *Political Culture of Democracy*, 3–28. www.LapopSurveys.org from p. 17. The question is: Have you been a victim of crime in the last 12 months?

3. World Bank, "Intentional Homicides per 100,000 People," accessed April 13, 2016, http://data.worldbank .org/indicator/VC.IHR.PSRC.P5.

TABLE 1.2: Crime and Insecurity in Latin America Compared to United States/ Europe/Antipodes

Country	Perception of insecurity, % (year)[1]	Victimization, % (year)[2]	Homicide rate 2012/2013 (per 100,000 people)[3]
Latin America			
Argentina	44 (2013)	15.8 (2013)	7/—
Brazil	37.5 (2014)	12.6 (2014)	27/27
Chile	40.2 (2011)	17.1 (2011)	3/—
Mexico	33.1 (2012)	20.2 (2012)	22/19
Peru	55.7 (2012)	23.6 (2012)	10/7
Uruguay	32.2 (2011)	15.7 (2011)	8/8
Europe/United States/Antipodes			
Australia	10.4 (2012)	10 (2012)	1/1
Germany	5.2 (2013)	4.2 (2013)	1/1
Netherlands	3.1 (2012)	3.6 (2012)	1/1
New Zealand	11.6 (2011)	12.7 (2011)	1/1
Spain	14.5 (2011)	5.2 (2011)	1/1
United States	16.4 (2011)	8.4 (2011)	5/4

Sources: World Values Survey, "Online Data Analysis," accessed June 8, 2016, http://www.worldvaluessurvey.org. World Bank, "Intentional Homicides per 100,000 People," accessed June 8, 2016, http://data.worldbank.org/indicator/VC.IHR.PSRC.P5.

1. Question: Could you tell me how secure do you feel these days in your neighborhood? Percentages shown are combined responses of "Not very secure" and "Not at all secure." From World Values Survey.
2. Question: Have you been a victim of crime in the last year? From World Values Survey.
3. World Bank, "Intentional Homicides per 100,000 People."

In turn, surveys that ask specific questions make choices regarding which crimes they ask about. For example, the crimes used in the LAPOP/AmericaBarometer survey are "robbery, burglary, assault, fraud, blackmail, extortion, violent threats or any other type" (Hinton et al. 2014, 15). Due to the normalization and justifications associated with some crimes, a respondent, for example, may not view rape, domestic violence, or police violence as a criminal act of "assault." Indeed, Marcelo Bergman notes that victimization surveys tend to overreport theft and underreport violence (2006, 221).

Putting aside these limitations, we find that overall, victimization is higher in Latin America than in Europe, Canada, the United States, and the Antipodes, yet there is significant variation (see tables 1.1 and 1.2). In 2014 in Latin America, victimization was highest in Peru (30.6 percent), Ecuador (27.5 percent), Venezuela (24.4 percent), and Argentina (24.4 percent). However, in that same year, some countries in Latin America had similar or lower rates of victimization than in the United States (16.7 percent) or Canada (11.6 percent), such as Panama (8.2 percent), Chile (11.9 percent), Costa Rica (12.5 percent), Paraguay (12.8 percent), Belize (13.8 percent), and Brazil (16.4 percent).

Together, statistics on reported crimes, homicide, and victimization can confirm the public's impressions of high or increasing crime. However, the methodological limitations and variation in results mean that they are vulnerable to media and political actors' selective use and interpretation. These interpretative choices structure the definition of crime. That is, most evaluations of crime emphasize homicide, theft, and robbery. They deemphasize white-collar crime, and crimes that may appear "normal" to a given community such as corruption, police abuse, vigilantism, domestic abuse, sexual assault, and rape. Such crimes may go unreported to the police, unreported in victimization surveys, and uncaptured in homicide statistics.

The available statistics also ignore problems around the criminalization of certain types of people (based on class, race, sex, political orientation, etc.) and uses of public spaces (such as public protest, the informal market, or prostitution). Thus the very act of trying to measure increasing crime shifts the conversation away from its more subjective class, gender, racial, and political dimensions. In what follows I provide two examples of the subjectivity of crime from the case studies used in this book in order to illustrate this challenge. The Argentine example highlights the issue of gender, and the Chilean example highlights class.

Argentina

In Argentina, journalists and political leaders do not rely on crime statistics to the extent that they do in Chile. This is the result of various political and pragmatic issues. However, the lesser use of crime statistics does not prevent mass media from reporting on "crime waves" and increased "insecurity" linked to crime. As many journalists have described, these labels are used when a series of similar crimes appear over a short period of time and the working definition of crime is homicide, theft, and robbery. In interviews with me, female police journalists noted gender biases in crime reporting and that they have been fighting to change these practices.

One female journalist noted that all the heads of police news sections are male and so are most of the police journalists, the police, and judicial actors. When she began working as a police journalist in about 2004 (after most of the neoliberal media reforms had been implemented), she explained that gender-based violence was covered mainly for its morose and sexual nature. It was often labeled "crime of passion" and she described the coverage as almost favorable to the perpetrator. She gave the example of Ricardo Barrera (among others). Barrera was found guilty of killing his wife, mother-in-law, and two daughters in 1992. The media emphasized *his* testimony and version of events, which at the time led audiences to conclude that the murders were justified due to the "27 years that Barrera suffered at the hand and mouth of the four women in the house."[3] The women's side of the story was not told.

As more female police journalists emerged (and their numbers are still small), they joined together to fight for these stories to be reframed as "sexual abuse" or "gender violence." Together a group of them (including some male police journalists) published a book on the topic (Di Lodovico et al. 2014), and in 2015, women from this group helped lead a campaign and now yearly demonstration that brings hundreds of people to protest in front of the Congress building under the slogan "Ni una menos" (Not one less), demanding an end to gender based violence.[4]

The movement was successful in changing the frame of news stories. Police journalist María Helena Ripetta explained that before this movement she could not publish stories on rape because there were no photos of beaten or murdered women, now she can write stories on rape.[5] However, many police journalists explained that gender-based violence is now often addressed in the "society" section of newspapers so that the social aspects of the crimes can be explained rather than the criminal/police aspects.[6] Of course, most crimes are of a social nature. The change of sections highlights how the structure of police news (along with statistics) limits the ability of journalists to address these more complicated, subjective, social, and political aspects of crime.

Chile

In Chile, political leaders and journalists rely on statistics much more pervasively than in Argentina. However, they are used in a selective manner that often emphasizes the class dimensions of crime. Many interviewees I spoke with in 2015 explained that crime (mostly theft) is higher in the more well-off neighborhoods of Santiago and has become increasingly violent. This perspective was mirrored in the news coverage. For example, on July 1, 2015, the organizer of a protest against crime explained: "There are neighborhoods like Lo Barnechea [a well-off neighborhood] where violent robbery is strongly increasing."[7] As the homicide rate in Chile is relatively low (see table 1.1), victimization surveys are the most relied upon sources for crime statistics.

In particular, the nongovernmental organization Citizen Peace produces the most frequently referenced victimization surveys. These surveys have the advantage of being longitudinal (and use the same question over time). However, the survey's weaknesses include that: in its first years it was not national; it is often conducted by phone (which is less reliable than the in-person method used in later polls); and it continues to include both criminal acts and *attempted* criminal acts (Dammert 2009, 231). Increasingly, most notably since 1999, the media are producing their own victimization polls with greater (or unpublished) methodological weaknesses (Cordero 2009a, 81–82; Dammert 2009, 233). In any case, the media emphasize those aspects of the polls that show an increase in crime, downplay the broader context of this increase (Dammert 2009, 232–233), and emphasize crimes that occur in the more economically well-off neighborhoods of Santiago.[8] Theft and robbery are also often portrayed as violent.

Yet the statistical evidence to support these evaluations is uneven. For example, the Chilean government's National Urban Survey of Citizen Security (ENUSC) found that all crimes decreased significantly from 2003 to 2014, including violent crimes. For example, robbery with violence or intimidation decreased from 8.9 percent of crimes in 2003 to 3.9 percent in 2014, although they note an increase in 2015 to 4.6 percent (ENUSC 2014, 9; 2015, 26). ENUSC does not disaggregate its results based on socioeconomic class.

In contrast, Citizen Peace's 2015 victimization poll finds that violent versus nonviolent robbery remained stable between 2004 and 2015, with approximately 30 percent being violent (Citizen Peace 2015, 12). Thus we immediately see a significant discrepancy between the numbers offered by ENUSC and Citizen Peace both in terms of dynamics and proportion. Citizen Peace suggests that violent crimes are six times more common than does ENUSC. Unlike ENUSC, Citizen Peace disaggregates by socioeconomic class, but its results are somewhat contradictory. It notes that Santiago's wealthier neighborhoods had lower levels of victimization than the rest of the city from 2010 to 2015 (Citizen Peace 2015, 13). For example, in October 2015 the victimization rate in the northeastern (wealthier) neighborhoods of Santiago was 31.6 percent and in the southeastern (poorer) neighborhoods it was 41.2 percent (Citizen Peace 2015, 13). Yet when sorted by "socioeconomic level," victimization appeared to be consistently higher for the upper and middle class until 2015, when there was "a significant reduction in the percentage of victimizations (from 48.7 percent to 36.8 percent and 44.8 percent to 39.5 percent, respectively)" for "high and middle levels" (Citizen Peace 2015, 4, 9). Victimization for the "low levels" was 36.6 percent in 2014 and 39 percent in 2015 (Citizen Peace 2015, 9).

To some extent, the variation in these two polls reflects the limited reliability of victimization studies and the choices made regarding what questions to ask and how to present the data. Indeed, both Chilean national victimization polls show two to three times the rate of victimization found by LAPOP or the World Values Survey (see tables 1.1 and 1.2). However, this also highlights that, even when statistics are used to confirm citizens' fear of crime, they can be used a manner that reflects, rather than challenges, existing biases.

In sum, crime is generally but not consistently higher in Latin America than in Europe, the Antipodes, the United States, and Canada. Yet the statistics we have available are open to significant interpretation. The stories told by the media and political leaders shape the types of crimes deemed problematic and their saliency as a policy issue. However, the public's "feeling" of insecurity (Garland 2001, 10; Roberts et al. 2003, 12) is more important to punitive populism than crime is.

INSECURITY

In many countries the terms "insecurity," "security," "citizen security," and "public security" are used in media and colloquially to refer to crime, particularly homicide, robbery, and theft. This conflation is consistent with punitive populist rhetoric that draws on the public's feeling of insecurity, identifies the problem as crime (homicide, robbery, theft), and the answer to be more police, greater police powers, and tougher laws. Thus it might appear redundant in this chapter to separate crime from insecurity. Yet there are three important reasons to do so. First, there is no necessary connection between insecurity and crime. Second, there is a stronger correlation between insecurity and socioeconomic issues. Third, there is a particular relationship between insecurity and the media.

INSECURITY AND CRIME

Public opinion and victimization polls as well as homicide rates reveal a significant disconnection between levels of crime and perception of insecurity (see tables 1.1 and 1.2). To begin, whereas some countries in Latin America have homicide and victimization rates similar to those in the United States or even Canada, Europe, and the Antipodes, the perception of insecurity is significantly higher across Latin America. Thus while crime is a very important problem in some countries and in some subnational areas of Latin America, the perception of insecurity is a far more pervasive problem.

Moreover, as tables 1.1 and 1.2 reveal, the countries with the highest homicide and victimization rates are not necessarily the countries with the highest perceptions of insecurity. Table 1.1 shows that Chile has one of the lowest victimization rates in the Americas and the second lowest homicide rate (both similar to Canada). Yet, at 42.2 percent, Chile's perception of insecurity is quite high (Canada is at 22.0 percent and the United States is at 27.4 percent). If we compare Argentina and Honduras we might conclude that robbery and theft are more correlated with perceptions of insecurity. Statistics in table 1.1 show Argentina to have the fourth lowest homicide rates in the Americas (after Canada, Chile, and the United States), but high rates of victimization (robbery/theft) of 24.4 percent. Perceived insecurity in Argentina is high, at 46.2 percent, just above that of Chile (42.2 percent). In contrast, Honduras has the highest homicide rate in the region (and one of the highest in the world), yet Hondurans' responses to surveys show relatively low victimization at 18.3 percent, and perceptions of insecurity are considerably lower than in Argentina or Chile at 38.6 percent. Yet, of course, the conclusion that victimization rates determine perceptions of insecurity does not explain Chile or Costa Rica, where both victimization and homicide rates are relatively low, but the perception of insecurity is high (42.2 percent and 48.7 percent, respectively). These numbers may indicate other potential conclusions.

It is possible that perceptions of insecurity are higher with changes in the type or quantity of crime. For example, in Chile while overall victimization rates have decreased from 2003 to 2014 by 42 percent, theft increased from 7.8 percent 2013 to 8.7 percent in 2014 (ENUSC 2014, 5–7). As theft increased, a Chilean government public opinion poll reported an increase in respondents' fear that they will become a victim of crime from 38.3 percent in 2013 to 43.8 percent in 2014 (ENUSC 2014, 22). In contrast, for citizens in Honduras, high levels of violence may have become normalized and this might contribute to lower perceptions of insecurity. In sum, there is no necessary correlation between crime rates and public feelings of insecurity.

INSECURITY AND SOCIOECONOMIC ISSUES

In contrast, many scholars and international organizations argue that insecurity is more highly correlated with socioeconomic and cultural anxieties than crime (Chevigny 2003, 79; Dammert 2012; Dammert and Malone 2006; Garland 2001; Roberts et al. 2003, 68; Seri 2012, 69; Wacquant 2009, 4; UNDP 2013a, 2013b), yet polls assume or structure questions that presuppose crime to be the cause. These studies all point in various ways to how neoliberal social and economic restructuring (privatization, deregulation, and cuts to state spending, especially to social services) as well as what Wendy Brown (2006) calls the "neoliberal political rationality" (work and governance organized around market rationality and citizens' individual responsibility for "self-care") have contributed to increased public anxieties. These anxieties include the following issues: precarious job situations; decreased access to quality social services such as health, education, and pensions; financial insecurity (loss of savings and property); restructuring of the family household; increased individualism/loss of egalitarian values/decreased interpersonal trust and trust in authority; and technological changes that have affected the shaping of news and democratic dialogue (see introduction; Chevigny 2003, 79; Dammert 2012; Dammert and Malone 2006; Garland 2001; Goldstein 2012; Müller 2016; Roberts et al. 2003, 68; Seri 2012, 69; Wacquant 2009, 4).

In addition, neoliberal economic polices have produced increased socioeconomic inequality, which has been shown to increase both homicides and victimization rates (Ostry, Loungani, and Furceri 2016; Fajnzylber, Lederman, and

Loayza 1998, 2002; Seri 2012, 69). According to the World Bank's GINI index (where 0 is perfect equality and 100 is perfect inequality), Argentina went from 42.8 in 1986, when only some neoliberal economic restructuring had occurred, to 53.8 in 2002 when President Menem had completed extensive restructuring. Chile implemented neoliberal economic reforms during the Pinochet regime and entered democracy in 1990 with a GINI index of 57.3 (which has since remained stable). Similarly, the United States has seen inequality increase from 37.7 in 1986 to 41.1 in 2013, and Australia went from 31.3 in 1981 to 34.9 in 2010. In comparison, Norway and Sweden have implemented far fewer neoliberal economic reforms and had scores of 25.9 and 27.3, respectively, in 2012.[9]

These studies have influenced the work of international organizations such as the United Nations Development Programme (UNDP). The term "citizen security" is commonly used in Latin America to refer to crime control. However, the UNDP draws on its definition of human security to redefine it as "consisting of the protection of a basic nucleus of rights, including the right to life, respect for the physical and material integrity of the whole person, and his or her right to have a dignified life. . . . Thus lack of work, poverty, inequality or lack of liberties, to name a few examples, are direct obstacles to peaceful coexistence and citizen security" (UNDP 2013b, 5). Other international organizations working on citizen security in Latin America, such as the International Centre for the Prevention of Crime (ICPC), the Washington Office on Latin America, Inter-Peace, and the International Development Research Centre (IDRC), use similarly broad definitions.[10]

Indeed, if we expand our understanding of insecurity beyond crime, we find significantly higher public anxiety around socioeconomic issues. For example, whereas the World Values Survey found perceptions of insecurity (defined in relation to crime) in Argentina and Chile to be at 44 percent and 40.2 percent, respectively, the public is much more worried about job security (45.2 percent and 56.1 percent) and the education of their children (47.4 percent and 65.1 percent) (see table 1.3). This applies even more to the cases of Mexico, Brazil, and Peru. In the United States, Europe, and Antipodes, although the overall numbers are lower, concerns for socioeconomic issues are also significantly higher than perceived insecurity (see tables 1.2 and 1.3). For example, the perception of insecurity in the United States is 16.4 percent (see table 1.2), but worries about job insecurity affect 40.6 percent of respondents (see table 1.3). Moreover, in many countries, people's experience with crime occurs at a similar rate to their experience with "police/military interference in private life." This was the case for Argentina (15.8/13.2 percent), Brazil (12.6/19.4 percent), Mexico (20.2/19.6 percent), the United States (8.4/8.0 percent), the Netherlands (3.6/2.5 percent), Germany (4.2/7.9 percent), and Spain (5.2/5.5 percent) (see table 1.3).

TABLE 1.3: Socioeconomic and Other Anxieties

Country	Worry about joblessness, % (year)[1]	Worry about education, % (year)[2]	Inadequate health care, % (year)[3]	Lack of money, % (year)[4]	Police/military interference in private life, % (year)[5]	GINI coefficient (2005–2013)[6]
Latin America						
Argentina	45.2 (2013)	47.4 (2013)	12.8 (2013)	18.1 (2013)	13.2 (2013)	43.6
Brazil	64.4 (2014)	82.0 (2014)	22.0 (2014)	19.4 (2014)	14.0 (2014)	52.7
Chile	56.1 (2011)	65.1 (2011)	23.0 (2011)	20.3 (2011)	9.4 (2011)	50.8
Mexico	90.6 (2012)	92.0 (2012)	30.6 (2012)	44.3 (2012)	19.6 (2012)	48.1
Peru	84.1 (2012)	82.8 (2012)	36.6 (2012)	34.1 (2012)	6.7 (2012)	45.3
Uruguay	59.5 (2011)	64.3 (2011)	16.7 (2011)	17.3 (2011)	9.2 (2011)	41.3

Sources: World Values Survey, "Online Data Analysis," accessed June 8, 2016, http://www.worldvaluessurvey.org. UNDP, Human Development Report 2015, accessed June 8, 2016, http://report.hdr.undp.org/.

1. Question: "To what degree are you worried about the following situations? Losing my job or not finding a job." Percentages shown are combined responses of "Very much" and "A great deal." From World Values Survey.
2. Question: "To what degree are you worried about the following situations? Not being able to give my children a good education." Percentages shown are combined responses of "Very much" and "A great deal. From World Values Survey.
3. Question: "In the last 12 months, how often have you or your family: Gone without medicine or medical treatment that you needed?" Percentages shown are combined responses of "Very much" and "A great deal." From World Values Survey.

The challenge with these broader socioeconomic definitions of insecurity is that the solutions they imply are in direct opposition to neoliberal economic policies that advocate for a smaller state and less public investment in social services. As discussed in the introduction, definitions of insecurity as crime and punitive populism as the solution for crime, while more costly than social programs and rehabilitation (Waller 2008, xvi), are more compatible with the practice of neoliberalism and the role it envisions for the state. Thus the very definition of insecurity and its appropriate solutions is highly politicized and shaped in part by one's preferred economic model.

INSECURITY AND THE MEDIA

Numerous studies and political leaders have identified the mass media as responsible for constructing citizens' feelings of insecurity (Garland 2001; Green 2008; Roberts et al. 2003; Seri 2012; Wacquant 2009; Walsh 2015). For example, Loïc

Country	Worry about joblessness, % (year)[1]	Worry about education, % (year)[2]	Inadequate health care, % (year)[3]	Lack of money, % (year)[4]	Police/military interference in private life, % (year)[5]	GINI coefficient (2005–2013)[6]
Europe/United States/Antipodes						
Australia	37.2 (2012)	37.9 (2012)	9.1 (2012)	12.7 (2012)	3.3 (2012)	34.0
Germany	32.4 (2013)	31.1 (2013)	3.7 (2013)	3.8 (2013)	7.9 (2013)	30.6
Netherlands	17.9 (2012)	12.0 (2012)	1.8 (2012)	3.5 (2012)	2.5 (2012)	28.9
New Zealand	34.0 (2011)	30.1 (2011)	11.8 (2011)	14.7 (2011)	5.9 (2011)	n/a
Spain	64.4 (2011)	51.3 (2011)	3.7 (2011)	14.5 (2011)	5.5 (2011)	35.8
United States	40.6 (2011)	35.1 (2011)	20.8 (2011)	21.6 (2011)	8.0 (2011)	41.1

4. Question: "In the last 12 months, how often have you or your family: Gone without a cash income." Percentages shown are combined responses of "Very much" and "A great deal." From World Values Survey.
5. Question: "How frequently do the following things occur in your neighborhood? Police or military interfere with people's private life." Percentages shown are combined responses of "Very much" and "A great deal." From World Values Survey.
6. Gini coefficient is from 0 to 100, where 0 represents absolute equality and 100 is extreme inequality. From UNDP.

Wacquant, in his study of the United States and Europe, maintains that media amplify public insecurity and focus it on crime "animated with martial images and broadcast to saturation by the commercial media" (2009, 2). In regard to Latin America, one UNDP report states: "Mass media has a crucial responsibility in transforming public perceptions about insecurity and offering legitimate and timely mechanisms for addressing it. Countries require media professionals that avoid sensationalism and the stigmatization of vulnerable groups—youths in particular. In order to achieve this, investigative journalism—that contextualizes the facts presented, while fully respecting the principles of media ethics, such as the presumption of innocence—is crucial" (UNDP 2013b, 15). Similarly a survey from LAPOP found: "Attention to the news is also related to feelings of insecurity; those who are more exposed to the news are more likely to report higher levels of insecurity. . . . The news media often portrays crime stories in a way that can heighten feelings of insecurity among viewers. The results here suggest that the media in fact plays a role in stoking fears of crime across the region" (Maldonado and Rodríguez 2014, 37).

To help remedy this situation, in 2011 InterPeace organized a regional forum for journalists on how to cover crime. Studies of punitive populism in the United States, Europe, and Antipodes have argued for a reform of journalistic culture and standards to provide a more pluralistic deliberative platform that treats audiences as citizens not consumers (Green 2008; Pratt 2007; Roberts et al. 2003). Certainly calls to improve the quality of journalistic coverage of crime are important, and some individual journalists have made vital (sometimes heroic) contributions to the public's understanding of criminal justice issues. However, to achieve these changes we need to address the structures and dynamics within which journalists work and state and civil society actors attempt to shape the news. Ultimately, if thought through carefully, media could play an important role in not only reframing the definition of crime and insecurity but also more positively framing solutions that emphasize the socioeconomic remedies, human rights, and preventive measures for crime control advocated in most criminological research.

In sum, public perceptions of insecurity are not synonymous with fear of crime. Socioeconomic issues can also produce public anxieties that political and media leaders might choose, intentionally or not, to reframe as a fear of crime. This is not to say that crime is not an issue in Latin America or countries in other regions. It is clearly very important in some countries and subnational regions. Yet punitive populist answers are unlikely to remedy the situation and, as we will see next, they expand opportunities for police violence.

POLICE VIOLENCE

Punitive populism sometimes explicitly advocates increased police violence, such as Carlos Ruckauf's call to "shoot criminals," as mentioned in the introduction. More often the connection is subtle. For example, Donald Trump's 2015–2016 "law and order" presidential nomination campaign downplayed police violence against African Americans as the acts of a few "bad apples" and, appealing to the "silent majority," pledged to "get rid" of gangs by increasing police powers.[11] In both cases, punitive populist rhetoric supports more police on the street with greater powers and discretion usually aimed at controlling the most marginalized sectors of society. These policies increase opportunities for police violence. This is not to say that all police officers engage in excessive violence. They do not. Rather such policies increase opportunities, expand the range of acceptable violence, and decrease accountability.

Yet in Latin America, punitive populism has emerged at the same time that national and international actors have been promoting democratization and, within it, corresponding police reforms. A significant challenge in the region is that the population does not trust the police (see table 1.4), which in turn un-

TABLE 1.4: Confidence in the Police, the Courts, and the (national) Government

Country	Police, % (year)[1]	Courts, % (year)[2]	National government, % (year)[3]
Latin America			
Argentina	25.0 (2013)	18.5 (2013)	31.6 (2013)
Brazil	45.0 (2014)	50.6 (2014)	41.0 (2014)
Chile	63.9 (2011)	26.2 (2011)	33.6 (2011)
Mexico	28.4 (2012)	30.8 (2012)	38.7 (2012)
Peru	27.9 (2012)	17.4 (2012)	21.8 (2012)
Uruguay	56.0 (2011)	50.0 (2011)	59 (2011)
Europe/United States/Antipodes[4]			
Australia	82.9 (2012)	58.1 (2012)	30.0 (2012)
Canada	80.8 (2005)	63.1 (2005)	36.7 (2005)
Germany	81.7 (2013)	71.3 (2013)	44.4 (2013)
Netherlands	65.5 (2012)	61.9 (2012)	33.0 (2012)
New Zealand	78. 5 (2011)	60.5 (2011)	44.7 (2011)
Spain	58.7 (2011)	39.7 (2011)	20.7 (2011)
United States	68.3 (2011)	53.8 (2011)	32.6 (2011)

Source: World Values Survey, "Online Data Analysis," accessed June 8, 2016, http://www.worldvaluessurvey.org.

1. Question: "I am going to name a number of organizations. For each one, could you tell me how much confidence you have in them: is it a great deal of confidence, quite a lot of confidence, not very much confidence or none at all?: the police." Percentages shown are combined responses of "A great deal" and "Quite a lot."
2. Question: "I am going to name a number of organizations. For each one, could you tell me how much confidence you have in them: is it a great deal of confidence, quite a lot of confidence, not very much confidence or none at all?: the courts." Percentages shown are combined responses of "A great deal" and "Quite a lot."
3. Question: "I am going to name a number of organizations. For each one, could you tell me how much confidence you have in them: is it a great deal of confidence, quite a lot of confidence, not very much confidence or none at all?: the government (in your nation's capital)." Percentages shown are combined responses of "A great deal" and "Quite a lot."
4. I have excluded Canada from the other tables because it did not participate in the World Values Survey in the most recent 2010–2014 wave.

dermines the ability of police to resolve crimes and contributes to public support in favor of replacing the police with military, paramilitary, private security, or even vigilantism (Müller 2016; Goldstein 2012). Often under the label of providing "citizen security," police reform projects in the region aim to professionalize police forces through, among other things, improving their investigation skills, relationship with the community, and accountability (e.g., Hinton 2006; Ungar 2011; UNDP 2013b). The goal is that together these changes will increase the effectiveness and legitimacy of the police by changing their practices and thus improving citizens' direct experience with them.

However, most people do not have direct experience with the police or the criminal justice system. Instead, as Justice Tankebe (2010) argues, in fact citizens' collective *perception* of the police is a stronger indicator of trust and legitimacy. Perception may come from word of mouth but more often from the mass media. Both sources of collective perception are shaped by the expected role of the police in democracy and the place of police violence within it. Thus citizens can have a high degree of trust or confidence in a police force regardless of the levels of violence used by the police if: (1) public knowledge of the violence is limited primarily to those directly affected; or (2) police use of violence does not exceed the level a particular society deems as acceptable.

As Neil L. Whitehead explains, "Violence is always a matter of degree, intensity, and culturally competent judgment, which constructs such vehement actions as violent" (2004a, 63). As he explains, the term has connotations of illegitimacy, but whether an act of violence is considered by a given society as legitimate or illegitimate depends on the cultural context and, he notes, mass media contribute to this cultural understanding (Whitehead 2004b, 11–17).

Moreover, as discussed in the introduction, police violence has always existed as part of democracy everywhere. Ideally, liberal democracy limits police violence through institutions of accountability, such as demands for resignations, trials against officers, official inquiries, ministerial responsibility, police internal affairs departments, civilian oversight bodies, or ombudsmen. Yet all these institutions rest on the premise that police can legitimately use violence (including homicide) against citizens as long as those actions can be justified as within the realm of police discretion.

Of course, many acts of violence or abuse by police will never reach institutions of accountability because they are considered by the affected person, community, or society in general as "normal." This is particularly true for members of marginalized communities in most countries. Society (including police, mass media, and political leaders) may view certain marginalized communities as inherently dangerous or criminal. In turn, members of these marginalized communities may perceive police abuse and violence as a regular part of their interactions with the police. For example, the cofounder of Vancouver Cop Watch, Jennifer Allan, describes the police in the (well-off) West Side of Vancouver as "part of the community," but in the Downtown Eastside (one of the poorest areas of Canada) the organization receives many complaints about police beating people before taking them to jail.[12]

However, despite the subjective nature of police violence, I am not advocating a cultural relativist approach (that might accept police violence as part of a country's culture). Nor do I view policing in the Global North (or any extant democracy) as the ideal to strive for. Rather I hold that it is important to understand current forms of police violence in a given country and the public debates (or lack of debate) regarding these levels of violence, in order to find the opportunities and innovations specific to that country that will most likely reduce violence.

Statistics on police violence and how (or if) they are used in the media can contribute to whether dominant narratives extol the police as the answer to crime (extending their powers) or favor nonpolice solutions and human rights. That is, I am less interested in police violence as an outcome or measure of punitive populism and more interested in how knowledge and the construction of knowledge around police violence can support punitive voices or hold them to account. Below, I assess statistics on police violence in Argentina and Chile. The aim is not to sensationalize but to bring police violence (and thus human rights) into the discussion of crime, security, and punitive populism. The most different comparison reveals two similar challenges. The first concerns the availability of statistics on police violence. The second is that neoliberal media systems favor a positive image of the police and thus have less journalistic interest in statistics on police violence, even if available.

Argentina

High levels of police violence in Argentina are widely acknowledged and often criticized by the public, civil society, mass media, and political leaders. Police violence includes arbitrary arrests, beatings, torture, arbitrary killings, and disappearances. The Coordinator against Police and Institutional Repression (CORREPI) reports 4,644 people killed by security forces in Argentina between 1983 and 2015 (CORREPI 2015, 9), with 52 percent of those occurring in the city and province of Buenos Aires (CORREPI 2015, 11–12).[13] Similarly, the Center for Legal and Social Studies (CELS), another Argentine civil society organization, reports 3,091 cases in the Metropolitan Region of Buenos Aires from 1996 to 2014 (CELS 2015, 269). For comparison, Killed by Police, a U.S. civil society organization, reports 3,093 police killings in the United States from May 1, 2013, to June 9, 2016.[14] Globally, few other civil society organizations consistently collect public statistics on police killings.

In Argentina, each province has its own police force. The Argentine Federal Police (PFA) are used for the national territory and, until 2017, the Autonomous City of Buenos Aires. From 2010 to 2017, the Autonomous City of Buenos Aires had an additional police force, the Metropolitan Police, but in 2017 it was combined with parts of the PFA to form a single Buenos Aires City Police. The military Gendarmería (Border Patrol) and Prefectura (Coast Guard) are sometimes used as additional federal police forces.

Provincial police forces are responsible for 52 percent of police-perpetrated deaths, which is not surprising given that these forces comprise more police officers than the other forces combined. The Argentine Federal Police are responsible for 10.42 percent of deaths, and the Metropolitan Police (2010–2017), which only operated in a limited number of neighborhoods in the city of Buenos Aires, were responsible for 17 deaths (0.37 percent) (CORREPI 2015, 14–15). Most deaths are the result of arbitrary police shootings (46 percent) or occur in police custody (39 percent), and the majority of victims are twenty-five years old or younger (52 percent) (CORREPI 2015, 10–11). Since 1995, security forces have been responsible for the deaths of 70 people at protests, most during the economic and political crisis of 2001–2002 (45) but 19 occurred from 2003 to 2015 (CORREPI 2015, 16). Over 200 people have been forcibly "disappeared" by security forces in Argentina since 1983 (CORREPI 2015, 10).

The Provincial Commission for Memory (CPM) registers 1,136 victims of 4,987 incidents of torture or mistreatment by security services officials in 2013–2014 (CPM 2015, 131). Many recorded incidents of torture or mistreatment pertain to prison conditions, but its category of "physical aggressions" is broader. It includes acts such as hitting, kicking, burning, electrical prod, sexual abuse, dry and wet submarines, and humiliating or degrading positions (CPM 2013, 126; 2015, 132). In this category most cases of torture or mistreatment by security services officials occur in prisons (71.9 percent of those interviewed by the National Register of Cases of Torture and/or Mistreatment, RNTS, in 2013–2014), however, police were involved in 26.1 percent of cases (CPM 2015, 131).[15] When police were involved, 56 percent of incidents occur during arrest and 44 percent while held in police custody (CPM 2015, 132).

The public repudiation of police violence in Argentina has its roots in two key experiences. First, there is a near consensus in Argentina that the last military dictatorship (1976–1983) was wrong and that police played a role in the violence and human rights abuses of the period. Police ran approximately sixteen to twenty-two clandestine detention centers, many police stations were used as transitory holding locations for those in the process of disappearing (CONADEP 1984; Vallespir 2002, 44). Police were often responsible for the disappearances, and they participated in torture. As of 2016, 865 police (provincial and federal forces) have been accused of committing human rights abuses during the dictatorship.[16] At the end of the military regime, chants during public protests included, "Policía Federal, la desgracia nacional" (Federal Police, national disgrace) (Andersen 2002, 292). The public, media, and political actors often condemn excessive police violence as a continuation of the rejected violence of the dictatorship. In 2013, only 25 percent of Argentines had confidence in the police, and this proportion has remained relatively stable since the return of democracy in 1983 (see table 1.4).

Second, in the 1990s, watchdog journalism contributed, with the work of leading social movement organizations, notably CORREPI and CELS, to exposing the ongoing violence and corruption of the police, particularly the Buenos Aires Provincial Police. This will be discussed more throughout the book, but it included critical public attention on police involvement in crime, disappearances, and arbitrary killings. Highly mediatized and emblematic cases contributed to police reforms aimed at reducing police violence, especially in the late 1990s and early 2000s.

Paradoxically, however, this rejection of police violence lies with public support for greater police presence and discretion in combating insecurity and crime. This has included strong support for political leaders who advocate for police violence, such as Carlos Ruckauf (governor of the province of Buenos Aires 1999–2002) and Luis Patti (ex-police officer, mayor of Escobar 1995–2003, elected to Congress in 2005, and in prison since 2011 for human rights abuses committed during the dictatorship). More recently, Daniel Scioli (governor of the province of Buenos Aires 2007–2015) and President Mauricio Macri (2015–) both went as far as suspending the democratic process in states of emergency in order to quickly increase the numbers and powers of police on the street.[17] Some researchers note a moderate increase in punitive populism (what CELS calls "punitive demagoguery") from 2007 to 2012 and a significant increase from 2013 to 2014 (CELS 2015, 250). Others have found a more consistent increase from 2001 to 2012 (Seri and Kubal 2018). Both time frames correspond to the unfolding of neoliberal media reforms. The mass media, state, and civil society practices explored in this book aim, in part, to explain this seemingly contradictory public perception of police violence and the contributing role of neoliberal media reforms.

Chile

Police violence in Chile, in contrast to Argentina, is a relatively new topic of public debate in democracy. It gained attention during the student protests in 2006 and 2011–2012. These protests prompted some civil society organizations (and since 2010, a new state institution, the National Institute for Human Rights) to begin collecting information on police violence in both protest management and crime control. However, the statistics remain significantly less than statistics available in Argentina.

Chile has only two police forces and both are national: the Carabineros de Chile and the Investigative Police (Policía de Investigaciones, PDI). The Carabineros are the uniformed police, the most numerous, and the only force involved in crime prevention. What we know about police violence in Chile is as follows. Unlike Argentina, Chile has no civil society organizations that collect statistics on the number of people killed by the police. There are qualitative descriptions of individual cases of excessive police violence leading to death. For example, on August 25, 2011, a Carabinero officer fatally shot sixteen-year-old Manuel Gutiérrez, who was watching a protest in Santiago. And on January 3, 2008, a Carabinero fatally shot twenty-three-year-old Matías Catrileo, a Mapuche university student, who was participating in a land occupation with members of his community in the region of Araucanía. In both cases the individual officers responsible for pulling the trigger were sentenced in military court and asked to resign from the Carabineros. Although we have no statistics that could tell us how common police killings are, most human rights organizations emphasize the more prevalent problem of persistent and pervasive police abuse and torture, particularly against protesters, those held in police custody, and members of vulnerable communities, such as students, workers, indigenous people, and common criminals (notably from the lower classes) (CECT 2013; Diego Portales University 2015; INDH 2015a, 2015b, 2015c; Observatorio Ciudadano 2008).

In Argentina, civil society organizations derive statistics on police abuse primarily from mass media reports and, for some organizations, a close working relationship with vulnerable communities. In Chile, most mass media do not publish information on police abuse unless it is unavoidable, either because there is photographic evidence from a reputable source or because the police admit to it. Thus human rights organizations in Chile cannot rely on the mass media. Most organizations that attempt to assess the state of policing in Chile collect information from those affected who approach their organization with incidents, from their members' own observations, or by using numbers from the courts (which of course only capture those cases brought to the courts). Most reports provide qualitative descriptions of individual cases of police abuse and torture, not statistics.

However, some researchers have taken on the laborious task of putting together statistics from court documents. Claudio Fuentes found 3,877 legal complaints by citizens against police filed in courts just for the central part of Chile (65 percent of the country's population) from March 1990 to December 2000, with the number of cases increasing significantly from 1990 (194) to 1998 (494) (Fuentes 2005, 58). The annual report of the Human Rights Center at the Diego Portales University found that although the number of cases of "unneccesary violence" or "torture and ill-treatment" by police from 1998 to 2005 decreased, this likely reflected a period of adjustment for the police to the new penal procedures reform, which completed its implementation in 2005 and included increased civilian oversight of the police (2015, 128–132). From 2006 to 2014 the number of cases significantly increased again. Cases of "torture and ill-treatment" brought to civilian courts went from 14 in 2006 to 204 in 2016 (Diego Portales 2015, 133). Cases of unnecessary police violence reported to military courts went from 675 in 2004 to 1,797 in 2011 (Diego Portales 2015, 134). Similarly, the National

Institute of Human Rights conducted its own inspections of people held in police custody in 29 police stations across the country and found that while 34.33 percent reported arrests with violence in 2013, reports rose to 82.75 percent in 2014 (INDH 2015b, 59). Unfortunately, the statistics available before and after the penal procedures reform are not exactly comparable but they do show trends, which the study by Diego Portales University Center for Human Rights triangulates with extensive interviews with public prosecutors and judges who also note a significant increase in cases of excessive police violence after 2005 (Diego Portales 2015, 132–138).

The interviewees offered some explanations for the increase in cases of police violence. First, beginning in 2007 there was increased mass media, political, and public criticism of the judicial system for being too lenient and letting "criminals" go free. This contributed to the presentation by the Bachelet government of a draft anticrime law called "Short-term Anti-Crime Agenda" (Agenda Corta Antidelincuencia, Law 20.253, 2008, passed into law in 2016), which proposed to increase police powers and decrease judicial oversight. Interviewees described this as a law giving police "confidence" that they had public and political support to apply high levels of abuse (Diego Portales 2015, 135–136). Second, interviewees argued that police became acclimated to the new penal procedures reform and learned that public prosecutors did not in the end have the time and resources, and did not see it as a priority, to provide oversight of police conduct. Finally, the increase in social protests, beginning with the 2006 student protests, contributed to a significant rise in the number of complaints of police abuse noted not only by interviewees but in many human rights reports, including those of the National Institute of Human Rights (INDH 2012; 2015a, 2015b), Amnesty International (2007, 2012), Human Rights Watch (2013), and the Inter-American Commission on Human Rights (2011).

From various sources it can be pieced together that police abuse, perpetrated by the Carabineros and the PDI, consists most commonly of hitting (with fists and batons) and kicking (sometimes by more than one officer and sometimes leading to injuries serious enough to require hospitalization). There are also many reports of sexual abuse, forced undressing, and threats of violence. Other reports mention tear gas fired into confined spaces or directly at people during protests or against members of vulnerable communities such as the Mapuche and people in shantytowns (*poblaciones*) (CECT 2012, 2013; Diego Portales 2015; INDH 2015a, 2015b;). Similarly, reports indicate that tear gas, pellet, and paint pellet gun projectiles were used by police in such a way that the projectiles hit those nearby in the eye, in some cases causing loss of the person's eye. This last issue was the focus of a 2013 student protest, "Marcha de los Tuertos" (The one-eyed march), which demanded a ban on police use of these weapons.[18] Although such accounts are rare, one human rights organization noted that it had contact with youth who had been subjected to wet submarines (head held underwater) and forced to eat their own vomit.[19]

As in Argentina, two key experiences have shaped public perception of police violence in Chile. First, as in Argentina, the police in Chile were involved in the last military regime. The Carabineros participated in the regime's governance through their seats on the National Security Council and Senate. The Carabineros, with the military, were responsible for disappearances in the first few months of the dictatorship. This task was then transferred to the National Intelligence Directorate, which was composed of many Carabineros officers (Maldonado 1990, 22; Policzer 2009, 90). The Carabineros were also responsible for the repression of protests during which police action led to the injury and deaths of hundreds of people (Maldonado 1990, 22).

However, unlike in Argentina, the Chilean population was not united in its initial rejection of the dictatorship. Certainly, the proportion of the population supporting Pinochet has declined over time. In the 1988 plebiscite, approximately 44 percent voted yes to Pinochet's continuation in power. In 2000, a public opinion poll found that 31 percent of Chileans thought Pinochet was "one of the best governors" of the country and by 2015 only 15 percent held this position.[20] Yet, as recently as 2015, a Mass in homage to Pinochet brought together approximately four hundred supporters, including Cristián Labbé (the mayor of Providencia, 1996–2012).[21] Those who support Pinochet view the violence and human rights abuses perpetrated by the regime as unfortunate but legitimate given the perceived threat they faced (from social unrest and the Socialist ideas and policies of Salvador Allende) and the economic improvements achieved. Moreover, throughout the 1990s, political leaders asked those who viewed the violence as illegitimate to reconcile and move on. While there was resistance to these policies, President Patricio Aylwin (1990–1994) declared the transition to democracy "closed" and President Eduardo Frei (1994–2000) emphasized *convivencia* or living together in peace (Phelps 2004; Stern 2010, 16–17).

Second, as we will see throughout the book, the market-based mass media in Chile, in combination with the proactive communications work of the Carabineros, have favored a positive image of the police and have omitted, downplayed, or legitimized their use of violence (Bonner 2013).[22] Social movements have struggled to include alternative perspectives on police violence in mass media debates. Indeed, in 2015 and 2016, the Carabineros, political leaders on the right, and key mass media strongly criticized the National Institute for Human Rights for undermining the legitimacy and work of the police by collecting statistics and reporting on police violence. In 2015 Senator Alberto Espina (National Renovation Party) explained that this work "is an insult to Carabineros and causes enormous damage to the institution."[23] In 2016, the Carabineros' director general, Bruno Villalobos stated (referring to the National Institute of Human Rights): "Organizations with unfounded accusations, all of this has to do with Carabineros actions, it limits them, it restricts their actions."[24] Public confidence in the police is high in Chile compared to other institutions in the country and police in other countries in Latin America (see table 1.4).[25] Yet public confidence in the police is not necessarily synonymous with a police force that is held accountable for its use of violence. Mass media contribute to the public's perception of the appropriate role of the police in crime control and the degree of violence deemed legitimate to achieve this goal.

THE LIMITS OF STATISTICS

At first glance, crime and security appear to be concrete issues that can be corroborated with statistical evidence. Yet when we unpack these concepts and their corresponding statistics we find that they are much more subjective. Moreover, with existing official measures, and in the absence of the work done by dedicated civil society organizations, it is difficult to statistically show the connection between police violence and proposed definitions of and solutions to crime and insecurity. In this manner, the available statistics on crime, security, and police violence require that interested parties construct a story or narrative. These narratives choose particular frames for understanding the problem of crime and security and corresponding solutions. They contain what Bal (1988) calls structures of attention and inattention, which may include or omit police violence and socioeconomic issues.

Mass media play a central role in the construction of dominant narratives. As a result, they have the potential to act as an important check on punitive populism. However, as this book reveals, the role of the mass media in the provision of accountability and as a platform for civil society voices is shaped by very particular media routines. The media system, combined with the corresponding practices of journalists, state actors, and civil society, affects journalists' selection of facts (see figure I.1). These choices, in turn, have consequences for how mass media portray the problems of crime, insecurity, and police violence.

Chapter 2

THE MASS MEDIA'S ROLE IN EMOTIONS AND PUBLIC OPINION

Punitive populism challenges liberal democracy. It places emotion at the center of politics and this lies in direct tension with Enlightenment arguments for rational legal authority as the cornerstone of liberal democracy. Indeed, many populists (punitive or otherwise) contend that this is the problem with liberal democracy; its rational legal authority is elitist and denies a place for emotions and the voice of the masses.

Of course, punitive populism draws on particular types of emotions, such as anger, most notably voiced in the personal accounts of victims whose pain is extrapolated as a collective experience rather than an exception. Punitive populism offers simple solutions that feed our emotional desire for order and revenge (Connolly 1995; Valverde 2006) and provides an outlet for our suppressed aggression (Matravers and Maruna 2005). It also creates a feeling of belonging by borrowing from populism the rhetorical device of dividing society into two irreconcilable groups. On the one hand, "us," "citizens" or "the people" are presented as facing a significant threat from "them," "criminals," or "enemies of the people." Similarly, punitive populism frames the political debate in such a way that a political leader is either "tough on crime" or perceived as "soft on crime"; the latter suggests a lack of care about crime or victims of crime. It is zero sum.

Importantly, punitive populism also articulates and emphasizes the emotion of fear. Fear can correspond to actual crime rates, but not necessarily. For example, crime rates were going down *before* Rudolph Giuliani was elected mayor of New York City in 1993 on a zero-tolerance platform. Similarly, in Latin America, Chile and Uruguay have much higher fear of crime than Honduras and Mexico, yet these latter two countries have among the highest homicide rates in the world (see chapter 1, table 1.1). While crime statistics are notoriously imperfect, especially in Latin America, fear of crime is a separate issue that can emerge from a variety of situations, including socioeconomic anxieties, that are transferred to the more concrete ordering and revenge provided by crime control (Connolly 1995, 42; Dammert 2012; Dammert and Malone 2006; Garland 2001; Walsh 2015). Thus criminologists widely regard punitive populism as a misdiagnosis of the problem (sometimes) and the solution (always), but it provides a place for emotion in politics.

The emotions evoked by punitive populism are rooted in values or morality. George Lakoff contends that, in the case of the United States, support for tough-on-crime rhetoric and policies is based on a "strict father morality" in which (in its pure form) the cure for crime is punishment because it is either in the criminal's self-interest to commit crimes if the costs are low (moral self-interest) or the criminal is simply a bad person (moral essence) (Lakoff 2002, 200–201). Stuart Hall et al. use a similar category of "family, discipline and morality" to describe the arguments in public debate on a crime crisis in Britain (1978, 139). Statistics on which policies actually reduce crime are irrelevant to morality-based discourse (Lakoff 2002, 201). It is an emotional issue, not a rational policy discussion. In this context it becomes much more challenging for a political leader or civil society group to change the conversation to a technical discussion framed in terms of what policies will actually reduce crime (Green 2008, 130–131) or for advocates to raise issues of human rights.

Hence, Tim Newburn and Trevor Jones argue that symbolic politics becomes very important (2005, 77). They posit that when confronted with punitive populism, it is possible for a candidate to support social welfare approaches to address crime and police violence. However, the candidate has to appear tough on crime by using tough-on-crime rhetoric and supporting tough-on-crime policies, at least for symbolic cases. This leads many political leaders on the left, like Mauricio Funes (El Salvador), Bill Clinton (United States), and Tony Blair (United Kingdom) to "compromise" by adopting a combination of repression/tough-on-crime measures with preventive policies—even if in practice the former strategies undermine the latter.

This appears to present a significant conundrum for liberal democracy. How can the emotions of the many be included in democratic debates without these emotions eroding democracy? I propose that rethinking the media system and its resulting communicational dynamics holds an important part of the solution.

The mass media ideally play a number of key roles in balancing emotion and rational legal authority. First, they ideally offer a forum for debate where the emotions of punitive populism can be expressed rather than stifled. As Ian Loader (2011) points out, excluding public emotion from criminal justice debates, as some scholars of punitive populism support (Campbell 2008; Lacey 2008), could potentially lead to resentment and backlash, further fueling punitive populism. Thus the public expression of emotion is important to democracy. Yet this emotion cannot go unchecked if democratic debate is to prevail. The debate presented in the media is ideally a *full* debate. That is, not only are punitive populist emotions presented, but so too are contending emotions of solidarity, understanding, care, nurture, and collectivism, as well as an array of rational legal diagnoses and solutions to the problem. That is, as Loader (2011) stresses, "the public" cannot be essentialized in a Hobbesian manner as naturally punitive. It is not. Public emotion and rationality are necessarily pluralistic. Mass media should ideally reflect this diversity.

Second, mass media also ideally provide a forum for discursive accountability (Bonner 2014a, ch. 2). That is, both watchdog journalism and the plurality of sources used by journalists should allow media to expose (or shame) wrongdoers or problematic ideas, require the wrongdoer or espouser of such ideas to answer for the wrongdoing or ideas, and, if applicable, advocate appropriate consequences (or punishment). In this way, for example, if a punitive populist policy incites greater police violence, this violence would ideally be fully exposed and connected to punitive populism; advocates of punitive populism would need to answer for the consequences of their policies; and, if deemed relevant, space would be provided for the articulation, advocacy, and debate of appropriate consequences or punishments, such as a change in policy, police reform, resignation(s), or electoral defeat. Certainly mass media-based discursive accountability does not guarantee the elimination of punitive populism but it may reduce the risks by holding emotions, ideas, and policies to account for their consequences.

To be sure, the mass media do not play this ideal role fully in any country. However, particular mass media structures and practices can shape how close or how far from this ideal a given media system is situated. As the above ideals highlight, key questions when assessing a media system's role in encouraging or dissuading punitive populism are:

1. How diverse are the sources used by journalists?
2. How homogeneous or pluralistic is their representation of public opinion? and
3. What are the possibilities for journalists to engage in watchdog journalism?

Of course, journalists' practices are not entirely individual choices. Their choices usually reflect the media system within which they work (discussed later in this chapter and in chapters 3 and 4). The media system may favor journalists' use of more or fewer sources and certain representations of public opinion over others; the system may encourage or discourage watchdog journalism. The media system will also affect *how* state and civil society actors engage with the media and *which* state and civil society actors are more likely to receive media coverage. Journalists are more likely to prioritize some sources (often punitive voices) when journalists use fewer sources, face greater time pressures, and have weaker incentives to pursue watchdog journalism. Such a media system also encourages state and civil society actors to engage the media using professional public relations (PR) and appeals to punitive emotions. This is because PR is quick and cheap for journalists (which cuts costs), and emotions provide drama that attracts large audiences (which increases revenue). This type of engagement with the media will favor some state and civil society actors over others. Taken together, these mass media, state, and civil society practices both favor and represent public opinion that supports punitive populism. These practices will be examined in progressively more detail throughout this book, assessing the influence of neoliberal media policies and drawing increasingly from the case studies of Argentina and Chile.

THE CONSTRUCTION OF PUBLIC OPINION

Public opinion is central to punitive populism. Its claim to democratic legitimacy is premised (rightly or wrongly) on the idea that public opinion is calling for a "tough" response to crime. Public opinion polls often appear to reinforce this perception of public demand. For example, since 2004, public opinion polls have shown that Latin Americans view crime or security as the second most pressing issue facing their countries after the economy. In recent years, the importance of security has been increasing and is now almost on par with the economy (Maldonado and Rodríguez 2014). In 2014, 55 percent of Latin Americans identified "increasing punishment for criminals" as the most appropriate response to crime. In Argentina support was at the regional average and in Chile it was higher at 59 percent (Layton and Rodríguez 2014, 95–96). Indeed, a 2015 poll found that 50.4 percent of Chileans saw human rights as impediments to crime control.[1] Across the region, support for punitive policies increased 8.2 percent between 2012 and 2014 (Layton and Rodríguez 2014, 95).

In most countries, public opinion matters as a factor in public policymaking. Yet its weight, relative to the analyses of experts, varies between policymakers and political systems (e.g., Burstein 2003; Jacobs and Shapiro 2000; Lacey 2010; Page and Shapiro 1983). For punitive populists, as for populists generally, public opinion is fundamental. It is the basis on which punitive populists claim greater democratic legitimacy than those elected representatives who choose policy based on "elite" (or expert) ideas. Punitive populist leaders might ignore expert analysis because they actually believe that public opinion is correct (Bottoms 1995) or they may know that the expert analysis is correct but ignore it because the leader believes punitive rhetoric and policies will win votes (Roberts et al. 2003). In either case, expert analysis, especially from those within the criminal justice system, is discredited in punitive populist discourses, based partly on the argument that the institutions they represent have failed to provide security. This is reflected in public opinion polls in many countries with punitive populism that show a low level of confidence in the courts and sometimes the police (see chapter 1, table 1.4). This lack of trust in state institutions is attributed in studies of punitive populism to a decline in deference as a result of "late modernity" in established democracies (Garland 2001; Nevitte 1996). In Latin America this low level of trust in the criminal justice system is more often perceived as a reflection of low public trust in democracy generally or a legacy of the complicity of these institutions in the previous authoritarian regime or both. In either case, it is argued that a lack of trust in the state contributes to the rise of punitive populism.

Instead, punitive populism places public opinion as the driver of criminal justice policy. Rather than speak on *behalf* of the people, punitive populists claim to speak *with* the people by drawing on evidence of public opinion demand (Pratt 2007, 33–34). Thus, punitive populists purport to be profoundly democratic as they represent the will of "the people" or the "silent majority." The leader frames those who oppose the leader's interpretation of the popular will as opposing "the people" (Laclau 2007; Peruzzotti 2013). In this manner public opinion is used to expand "official discretion by immobilizing potential opposition" (Edelman 1977, 55).

Yet public opinion is never homogeneous or static. It is always diverse, multifaceted, and dynamic, shifting in response to new information and events. Thus public opinion in the singular is necessarily constructed, as much as it is consulted (Hall 1980). Understanding *how* public opinion can be constructed in the mass media to support punitive populism is vital to changing this pattern.

MEDIA'S INFLUENCE ON PUBLIC OPINION

To be sure, in many countries the mass media's role in creating fear of crime has been overstated. In 2015, Argentina's largest media group, Clarín, aired an advertisement on its television channel, in response to critiques from the government that it was causing people to fear crime. The ad began: "We told you it was going to rain, but you didn't bring your umbrella." It is true. People do not always believe what the media say.

The idea that media control what people think was popular in the early twentieth century and is referred to in media studies as the "hypodermic needle" model (Jowett and O'Donnell 2012, 166; Lasswell 1927). However, communications scholars had widely dismissed this theory by the mid-twentieth century in favor of the "minimal effects" model (Lazarfeld, Berelson, and Gaudet 1948; Scheufele and Tewksbury 2007). In reaction to the hypodermic needle model, scholars argued that in fact the media have a very minimal effect on public opinion. People's opinions are more affected by their personal relationships and conversations; media simply activate and reinforce preexisting opinions or ideas. Beginning in the 1970s, scholars began to find the minimal effects model to be insufficient. The media, they argue, do have an important influence on public opinion beyond activating and reinforcing preexisting ideas, but they do not completely control public opinion. The relationship between media and public opinion is more nuanced. In particular, media studies have reached a general consensus that the media affect public opinion in three key ways: agenda setting, priming, and framing (e.g., Iyengar 1996; McCombs and Shaw 1972; Scheufele and Tewksbury 2007).

First, the mass media affect public opinion in the sense that they can set the agenda of public debate and thus the issues facing their country that the public are most likely to identify as most important. The issues or stories they choose to place on the front page, in lengthy articles, in large broadcasting segments on television and radio, and disseminate widely through social media, set the agenda regarding what issues the public and political leaders will be talking about. Individuals may agree or disagree with what happened or how the mainstream media covered the topic but this is the issue they are talking about. Journalists ask political leaders to respond as part of these news stories. For example, in 1993, in the United States, despite decreasing crime, coverage of crime increased in the mass media and drew attention to spectacular cases. This contributed to making crime a top concern in public opinion polls and the implementation by political leaders of new laws to fight crime (Patterson 1998, 62; Roberts et al. 2003, 78).

Similarly, the mass media might ignore some topics or minimize their importance by placing them in the back of newspapers, in small articles, or in very brief segments at the end of news broadcasts. These items are less likely to be topics of conversation for the public, and political leaders may not be asked to respond. So, for example, if kidnapping is the front page cover story one day, it is likely the public will be talking about kidnapping and political leaders will be asked what they are doing about kidnapping, as opposed to other crimes or issues (such as police violence) that might be found in smaller news stories.

Priming involves repetition. While agenda setting might mean an issue is headline news one day, priming makes that topic headline news repeatedly over a long period of time (months or even years) and the issue is used again and again to analyze other matters. The topic is likely used as the basis for evaluating political leaders' performance. This frequency leads the public to become familiar with these issues and their importance as problems as well as offering ways for the public to understand or evaluate events, actions, or omissions. For example, if crime is often front page news and is used repeatedly by the mass media as a key issue on which to evaluate political leaders' performances, then, over time, those people with little knowledge on the topic outside the mass media are likely to evaluate crime as one of the most significant issues facing their country and use this as a measure to evaluate political leaders.

Finally, framing involves the way in which media tell stories. That is, news stories are never neutral conveyors of information. The information needs to be presented in a compelling manner that helps the audience interpret the information. This interpretive frame selects and shapes information in a manner that offers the reader a perspective on: the nature of the problem (why one should care about this news item); who the important actors are and how they are involved; and the possible solutions to the problem. Frames can be "thematic" by placing the new information into context (e.g., socioeconomic or historical context, etc.). Frames can also be "episodic" when they focus on the drama of what is happening now and omitting the context (Iyengar 1996). Thus framing involves the details of how a particular news story is told. In contrast, priming refers to the repetition of these frames over a longer time period.

David Green (2008) compared the media framing of a child-on-child homicide in Norway to a similar case in England. In Norway the murder was framed in news stories as a tragic accident in which social workers or health-care workers are assisting those involved to come to terms with the tragedy and prevent such incidents in the future. In contrast, in England, the homicide was framed as another example of an epidemic of out-of-control youth crime to which police are responding, but which requires that political leaders reply with tougher policies and penalties, such as increasing police powers and lowering the minimum age of criminal responsibility. The latter frame, if used repeatedly over time in agenda-setting news items, is more likely than the repetition of the former frame to encourage a public opinion that is open to punitive populism. Indeed, Green (2008) and many other authors (e.g., Lacey 2008; Tonry 2007) find punitive populism to be lower in Norway than in England. Norway and England also have different media systems, which contributed to the contrasting frames.

Of course, agenda setting, priming, and framing do not determine how each individual will respond to these news stories. To affect public opinion, the frames used must resonate with audiences and will not necessarily resonate with all audience members in the same way all the time. Frames are more likely to resonate with audiences when they comprise some or all of the following features (Benford and Snow 2000; Goffman 1974). First, they are familiar. Priming contributes to familiarity, but so does the use of frames that draw on selective aspects of the country's history, societal values, or political culture. The linguist George Lakoff (2002) argues that simple "tough on crime" frames resonate with more people because they appeal to familiar authoritarian family structures, for example, the punitive populist leader as "strict father" figure.

Second, to resonate, frames must be consistent with current and everyday events as well as the recipient's knowledge base. That is, the claims must appear empirically credible. Thus, someone who has been a victim of crime, is an expert in the criminal justice system, or someone who has been a victim of police abuse will use this experience to judge whether or not to accept media frames. Such a person will likely judge media frames differently from the way in which someone with far less experience or empirical knowledge on the topic will. Those with less experience and knowledge will rely more heavily on mass media frames to help them make sense of the problem, the actors, and the solution.

Finally, the credibility of the frame articulator is important to its resonance. Some media outlets and speakers are deemed more credible than others owing to factors such as their status, power, or assumed knowledge. Mass media can also bestow credibility on an actor by including the perspectives of the person or organization in news items and by using positive adjectives to describe the person or organization. Journalists tend to favor the frames used by high-level public officials and those who use their frames (Bennett 1996, 65–67; Gamson and Stuart 1992, 56–57; Gans 2003, 46–47). However, as we will see in chapter 6, it is possible for some civil society organizations to make themselves credible journalistic sources.

Thus, in sum, media affect public opinion on the problems of crime and police violence and their solutions in important but nuanced ways. While possibly affecting agenda setting and priming, the choice and diversity of journalists' sources will certainly determine the array of frames available to them for explaining the problem of crime, offering solutions, and addressing the relative importance of police violence. Yet, what is taken to be public opinion is equally significant in regard to punitive populism.

MEDIA AS A SOURCE OF INFORMATION ON PUBLIC OPINION

Journalists often refer to public opinion in the singular. Thus they construct public opinion using the indicators they use to measure or symbolize it. In turn, most democratic political leaders prefer to provide empirical evidence of public opinion demand to which the leader is simply responding (e.g., Garland 2001, 11–22; Pratt 2007, 13; Roberts et al. 2003, 26, 64). Public opinion polls and mass media news stories are the most common gauge of public opinion support for tough-on-crime policies.

Public opinion polls are used frequently as a tool for assessing what the public thinks about the importance of crime as an issue and the preferred solutions. However, these polls have some significant limitations. At the technical level, the quality of polls is inconsistent and can be affected by choices such as sample size, rate of response and the demographics of respondents, reliance on telephones or internet, the phrasing and order of questions that might favor a particular response, and the omission of some types of questions. Yet even the most technically sophisticated public opinion polls elicit people's *impressions* that are often gleaned from the media and vulnerable to significant change (Green 2008, 14–15; Roberts et al. 2003, 29–32).

Ideally, what is needed is an understanding of people's *informed* opinion. That is, respondents should be given the information they need regarding crime and the possible solutions as well as the benefits and drawbacks of each option. They need to be able to ask questions and deliberate with others. The deliberative poll promoted by Stanford University's Center for Deliberative Democracy is one example of an effort to do this (Fishkin 1995; Green 2008, 244–245). Compared to regular public opinion polls, deliberative polls have revealed informed public opinion to be less punitive (Green 2008, 14; Roberts et al. 2003, 29). Consequently, some scholars view deliberative polls as the antidote to punitive populism (Green 2008; Roberts et al. 2003). Yet collecting informed public opinion is a much more costly and time-consuming task than conducting regular polls and this does not guarantee greater mass media coverage. More commonly the polls that political leaders take to be public opinion and that the mass media publish are quick, cheap, based on impressions, and thus an inaccurate reading of public opinion.

Political leaders often take public opinion to be the dominant views presented in the mass media, especially the views that appear to represent the public. One of the media's ideal roles in democracy is to be a forum for public debate that contributes to the formation of a public opinion (Curran 2005, 120). The media then reflect public opinion to political leaders. Of course, in practice, many citizens' voices are absent in news media stories, although this varies between media systems. Instead, mass media use proxies for public opinion on crime, security, and police violence such as: victims of crime, family members of victims, or witnesses; civil society organizations (e.g., security-focused organizations or human rights organizations); public opinion polls; statements about public opinion; issues evaluated based on current social norms or laws; and interviews with people on the street being used as symbols of public opinion (Hall et al. 1978; McLeod and Hertog 1992, 260; Roberts et al. 2003, 26;). The choices mass media actors make as to which proxies they use can affect what political leaders (and the media themselves) take to be public opinion.

In sum, media practices affect actual public opinion as well as that which is considered public opinion. These practices include the degree to which mass media use and legitimize public opinion polls, the diversity of citizen sources included, and whom the mass media use as proxies for public opinion. In turn these choices shape the manner in which news stories are framed. Journalists, editors, and producers then make additional choices regarding the placement and size of stories and their frequency. Together, framing, priming, and agenda setting affect particularly uninformed public opinion, creating a circular relationship between mass media and public opinion. However, the manner in which mass media construct public opinion varies not only between media outlets but also between media systems.

DIFFERENT MEDIA SYSTEMS

Media systems are not uniform across countries. This point is lost in some studies that attribute the rising role of emotions in politics to mass media tabloidization and changes in media technology (Connolly 1995; Garland 2001; Lakoff 2002; Thrift 2004). For example, for George Lakoff, the "objective" media underappreciate the power of language and its inability to be neutral. And thus, media replicate and reinforce, often unintentionally, the "common sense" of strict father morality (2002, epilogue). For others, television has brought increased public exposure to image-based news that emphasizes drama and draws our attention to small facial and voice details that provoke emotion and come to symbolize the whole person or viewpoint (Thrift 2004, 65–66). Indeed, Nigel Thrift argues that "political presentation conforms increasingly to media norms of presentation which emphasize the performance of emotion as being an index of credibility. Increasingly, political legitimation arises from this kind of performance" (2004, 66). Such analyses suggest that mass media inherently favor emotion over rationality and thus contribute to punitive populism.[2] This returns us to the conundrum of how to include emotions in public debate without their undermining democracy.

Yet these characterizations of the mass media reflect the practices and structures of a particular media system. By not recognizing this location, the political economies that shape journalistic practices and the use of new technologies are obfuscated. For example, "objective" media are particular to (neo)liberal media systems, and not universal. Similarly, the use of television differs between countries and is shaped, among other things, by the degree and form of broadcast regulation. Drawing on the work of Daniel C. Hallin and Paolo Mancini (2004) and Manuel Alejandro Guerrero (2014), I briefly discuss three different media systems and their relative receptivity to punitive populism: democratic corporatist, (neo)liberal, and captured (neo)liberal. In particular, I assess the degree to which each system encourages journalists to use a wide variety of sources, present a heterogeneous public opinion, and engage in watchdog journalism. Table 2.1 summarizes the comparison and the details follow.

DEMOCRATIC CORPORATIST MEDIA SYSTEM

Northern Europe has relatively low levels of punitive populism. Consequently, many studies have explored the reasons for this and point to the countries'

TABLE 2.1: Media Systems and Public Opinion

	Democratic corporatist	**(Neo)liberal**	**Captured (neo)liberal**
Journalists' sources	Incentives to expand range and number of sources	Few sources used in order to cut costs	Few sources used in order to cut costs and clientelism shapes which sources
Representation of public opinion	Diversity is encouraged, regulated, and subsidized External pluralism	Scope of diversity is limited by the market Internal pluralism ("objective" journalism)	Scope of diversity is limited by the market, legacy of authoritarian regime on media ownership, and clientelism External pluralism
Watchdog journalism	Conditions are supportive	Avoided in order to cut costs	Limited by cost-cutting but used strategically as part of clientelism

electoral system (proportional representation), political system (consensus as opposed to majoritarian), political economy (social democratic or "coordinated"), or political culture (collectivist) (Green 2008; Lacey 2008; Tonry 2007). Yet less attention has been given to a country's media system as an explanatory factor.

Hallin and Mancini (2004) refer to the media systems found in Norway, Sweden, Denmark, Finland, Belgium, the Netherlands, Austria, Germany, and Switzerland as "democratic corporatist" (Hallin and Mancini 2004, ch. 6). The key features can be summarized as follows. First, while freedom of the press and access to government information are strongly defended, the state treats media as a social institution that contributes to the countries' progress and equality and is therefore subject to both state regulation and a system of state economic subsidies (Hallin and Mancini 2004, 160–165). These regulations and subsidies aim to ensure that diverse political parties and relevant social groups are represented either through their own media (newspapers, television, or radio) or their own segments within public broadcasting or "omnibus" newspapers. That is, "the public" is not taken to be homogeneous. Instead the representation of its plurality is regulated and financially supported. Journalists, especially in public broadcasting and "omnibus" newspapers, negotiate stories with other journalists who offer different political and social perspectives (Hallin and Mancini 2004, 170). Thus journalists are motivated to expand the number of sources they use. James Curran cites Northern Europe as an example of what he calls a media system with a "radical democratic" public sphere, in which many voices are included in a media public debate that aims to shape policies and hold power holders to account (1991, 30).

In addition, journalists have strong professional associations that effectively regulate journalistic ethics and defend professional autonomy vis-à-vis media owners and publishers—and the courts support them (Hallin and Mancini 2004, 170–175). Thus journalists have significant autonomy to write stories as they see them. Furthermore, a culture of "critical professionalism" encourages journalists' critical reporting of policies, even if these policies are not supported by the political party of their newspaper or broadcast company (Hallin and Mancini 2004, 177). This, combined with strong job security, facilitates watchdog journalism (Hallin and Mancini 2004, 174–177). Green notes that in Norway journalists compete with each other for the quality of their stories, rather than the speed by which they can produce a large number of stories (2008, 45–46).

Certainly commercial media (as opposed to political party or social group media), including tabloids and television, have expanded significantly in these countries since the 1970s and now compose the majority of print media. This reflects the adoption of some neoliberal media policies (Syvertsen 1997). Yet these countries have not experienced the same degree of tabloidization of media, which forefronts emotion and drama over context, seen particularly in (neo) liberal media systems. Due to pressures to produce quality news and strong journalistic ethics and regulation, tabloids are not as sensationalist when compared to those in Britain. As they often focus on culture, their readership tends to cut across classes and they are often read along with a quality newspaper (Hallin and Mancini 2004, 159). They are not a central part of the newspaper market (Hallin and Mancini 2004). Indeed, studies of crime coverage in these countries show these news stories to pay strong attention to context and socioeconomic issues, and exhibit less tabloidization than is found in the (neo)liberal media model (Green 2008; Lappi-Seppälä 2007, 271–272; Pratt 2007). Yet neoliberal media policies continue to expand and there is some evidence that they (particularly commercial tabloids) may be eroding these democratic strengths and contributing to an increasingly punitive discourse on immigration (e.g., Moore 2010). However, more research is needed on this topic to explore the similarities with and differences from crime coverage.

(NEO)LIBERAL MEDIA SYSTEM

Most studies consider punitive populism to be high in the United States and Britain. Research often points to the following explanations: both countries have a similar electoral system (first-past-the-post), political system (majoritarian), political economy (liberal or neoliberal), and political culture (individualist) (Garland 2001; Green 2008; Lacey 2008). Yet they also have a similar market-based media system. Hallin and Mancini (2004) contend that the most "liberal" (or neoliberal) media system is found in the United States but the system also fairly closely describes those found in Britain, Ireland, and Canada. This system has several key features (Hallin and Mancini 2004, ch. 7).

First, as in the democratic corporatist system, freedom of the press and access to government information is strongly defended. Yet, unlike state treatment of the media in Northern Europe, in the United States and Britain media are treated by the state as purely or predominantly businesses. The role of the state as funder and regulator of media is minimal. For example, the United States has no public broadcaster, and since the 1990s, its already minimal media regulations on ownership were cut to allow greater media holdings across mediums (e.g. owning both newspapers and radio stations) and within particular geographic locations. These cuts have reduced the number of media owners in the United States from fifty companies owning 90 percent of the media market in 1983 to five in 2014 (Sommer 2014). Similar increases in levels of media ownership concentration have resulted due to deregulation in Britain and Canada (Media Reform Coalition 2014; Winseck 2016). Where the state does play a role in liberal media systems, such as it does with the BBC in Britain or CBC in Canada, it is through arms-length governing boards with the goal of promoting national identity rather than the more heterogeneous external plurality of ideas between media or media programs found in the democratic corporatist system (Hallin and Mancini 2004, 75).

Press freedom in this system is understood as freedom from state or political actors (Curran 2002, 80). Thus, strong journalistic autonomy and professional standards emphasize "objective journalism" or what Hallin and Mancini (2004) call internal pluralism. The ideal is that news stories are "neutral" or "nonpolitical" reports that provide information (albeit selective), not political commentaries, and thus offer more than one perspective on an issue within each article. However, unlike standards in the other two systems, these standards are more likely to be compromised for commercial, rather than political reasons. That is, journalists and media companies in (neo)liberal media systems often select information, viewpoints, and accountability based on the potential effect on advertising, sales, and other business interests, rather than democratic goals (Curran 2002, ch. 3; Entman 1989; Gans 2003). The emphasis on "neutral" stories, often prefers that journalists use "neutral" or "apolitical" sources such as state actors, rather than a wide array of political party or organized civil society groups (Bennett 2005; Hallin and Mancini 2004, 142).

Although political parallelism (media outlets' overt ties to political parties) was common in the United States in the nineteenth century, as in many countries at the time, it faded with the emergence of press agencies such as the Associated Press (established in 1846). Press agencies aim to sell stories to as many different media outlets as possible, and this contributed to the initial production of politically "neutral" stories focused on information rather than ideas, which could be sold to a wide range of newspapers (Bennett 2005, 186–187).

As media concentration has increased, along with twenty-four-hour television and internet news, competition between outlets has focused on cost-cutting and sales to increase revenue (Gans 2003, 50; Paterson 2010, 103). Cost-cutting has meant that fewer journalists produce more stories for less money. This has increased journalists' reliance on fewer sources (usually official or state sources), on increased use of public relations and press agency material, and less watchdog journalism (Bennett 2005; Moloney 2006). In turn, tabloids and the tabloidization of once quality news sources have helped to increase audiences and advertising sales (Bromley 2010). Tabloids (media that emphasize entertainment, emotion, and drama) use crime (along with entertainment and sports) to attract audiences and, as a consequence, make crime an agenda-setting issue. The tabloidization of many news outlets in order to increase profits has subsequently increased overall crime coverage. Indeed, most studies of media and punitive populism suggest a correlation between increasingly (neo)liberal media systems and the rise of punitive populism (Chevigny 2003; Green 2008; Pratt 2007; Roberts et al. 2003).

CAPTURED (NEO)LIBERAL MEDIA SYSTEM

Punitive populism is common throughout Latin America, but it has not been studied to the same extent as in Europe and North America, and the region's political culture does not fit neatly into established categories. The electoral system of the region is generally proportional representation (as in Northern Europe), but despite coalition governments in some countries, the political systems can be described as majoritarian (as in Anglo-American countries), as well as, to varying degrees, clientelist (as in Southern Europe). The political economy, since the International Monetary Fund led structural adjustment in the 1980s, is predominantly neoliberal, despite attempts by left-of-center governments in the early 2000s to extend social welfare (e.g., Bakker 2013; Ruckert, MacDonald, and Proulx 2016; Seri 2012, 6–8; Terhorst, Olivera, and Dwinell 2013; Webber 2010). The political culture is individualist (in the sense that family ties supersede commitment to the greater societal good) but also hierarchical and often highly polarized (Calvert and Calvert 1989).

Hallin and Papathanassopoulos (2002) refer to Latin America's media system as similar to Southern Europe's. They emphasize the centrality of clientelism in both systems—however, Latin America's system has many unique characteristics. Most notably, Latin America has a much longer history of commercial media than does Southern Europe. Commercial media did not become significant in Southern Europe until the 1980s and 1990s, and even into the early 2000s, tabloids or sensationalist newspapers were virtually absent in the region (Hallin and Mancini 2004, 97). Thus, Guerrero (2014) better defines the Latin America's media system as a "captured liberal" media system.

The Latin American media system is composed of both the commercial media of the (neo)liberal system and the polarized, politicized, advocacy journalism found in Southern Europe (what Hallin and Mancini [2004] call "polarized pluralist") (Guerrero 2014; Waisbord 2000). Guerrero (2014) argues that this combination has led to the "capture" of the commercial media system by both political (government) and economic powers. He uses the term "capture" to "underline the capacity of groups to twist the rules in their favor to make their application selective and ineffective, and the condition where extra-journalistic criteria shape, determine, and limit the watchdog role of the media" (Guerrero 2014, 56). While not a new phenomenon, the interacting and recent experiences of authoritarianism, neoliberalism, and clientelism in the region have led to the emergence of new forms of "capture" (Guerrero 2014, 44–45; Hallin and Papathanassopoulos 2002, 191).

As previously discussed, the liberal media model is defined primarily or exclusively by private commercial media organizations with minimal state regulation and funding. The United States promoted this model in Latin America as the model emerged in the early twentieth century and later through the Inter-American Press Association (established in 1943). However, the regions' political systems have shaped the manner in which the media system developed in Latin America. For years, in many countries in the region, authoritarian regimes nationalized, censored, or repressed (or all three) media outlets, particularly broadcast media, as well as journalists. Yet beginning in the 1980s most countries in Latin America underwent the dual processes of electoral democratization and neoliberal economic reform. By the 1990s, the Latin American media model was clearly (neo)liberal in the sense that most of Latin America's commercial media organizations are almost entirely private and largely deregulated. Yet this (neo) liberal model continues to be "captured" by powerful political and economic interests that further hinder both the state's regulatory capacities and journalists' ability to engage in watchdog journalism (Guerrero 2014, 43).

In particular, private media groups that were supportive of previous authoritarian regimes gained a significant amount of economic power during these periods. When democracy returned, the new ruling political elite, whose members depended on the media to convey their messages, forged alliances with these traditional commercial media. These alliances protected large media business interests and weakened the state's regulatory role (Guerrero 2014, 44). The simultaneous implementation of neoliberal media policies that further expanded media privatization and deregulation contributed to a dramatic rise in media concentration and in large media conglomerates focused on financial accumulation. For example, El Mercurio and Copesa media groups dominate the media market in Chile, Clarín Media Group dominates in Argentina, and Mexico's Televisa is the largest Hispanic media conglomerate in the world (Guerrero 2014, 48). Thus the commercial pressures placed on journalists' use of sources and opportunities for watchdog journalism are similar to those outlined in the (neo)liberal media system. Yet, in Latin America, the state (especially the authoritarian state) played an important role in determining which media companies have benefited most from neoliberal market reforms, and thus which viewpoints are most likely to dominate.

In addition, like Southern Europe, Latin America has a long and persistent history of clientelism. Clientelism refers to a system of private exchange "in which access to social resources is controlled by patrons and delivered to clients in exchange for deference and various kinds of support" (Hallin and Papathanassopoulos 2002, 184–185). While clientelism exists in all societies and is almost always viewed as illegitimate, it is a common practice in Southern Europe and Latin America, stronger in some countries such as Greece, Mexico, and Argentina and weaker in others such as Italy and Chile (Hallin and Mancini 2004, ch. 5; Hallin and Papathanassopoulos 2002, 176).

Clientelism plays an important role in the political and economic capture of media as it involves media owners making private political alliances that include, on the part of the state, information exchange, state advertising, or the differential application of laws and regulations (or all of these), for uncritical or even openly supportive news reporting (Guerrero 2014, 44–45). In turn, media outlets use selective watchdog journalism to fortify clientelist commitments or strengthen their own negotiating power with the government, or both (Guerrero 2014, 51; Hallin and Papathanassopoulos 2002, 91). That is, advocacy journalism dominates in this media system and is an integral part of the political and economic system. Advocacy journalism views the "neutral" news story as an impossibility. Instead, opinion or commentary is common in news analysis and most media take a political position, providing what Hallin and Mancini (2004) describe as "external pluralism." Thus, the state plays an important role in the media market but not as a regulator of public external plurality (as it does in Northern Europe). Its role is to negotiate acceptable and unacceptable political viewpoints and their corresponding rewards and punishments.

This media system offers important possibilities as well as limitations in journalists' practices. On the one hand, without the strong professional associations (weakened by clientelism and job instability) or the consistent court support for journalistic autonomy and freedom of the press enjoyed in democratic corporatist media systems, journalists in Latin America may find that the sources they can use are limited by *both* commercial and political interests (Guerrero 2014, 52; Hallin and Papathanassopoulos 2002, 182). Yet, depending on the exact combination and degree of homogeneity of these pressures, there can be greater or fewer opportunities for watchdog journalism and the expansion of journalists' sources, compared to those found in the liberal media system. For example, newspapers whose clientelist networks oppose the government might encourage their journalists to pursue watchdog journalism that exposes government wrongdoing. Or the government might close off a media outlet's access to government sources or information, forcing these journalists to expand their use of civil society sources. Or civil society organizations involved in or opposed to the same clientelistic networks as a given news outlet might be used to represent "public opinion."

Yet as Latin American countries have pursued the implementation of a wide range of neoliberal media policies, it has had an important influence on the strength of the commercial limits within which these journalistic opportunities can be pursued. Crime is a great topic for opposition media to use in criticizing the government without compromising commercial interests (Hallin and Papathanassopoulos 2002, 51). Thus, as we will see in more detail in the following chapters, the neoliberalization of the "captured" liberal media systems in Latin America has favored the rise of punitive populism in similar but unique ways compared to (neo)liberal media systems.

Chapter 3

COMPARING MEDIA SYSTEMS
ARGENTINA AND CHILE

Some studies of punitive populism argue that what is needed to curb it is more journalists willing to pursue watchdog journalism (UNDP 2013b), or more criminal justice experts willing and better able to speak to the media (Green 2008; Roberts et al. 2003). Yet it is not courage or information that is lacking. Courage is always exceptional, and information holds little weight in debates led by emotion. Rather, particular media systems favor some journalistic practices over others, and these more routine practices have an important influence on media's receptivity to punitive populism.

This is not to say that some journalists or media outlets will not defy the norms and expectations of their domestic media system. Some do so almost always. Rather, media systems shape the most common practices of journalists and media outlets that in turn affect what becomes agenda-setting news, the range of available news frames, and the presentation of public opinion. Thus reducing the prominence of punitive populism requires rethinking the media systems that favor it.

This chapter provides a brief historical overview of the contrasting media systems of Argentina and Chile. In so doing, it offers a most different comparison between the two countries and a most similar comparison across time within each country. These comparisons reveal how neoliberal media reforms reshaped their respective media systems in a similar manner that favored greater receptivity to punitive populism.

ARGENTINA

Argentina was an early adopter of the liberal media system (1880–1920), which was then "captured" by powerful political interests in different ways over time. However, recent media democratization (defined as an expansion of journalistic sources and watchdog journalism) followed by neoliberal media restructuring (privatization and deregulation) has ruptured this capture in particular ways that have broadened the scope for commercial-based media decision making and contributed to the expansion of communicational practices favorable to punitive populism. Three key historical and contemporary features characterize Argentina's media system: populism, military regimes, and media neoliberalization.

POPULISM

Argentina has a long history of populist governments and an enduring classical populist movement (Peronism). This might be assumed to predispose the country to punitive populism. Yet, according to public opinion polls, support for punitive populism is in fact higher in Chile, which has never had a classic populist movement (Layton and Rodríguez 2014, 95–96). That said, populist Peronist governments (1946–1955; 1973–1976; 1989–1999; 2003–2015) in Argentina have shaped the media system in a particular manner that is not inconsistent with punitive populism.

By the early twentieth century, Argentine media production and consumption were among the highest in Latin America (Cane 2011, 7; Fox 1988b, 36). These were influenced early on by the emergence of tabloid journalism in the United States (in 1919) and sensational crime stories through the press agencies United Press and Associated Press, as well as in Hollywood films (Caimari 2017, 45, 52).[1] Crime reporting in the nineteenth century was covered in detective-story style using "natural-scientificist" language to explain the human biology that caused the perpetrator's criminality; now coverage was focused on entertainment and the action of the moment that assessed *how* the crime was committed and with cars and guns featuring prominently (Caimari 2017, 1, 43–44). Police were minor characters in these stories until they learned to effectively engage the mass media fascination with new technologies and drama (Caimari 2017, ch. 6).

After the Second World War the United States began actively promoting its market-based "professional" and "nonpolitical" style of journalism in the region (Waisbord 2000, 14). Many Argentine newspapers, including the prominent *La Nación* and *La Prensa*, adopted this rhetoric along with many U.S. organizational practices and newspaper layouts. However, this was around the same time Peronism emerged. Juan D. Perón assumed the presidency for the first time in 1946 (until 1955, and again 1973–1974). These changes affected the media system in particular ways.

First, the limits of the liberal media system were beginning to be exposed. Market-based media systems rely on large audiences and ample sources of private advertising. While readership was strong in Argentina compared to other Latin American countries at the time, the economic crisis of the 1930s and the world wars weakened this financial base as well as advertising revenue. This provided an avenue for political capture. Moreover, the ideal liberal media system promotes "nonpolitical" or "objective" journalism that includes a watchdog or critical approach by all media in their reporting on state actors (although, in practice, commercial interests have always superseded these goals). Yet from 1930 to 1946, practices increasingly contradicted this ideal. For example, a working-class movement was growing, but their voices were excluded from the public opinion articulated in the major newspapers. Newspapers were also experiencing new and growing commercial pressures to prioritize profit over democracy. This led many political actors and members of the public to question the legitimacy of the press and call for an increased role of the state in its regulation (or even control) (Cane 2011). Perón offered an answer to these contradictions that favored quasi-state control and polarized public debate.

As with punitive populism, classic populist movements divide the population into two irreconcilable groups, "the people" and "the elite" (Laclau 2007). The will of "the people" is not expressed through public opinion polls or a diverse civil society but through the executive (or president) who, via the legitimacy of elections, represents the will of "the people." Those who oppose the president, oppose the people, and are deemed part of "the elite." For the executive, the media are a central vehicle through which the leader communicates directly to "the people," unmediated by the "elite" or the "foreign" interests of media companies. Moreover, populism perceives the media to have an enormous amount of power over public opinion, similar to the hypodermic needle model long rejected in media studies (chapter 2; Waisbord 2013, 46). Media communications within the state are centralized in the executive. Private and public media are expected to uncritically support the government and, in return, private media receive economic benefits such as significant government advertising. Media that oppose the government may be targets of various forms of punishment such as lack of state advertising, rigorous enforcement of regulations, and unfavorable policies.

The image of the police promoted in the mass media by Juan Domingo and Eva Perón was the "police of the people" and defenders of the working class against foreign agitators (communist, anarchist, etc.) (Caimari 2017, 164, 188). Thus, within this framework, "public safety" primarily involved defending "the people" against "the elite," not against common crime.

Perón justified the centralization and nationalization of many media (as well as the repression of opposition media) as necessary to combating the dominant ideas of commercial and foreign interests. For example, in 1944, after suspending *La Prensa* (at the time Argentina's most important national newspapers) for five days by executive decree, then-vice president Perón explained the action as vital to stopping "the arbitrary invocation of freedom of expression to cover up campaigns aimed to confuse and disorient public opinion. Printing presses cannot be converted into arms of economic disturbance, social dissociation, nor into vehicles of foreign ideas, political ambitions, or personal opinions with impunity" (quoted in Sirvén 1984, 32). In 1951, then-president Perón was able to pressure the owner of *La Prensa* to flee the country, leaving his business to the state (Sirvén 1984, 103, 107–108, 112, 114; Waisbord 1998, 43). In contrast, the newly established (1945) national newspaper *Clarín*, to its economic advantage, was careful to remain supportive of Perón for most of his time in office (Sivak 2013, 54–119).

When Argentina received its first television station there was only one channel. It was state owned and the content was entirely Peronist; the first broadcast was of Eva Perón on October 17, 1951 (Loyalty to Perón Day) (Waisbord 1998, 44). However, media were never entirely nationalized; most expropriated newspapers were run by the private media holding, Editorial ALEA. Media that remained commercial (mostly newspapers) functioned under high levels of scrutiny and control. Radio and television were easier for the state to nationalize because the government could take over their broadcast licenses and these media gave in more readily to harassment (Sirvén 1984, 117).

Peronist accusations of commercial and foreign interests in Argentine media were not unfounded. *La Prensa* did receive significant international funding and the United States was actively promoting its ideas in the region through: the Inter-American Press Association; substantial funds for advertising; and its news wire services such as the Associated Press. Yet state control and nationalization of the media also aimed to silence opposition to the governments' goals, actions, and omissions, and thus limit watchdog journalism.

MILITARY REGIMES

Argentina's twentieth-century political history was also punctuated by many military regimes (1930–1932, 1943–1946, 1955–1958, 1962–1963, 1966–1973, and 1976–1983). The last military regime from 1976 to 1983 has had the most profound influence on Argentina's media system. As prior Peronist governments had battled "foreign" and "elite" ideas, the last military government also perceived itself as engaged in a war in which it required full media support.

Rather than being at war with the "elite" or common criminals, the military regime was battling "subversives," broadly defined, to which the dictatorship promised to bring "order" (understood as "public safety"). According to the military's 1980 Broadcasting Law (Law 22.285), media were expected to support this "national security" objective and could be restricted by the government for this reason (Mauersberger 2012, 591). While appropriating the centralized and nationalized broadcast media inherited from Perón in 1976, the military in this period took repression of media to new heights. On March 24, 1976 (the day of the coup), the military issued Press Release No. 19, which stated: "Any media that circulates, divulges, or propagates news, communications or images, with the objective to upset, prejudice, or defame the activities of the armed, security, or police forces shall be punished by up to ten years' imprisonment" (quoted in CONADEP 1984, 367). Threats of imprisonment were supplemented with high levels of repression. At least eighty-four journalists disappeared between 1976 and 1983,[2] hundreds more were jailed and many were killed or went into exile (CONADEP 1984, 369–374; Muraro 1988, 117; Waisbord 2000, 23).

The military government was certainly interested in implementing neoliberalism at the time and did so in some policy areas, but complete consensus on this economic program within the regime was lacking (Sivak 2013, 272–378; Teichman 2001, 30). Even *Clarín*, then one of Argentina's most circulated national newspapers, did not support neoliberal economic reforms (Sivak 2013). Neoliberal reforms that did occur were not generally directed at the media. Broadcast media were under direct military (state) control. Print media remained commercial (Postolski and Marino 2005). Print media that were supportive, or at least not critical of the regime, benefited from an important increase in state advertising and the restructuring of Papel Prensa (Press Paper).[3]

In 1972, under the previous military regime (1966–1973), General Alejandro Lanusse established a national newsprint company called Papel Prensa. By 1976, the majority of Class A stocks were held by Graiver Group. The military accused the president of the company, David Graiver, of being connected to the Peronist guerrilla group the Montoneros and seized his goods, including his stocks (Postolski and Marino 2005, 173). The state retained 25 percent of the stocks and sold off the rest to media groups supportive of the regime, *La Nación*, *La Razón*, and *Clarín*.[4] In 1980, *La Razón* went bankrupt and its stocks were sold to *Clarín* (Blanco and Germano 2005, 35; Postolski and Marino 2005, 174). Papel Prensa gave these companies access to subsidized newsprint 50–60 percent cheaper than the cost of newsprint available to other newspapers (Waisbord 1998, 46; Blanco and Germano 2005, 34). In this manner *La Nación*, and especially *Clarín*, benefited economically from the military regime and the controlled commercial media spaces it permitted.

What is interesting about this history for our purposes is that, first, state intervention and political "capture" of the media have been consistent features of the media system, despite the early adoption of the liberal media model. Second, state intervention and political capture have been very polarizing and seemingly based on both populist and military state actors' acceptance of the validity of the academically rejected hypodermic media model (Waisbord 2013, 46). That is, if the media say something, people will believe it. Thus, while public relations (PR) and public opinion poll companies began to form in Argentina in the 1950s and 1960s, their spread beyond the private sector remained limited (Aparecida Ferrari and França 2011, 54–58; Mora y Araujo 2009). If the leader embodies "the people" or "national security," and can control public opinion through the media, there is limited need for polls or PR. Thus the political "capture" of the media limited the degree to which media pursued practices based purely on commercial logic. Moreover, neither Peronist nor military governments had an interest in promoting common crime as being out of control; instead they emphasized the threat of "the elite" and "subversives." In this manner political capture reduced media outlets' incentives to sensationalize crime.

MEDIA NEOLIBERALIZATION

This media environment began to change with the return of electoral democracy in 1983. The end of the last military regime in Argentina was not negotiated, unlike in Chile. The military had lost its legitimacy through its poor handling of the economy, its loss of the Malvinas/Falklands War, and the exposure of human rights abuses. The first democratic government led by President Raúl Alfonsín (1983–1989) lifted official censorship, replaced military heads of radio and television stations with civilians, and journalists who had been in exile returned (Blanco and Germano 2005, 114; Fox 1988a, 29). Yet beyond these changes, Alfonsín did not pass any significant media reforms. The Broadcasting Law of 1980 was not replaced until 2009. Most broadcasting licenses remained unchanged and the government continued to control seventy-seven radio stations and seventeen television channels—a significant portion of the country's broadcasting media (Muraro 1988, 123). Of course newspapers, most of which had remained commercial throughout the military regime, were free to publish as they wished, yet remained cautious about criticizing the new democratic government, until 1987.

In 1987 the left-of-center national newspaper *Página/12* emerged as a critical voice, spearheading watchdog journalism, expanding the array of sources it used, and promoting democracy and human rights. It gained a broad audience, including elite decision makers (Waisbord 2000, 78). *Página/12*'s success also pushed the other national daily newspapers, *Clarín* and *La Nación*, to pursue watchdog journalism, a phenomenon that Juliet Pinto (2008) found, in her content analysis of the newspapers, to have lasted until approximately 2005.[5] Investigations into police violence and corruption were an important part of this new watchdog journalism (discussed further in chapter 4).

Yet as neoliberal media reforms expanded, watchdog journalism contracted. These reforms began in 1989, when President Carlos Menem passed the Law of State Reform (23.696/89) as part of his radical neoliberalization of the country's economy. Circumventing aspects of the military's 1980 Broadcasting Law, this law mandated the privatization of state-owned radio and television, allowed companies (first domestic and later foreign) to own across mediums (e.g., newspapers owning TV stations), and allowed unregulated foreign investment (Blanco and

Germano 2005, 141, 149; Park 2002, 244; Waisbord 1998, 49). Broadcast media were further deregulated through a 1992 bilateral investment treaty between the United States and Argentina, which eliminated limits on foreign investment. As a result, in the late 1990s Argentina experienced the third largest entry of foreign capital into its communications' market in the history of the country (Blanco and Germano 2005, 158). Foreign media conglomerates such as Telefónica, Prime, and Prisa, entered the market, as did foreign financing for national media companies from Citibank and Goldman Sachs (the latter associated with *Clarín*) (Becerra 2015, 93).[6] In 1999, a presidential decree (1.005) decreased regulations on the trading of frequencies and increased the maximum number of licenses from four to twenty-four per legal person (Mauersberger 2012, 591). In 2003, another presidential decree eliminated territorial restrictions on media ownership (Blanco and Germano 2005, 184).

All these changes contributed to substantial media concentration. Owing to the advantages it gained during the dictatorship, *Clarín*, then limited to a newspaper, was in a good economic position to take advantage of the neoliberal reform of the media market. During this period, Clarín Group (established in 1999) came to control TV and radio stations, a publishing company (Editorial Atlátida), and majority shares in the country's major telecommunications company, Telefónica. Their holding now comprised: 35 percent of the print media market; the top-selling national daily newspaper; and the two leading broadcast companies in Buenos Aires (Mastrini, Becerra, and Marino 2014, 205). Spanish-owned multinational Telefónica went on to own 85 percent of open television channels (Telefe Group), while Clarín Group owned 60 percent of the cable market (Becerra 2015, 94; Blanco and Germano 2005, 51–61; Mastrini, Becerra, and Marino 2014, 205).[7] Clarín Group is now the largest media conglomerate in Argentina. Thus the 1990s can be characterized as a period of "expansive media concentration" (Becerra 2015).

The significant media concentration that resulted from media privatization (private business acquisition of formerly public media outlets) and deregulation (reduced limits on ownership across mediums and territory, and on foreign investment) contributed to a decline in the diversity of perspectives found in the news. It did so in key ways, including: reducing the number of media owners; conforming content across mediums (to cut costs); concentrating media production in Buenos Aires at the expensive of local content (to cut costs);[8] renting space of large companies to small media companies with content restrictions; and expanding the room available to promote foreign and domestic business interests (Becerra 2015, 92–93).

Moreover, as the central role of media, profit was consolidated over any ideal role it might play in democracy. Media concentration coincided with a flourishing of new technologies and new broadcasting formats, facilitated in part through foreign investments. Satellite and cable TV expanded significantly, twenty-four-hour TV news channels Crónica TV and Todo Noticias (TN) began to air in 1994, and the (relatively unregulated) internet expanded as a news source in the 2000s. The drive for profit, combined with the new (largely deregulated) technologies, contributed to an increase in media market competition to cut costs (by reducing the number of journalists and expensive watchdog journalism), to increase the number and frequency of stories journalists produced (to fill time and space demands), and to increase audience sizes (to attract advertising and subscriptions). That is, media companies competed to produce more stories, more often, with less staff and more visuals and drama.

Crime is an easy way to meet this demand. It is cheap, plentiful, and dramatic. Thus it is not surprising that as the effects of the neoliberal media reforms were felt, crime news and the political use of punitive populist rhetoric began to expand (chapters 4 to 6; Fernández Roich 2017; Seri and Kubal 2018). Indeed, Cynthia Fernández Roich's (2017) careful discourse analysis of Argentine newspapers' coverage of crime, security, and order found 1999 to be a turning point in coverage of iron-fist or tough-on-crime policies. Guillermina Seri and Mary Rose Kubal (2018) trace its expanded use by political leaders across the political spectrum from 2001 to 2012.

Neoliberal media reforms also created a fertile environment for the explosive growth of public relations and public opinion companies as these both provide quick and cheap news stories (Aguiar 2009; Aparecida Ferrari and França 2011; Mora y Araujo 2009). However, the adoption and acceptance of these techniques for managing public democratic discourse have been different from and slower than in Chile. In particular, clientelism and the Peronist populist movement have been important intervening variables. These influences were amplified by the 2001 economic crisis.

The economic crisis severely affected the media industry; newspaper sales fell approximately 50 percent between 2000 and 2004 (Mauersberger 2012, 591). Clarín Group's debt reached US$1 billion (Liotti 2014, 105). This further decreased the funds available for watchdog journalism and increased the need to reach a broader audience. For example, one former crime editor for *Clarín* explained that around the time of the economic crisis, *Clarín* went through a redesign that included reducing the size of its written stories and increasing the importance of photographs (both practices associated with tabloid journalism).[9] In 2001 the government passed a law allowing the state to assist media groups with their debt. However, more than simply saving the industry from bankruptcy, Becerra argues that this began a period of what he calls "defensive concentration" (2001–2008) (Becerra 2015, 94–95).

The government (presidents Duhalde and Néstor Kirchner) and large media groups used the economic crisis as a justification for protecting them from competition, achieved in large part through the automatic ten-year extension of Clarín and Telefónica's broadcasting licenses in 2004 (some licenses were extended to 2025), and the lack of open competitions for licenses since that time (Becerra 2015, 97; Liotti 2014, 105). This came at the expense of many small and medium media outlets, many of which closed. Nonprofit organizations, which gained the right to own broadcast licenses in 2005, found they had no open competitions from which to buy licenses (Becerra 2015, 97). Thus the media market was "free" but captured in a manner that became increasingly polarized from 2008 onward.

Indeed, both the expansion of neoliberal media reforms and their defense were negotiated through clientelist relations between the government and large media companies. President Menem's neoliberal economic and media reforms stemmed in part from pressure due to the structural adjustment loans it owed to the International Monetary Fund, and also from domestic media groups that had acquired significant power from the economic benefits they gained during the dictatorship. This facilitated the negotiating strength of these businesses in their clientelist relations with the government. Thus Menem likely expected positive media coverage in exchange for the economic benefits these companies gained from his reforms. He was unpleasantly surprised by the critical watchdog journalism that in fact flourished in the 1990s (Blanco and Germano 2005, 230).

Similar negotiations took place between President Néstor Kirchner (2003–2007) and media companies, and included exchanges of increased official advertising for positive media coverage of the government (Becerra 2015; O'Donnell 2007). These negotiations likely contributed to the betrayal felt by his wife and successor president Cristina Fernández de Kirchner (2007–2015) when it appeared that *Clarín* had sided with landowners in the rural protests of 2008, arguably contributing to the Senate vote against her reform (Sivak 2013, 389–390). This tension between the executive and the news media escalated and became more polarized from 2008 to 2015 (although some journalists suggested it began earlier) and was increasingly targeted at Clarín Group.

For *Página/12* and other media supportive of the populist Kirchner government political capture through clientelism began to outweigh the influence of commercial interests in media choices (O'Donnell 2007). Eventually new and old media conglomerates, including Telefónica, open to supporting the government came to benefit (Becerra 2015). In contrast, for *Clarín*, and other media able to survive with limited government advertising, commercialization and a focus on profits provided them with the financial means to counter the government and defend their business interests. Crime and security then became news topics that both expanded profits and provided a platform for critique of the government. Thus, political capture is important in Argentina, but not absolute. It is negotiated, with varying degrees of success.

The deregulation of the media market and subsequent private media ownership concentration in the late 1990s prompted the formation in 2004 of a Coalition for Democratic Broadcasting. This coalition of civil society groups, academics, and journalists presented twenty-one points they identified as vital to the democratization of communication in the country (Mauersberger 2012, 592–593). Some of their points are similar to aspects of democratic corporatist media systems (see chapter 2). In early 2008, President Fernández de Kirchner drew on this movement's proposal to pass an impressive media reform package in 2009 that incorporated most of the demands of the organization including: the establishment of spaces for civil society voices in television and radio; the regulation of diversity of content; and, provisions to decrease commercial multimedia concentration (Becerra 2015; Mastrini, Becerra, and Marino 2014; Mauersberger 2012).

Yet the president retained the power of the executive to distribute state advertising, and the law's application under the Kirchner government was selective (aimed primarily at the breakup of Clarín Group) (Becerra 2015; Liotti 2014, 111; Mastrini, Becerra, and Marino 2014, 205). For example, while the law required 33 percent of new frequencies to go to nonprofit groups, 94 percent (1,176 of 1,256) of new radio stations were government owned (Becerra 2015, 105; Liotti 2014, 111). Moreover, little effort was made to break up Kirchner-supporting media conglomerates such as Telefónica and DirecTV (Becerra 2015, 105). When Mauricio Macri assumed the presidency in 2015, he modified the media reform in a manner consistent with the previous neoliberal policies of deregulation. He extended existing broadcast licenses for ten years, reopened the number of licenses one company can hold and the ability to transfer licenses, and reorganized the governing commission.[10]

In sum, the media system in Argentina is characterized, especially after 1989, as a *neo*liberal market-based media system with significant but not absolute political capture. The implementation of neoliberal media reforms *after* media democratization provided the opportunity for new media outlets and new journalists' practices to establish themselves in democracy and for media outlets to negotiate their capture by the state as the effects of the neoliberal media and economic policies were felt. Media coverage of crime, security, and policing issues has similarly and equally been influenced by (1) the order of media democratization and neoliberalization, and (2) the politicization of crime, security, and policing in state-media clientelist negotiations. This media system has favored competition between punitive populist rhetoric and policies and those of human rights, with the ascendancy of the former as the influence of neoliberal media reforms broadened (Seri and Kubal 2018). By 2015, all three top presidential candidates campaigned on getting tough on crime. On assuming office that year, President Macri declared a "public security emergency." This declaration of "emergency" gave the government extraordinary powers, which it has used to reinforce, mobilize, and extend the powers of military and police forces.[11]

CHILE

Similar to Argentina, the Chilean media system is characterized by the early adoption of the liberal media model, with persistent and high political parallelism. Media have been "captured" by political and economic interests through direct and indirect links to political parties or governments. These political links kept the media market relatively pluralistic (external pluralism) until 1973. Indeed, the state even made some attempts to use regulation to reinforce and expand this pluralism. Yet the state controlled application of neoliberal economic policies to the media market during the dictatorship of General Augusto Pinochet (1973–1990), greatly elevated the power of some media outlets (and their political and economic ideas) over others, limiting the potential for media democratization with the return of elections in 1990. Compared to Argentina, the Chilean media environment has been more consistently favorable to punitive populist rhetoric and policies since the return of electoral democracy in 1990. In what follows I examine some of the key historical and contemporary features of the media system in Chile: political polarization, the Pinochet regime, and media neoliberalization.

POLITICAL POLARIZATION

Unlike Argentina, Chile does not have a history of strong classical populist movements nor is clientelism as entrenched or accepted. For example, in 2016 Transparency International identified the corruption perception score for Argentina to be 36/100 (where 0 = highly corrupt and 100 = very clean) and ranked it 96/176. In comparison, Chile's score is 66/100 and its rank is 24/176, similar to France's score of 69/100 and rank of 23/176. Instead, Chile's media environment has been most affected by persistent political polarization that is rooted in significant class cleavages.

As in Argentina and in Europe, Chile in the early nineteenth century had a politically partisan and literary press, supported by laws that strongly protected freedom of expression (HRW 1998, 20). Similarly, when crime was covered in the media it reflected the biological determinism popular in scientific criminology at the time, which examined the ascriptive characteristics that explain an individual's criminality (Palacios and Leyton 2014). These physical and mental traits corresponded to those held by particular marginalized social groups and were used to account for these people's proclivity to disrupt "the natural economic order" (Leyton and Palacios 2014, 7–8). As César Leyton and Cristián Palacios argue, this class-based deterministic analysis of crime has persisted in Chilean public discussions of insecurity and its solutions (2014, 9).

Indeed, for much of the twentieth century, media portrayals of crime and disorder were associated with class-based strikes and protests. The Carabineros de Chile, established in their current form in 1927, were central protagonists in this struggle for "public order" (Bonner 2014a, 122–126; Candina 2006, 81; Maldonado 1990, 18). Unlike in Argentina, where the police used media to portray themselves as supporters of the working class, in Chile the Carabineros promoted themselves as defenders of "the public" (assumed to be the middle and upper classes) against "public disorder" (assumed to be caused by protesters and the popular sectors).

The number of newspapers expanded substantially by the early twentieth century. However, unlike other newspapers of the time (mostly founded by political parties and of short duration), the commercial *El Mercurio* (established in Valparaíso in 1827 and Santiago in 1900) endured and for a time became the country's only daily newspaper (Campbell 1962, 548; HRW 1998, 21). At its centennial celebration, then president Lagos stated: "It is difficult to understand Chilean history without *El Mercurio*" (quoted in Lagos Lira, Salinas Muñoz, and Stange Marcus 2009, 176). While firmly supporting the conservative elite, it initially aimed to detach itself from political struggles (HRW 1998, 21). Similarly, radio, which began in 1923 (Radio Chilena), was not as connected to politics because it was primarily conceived as a medium for entertainment, not news. It thus had weak connections with political parties and the political conflicts of the time (Léon-Dermota 2003, 49; Tironi and Sunkel 2000, 168).

However, the 1920s and 1930s brought social protests and economic instability in Chile, followed soon afterward by the tensions of the Cold War. Class cleavages were central to these political tensions up to and through the 1970s. Thus while *El Mercurio* was adopting the format and many of the practices of U.S.-style market-based journalism, it simultaneously became increasingly involved in politics. Indeed, Guillermo Sunkel argues that as early as the 1920s and early 1930s, *El Mercurio* began to question democracy, and its owner Agustín Edwards used *El Mercurio* to unsuccessfully promote a state corporatist regime (1986, 111).

Instead, within a democratic political system that favored the political Right and economic elite, political leaders implemented import substitution industrialization (ISI) from 1939 to 1973 (Collier and Sater 2004, 237). This contributed to the creation of what Manuel Antonio Garretón calls a "compromise state" in which economic growth was achieved while some sectors of society were structurally excluded, notably peasants and the urban poor (1989, 6). In fact, even the urban working class, whom ISI was intended to benefit and whose employers saw substantial profits, did not see significant wage increases (Collier and Sater 2004, 272). This structural exclusion was supplemented with state violence (often led by police) aimed particularly against those members of the popular sectors who challenged the established system—notably in response to their strikes and public protests (Bonner 2014a, 122–126; Garretón 1989, 6; Salazar 1994, 94–95).

Control of the mass media was an important means through which the dominant economic sectors exerted their influence over the state and resisted greater economic and political inclusion (Garretón 1989, 12), as remains the case today.[12] Criminalizing the marginalized classes was a persistent strategy. Indeed, one author who analyzed *El Mercurio* news coverage at the height of the class and political conflict during the parliamentary election from 1972 to 1973 found that news items previously framed as "Marxist" and "Popular Unity" violence were reframed for this election as a rise in "criminal gang" violence (Duran 1976, 8–9); during this period, the newspaper published 183 items on organized crime, a quarter of which referred to "aggressions against children" (Duran 1976, 10). Yet there was no rise in such crimes (Duran 1976, 9). However, unlike after the coup, competing voices in this media system supported Allende and challenged the Right's discourse of rising crime.

In an attempt to decrease the role of the media in escalating political tensions, governments passed increasingly restrictive laws aimed at limiting press freedoms. For example, laws passed between 1931 and 1937 linked certain press acts with state security. These laws "made it a crime against state security to publish tendentious or false information, to defend violence or to propagate subversive doctrines" (HRW 1998, 22–23). These laws were reorganized and expanded culminating in the passage of the 1958 State Security Law (no. 12.927), which remains in effect today, albeit reformed significantly in 2001. However, rather than being aimed to reduce problematic coverage of "crime," these laws sought to decrease favorable news coverage of protests and strikes. In this manner, journalistic autonomy was increasingly limited by legal as well as political and economic restrictions.

In the 1950s, the media environment changed as television emerged and *El Mercurio* assumed a more assertive political role. Due to disagreements regarding whether to place television under state control or to let it be run by the private sector, a compromise was struck. Similar to public broadcasting in Europe, in Chile television was placed under the control of two of the country's most prestigious universities, the Catholic University (which acquired channel 13) and the University of Chile (Red de Television de Universidad de Chile, RTU, channel 11 in Santiago) (Catalán 1988, 48; Fox and Waisbord 2002, 5). Funding came from both the state and advertising revenue. The channels were politically pluralistic, but not national. Until 1969, only Santiago and Valparaíso had full television coverage (Fox 1997, 119). In 1969 President Eduardo Frei established Chile's first national television network, Televisión Nacional de Chile (TVN). TVN was state run but kept at arm's length through a politically plural governing board (Davies 1999, 130). The emergence of a national television station meant that in 1970, for the first time, television was a factor in a presidential election, to the benefit of Salvador Allende (Popular Unity).

However, print was and remains the agenda-setting medium, within which *El Mercurio* plays a prominent role. In the 1950s, *El Mercurio* began to build its own political agenda, independent of a particular political party. Ken Léon-Dermota attributes this change in direction to the death of Agustín Edwards Bulge in 1955 and his replacement by his conservative and authoritarian son Agustín Edwards Eastman (Léon-Dermota 2003, 6). Certainly, from 1964 to 1973 most newspapers in Chile, as well as many radio stations, were highly politicized and polarized. *El Mercurio* was not an exception.

El Mercurio took a decidedly antidemocratic and economically neoconservative shift. Its editorials began to question the role of political parties and democracy (Léon-Dermota 2003, 14–15). In 1968 it established an economics section in its newspaper, and Edwards put Chicago Boys in charge of teaching Chileans about neoliberalism (Léon-Dermota 2003, 9).[13] These efforts and those of other conservative newspapers were supported by the United States government through money the CIA channeled to the anti-Allende Chilean press both before and after the 1970 presidential election. More than $12 million was provided between 1963 and 1973 (HRW 1998, 27).[14]

In an effort to mediate growing political tensions, the Christian Democrats, who were governing the country under President Frei (1964–1970), increased state ownership of and subsidies to the media, with the objective of better representing a broader spectrum of society, combating commercialism, and increasing cultural and educational content (Fox 1988, 21). However, the Christian Democrats were not eager to allow a potential Popular Unity (Unidad Popular, UP) government, led by Allende, to control the media. Thus, before the 1970 election, and as a condition for Christian Democrat support for UP, the two parties established an agreement titled "Statute of Constitutional Guarantees." The statutes were a series of constitutional reforms that ensured private media ownership and limited government's use and access to the media (Catalán 1988, 51; Fagen 1974, 63; Fox 1988, 21–22; HRW 1998, 25).

While confined by the constitutional changes, Allende did try to defend himself against the opposition media. He attempted to nationalize *El Mercurio*'s newsprint (unsuccessfully), harassed the newspaper with tax and weapons inspection, withheld government advertising, and pressed legal charges (using the State Security Law) (HRW 1998, 25; Léon-Dermota 2003, 3, 16). These tactics were not new; all Chilean governments have used them since 1958. Moreover, some large national dailies supported Allende, in particular *Clarín* (Léon-Dermota 2003, 6); in 1963 *Clarín* was the second most popular newspaper in Chile after *El Mercurio* (Carter and Sepúlveda 1964, 219). *La Tercera*, the third most popular newspaper in 1963, was one of the few dailies that managed to continue to represent all sides during this very polarizing period and, as a consequence, was able to increase its circulation rate between 1971 and 1973 (Reyes Matta 1986, 65).[15] However, the extent of media polarization and politicization was such that later Chile's truth commission report would hold the press partly accountable for the coup that followed (HRW 1998, 27). Indeed, in July 1973, an *El Mercurio* editorial called for military intervention (Léon-Dermota 2003, 19).

In sum, as in Argentina, Chile's media environment has seen the coexistence of a liberal media system with significant political polarization, albeit based on class rather than a populist movement. Until the 1973 military coup, this polarization contributed to a diversity of mass media political perspectives (external pluralism), some government attempts to broaden the pluralism of ideas through state regulation and subsidies, and various attempts through legal restrictions and state control to limit political pluralism. Both before and after the coup, the economic elite used the mass media as a political tool in negotiations with the state on economic policies.

THE PINOCHET REGIME (1973–1990)

The military government that followed reshaped the media environment in Chile. The regime closed all media that supported Allende's Popular Unity party (under threat of bombardment) and permitted only two newspapers, *El Mercurio* and *La Tercera de la Hora* (Knudson 1981, 5; Krohne 2005, 89). Media outlets that were seized were either kept by the state or sold to regime-supporting private firms. By April 1975, the Chilean Journalists Association reported that four hundred journalists had lost their jobs, two hundred had left the country, and fourteen were in prison (HRW 1998, 29). In total, the regime killed or disappeared as many as twenty-three pro-Allende journalists and forty-six other press workers between 1973 and 1990 (HRW 1998, 29).

As was done in politically conservative media before the coup, the mass media that survived continued to elide the difference between political opposition and "criminals." The 2004 Valech Report on torture during the Pinochet regime states: "The press presented acts of state repression as crusades against crime, denigrating in this way opposition figures through their presumed association with criminal acts" (188). One study of *El Mercurio*'s coverage of dramatic human rights cases during the dictatorship describes how this reframing of state-led human rights abuses as common crime allowed journalists to avoid the need to lie or omit information; they simply had to do as they do today, put such cases in the police section of the newspaper, report what the judge says, and not bother interviewing human rights organizations such as the Vicaría de la Solidaridad (Lagos Lira, Salina Muñoz, and Stange Marcus 2009, 183; see chapter 4).

In 1978 the state of siege ended and a large and diverse trench media gradually emerged, funded by international solidarity organizations. Initially, alternative print media lacked the capacity for national distribution, but radio, notably Radio Cooperativa, was able to reach this broad audience. Media not only covered the spectrum of political views but many outlets delinked themselves from political parties and aimed to represent all perspectives (Bresnahan 2003, 46; Tironi and Sunkel 2000, 173). By 1987, two national daily center-left newspapers, *La Época* and *Fortín Mapocho* expanded the reach of the alternative media.[16] However, all media remained under the control of laws that limited freedom of speech (Léon-Dermota 2003, 76).

Yet the gains made by the conservative media under the Pinochet government far exceeded the success of the reemergence of the alternative press. In 1973, when Pinochet came to power, the *El Mercurio* chain owned 22 percent of all Chilean newspapers; by 1988, they owned more than 50 percent of all newspapers with a national circulation (Aparecida Ferrari 2003, 389; Krohne 2005, 91; Léon-Dermota 2003, 53–54). The gains in percentage of ownership occurred in part due to the closure of opposition papers but also as a result of the acquisition of newspapers by El Mercurio Group. During the dictatorship, El Mercurio increased its ownership of regional newspapers from eight to fourteen (Léon-Dermota 2003, 53).

While *El Mercurio* and *La Tercera* benefited from increased government advertising and significantly reduced competition,[17] the economic crisis of 1982 required them to seek loans. In 1980 *El Mercurio* was $13 million in debt (but its profits were $14.5 million), by 1984 the newspaper was approximately $100 million in debt and was operating at a loss of $22.5 million (Léon-Dermota 2003, 43–44). The debts of COPESA (Chilean Newspaper Consortium), the media group that owns *La Tercera*, also ballooned during this period (Léon-Dermota 2003, 46). While other media were suffering economic hardships, only *El Mercurio* and *La Tercera* received state-funded loans saving both newspapers from bankruptcy.

By the end of the dictatorship, *El Mercurio* and *La Tercera* owed large amounts of money to the State Bank. This gave Pinochet a great deal of control over these media groups because he could, at any time, ask that the debts be repaid. However, with the impending return to electoral democracy this power meant that the new government could do the same. So he transferred the debt to private banks and bought millions of dollars worth of prepaid advertising from *El Mercurio* and *La Tercera* (Léon-Dermota 2003, 35, 63–66). Even in 2007, *El Mercurio* still received almost half of all newspaper advertising (Lagos Lira, Salinas Muñoz, and Stange Marcus 2009, 176).

In sum, whereas political capture of the media before Pinochet favored those representing the interests of the dominant classes, the politicized mass media environment was still relatively pluralistic. Yet by the end of the Pinochet regime, the media system had been significantly altered in favor of pro-Pinochet media.

MEDIA NEOLIBERALIZATION

Despite Pinochet's political capture or control of the mass media, it was his regime that initiated an extensive implementation of neoliberal economic policies in Chile, which eventually included the media. While newspapers had remained privately owned, television was the most controlled medium during the Pinochet regime (Bresnahan 2003, 54). Only a few channels existed. The government administered TVN, and the University of Chile and the Catholic University continued to run their channels within the parameters set by the military and with state funding that favored the Catholic University (which was more supportive of the regime).

Neoliberal reforms of television began with the opening up of trade regulations, particularly transnational advertising, investment, entertainment, and technology transfers (Crofts Wiley 2006, 671). Cable television began in 1986 and the first provider was Intercom, owned by the El Mercurio Group. Eventually government funding of the university channels ended and Pinochet privatized television in 1989. The first noncable private TV channel, MEGA, aired in 1990 and was owned by Pinochet supporter Ricardo Claro. Due to financial difficulties resulting from state underfunding during the dictatorship, in 1992 the University of Chile gave the international business group Cisnernos a twenty-five-year lease on its channel. Also in 1992, the newly elected Aylwin government made TVN legally and financially autonomous from the state (although six of the seven board members are appointed by the president of the republic and approved by the Senate).[18]

Almost all the alternative media from the dictatorship closed in the 1990s as international solidarity funds were withdrawn, businesses were reticent to advertise in these outlets, and the government did not provide even temporary assistance with the transition (Bresnahan 2003, 48, 51; Krohne 2005, 93–94; Léon-Dermota 2003, 29–37). Thus in Chile neoliberal economic policies were applied to the media in a manner heavily orchestrated by the state. Privatization favored media that supported the military regime and, to a lesser extent, international media conglomerates. The democratic governments that followed equated a market-based media system with a democratic media.

This new conservative market-based neoliberal media system, with significantly concentrated ownership, encouraged the continuation of journalistic practices from the dictatorship that favor story frames criminalizing political opposition and the popular sectors (e.g., Ramos A. and Guzmán de Luigi 2000, 34–35). This is because conservative media in Chile had a long history of such framing, because media ownership concentration significantly reduced the external pluralism of ideas, to the benefit of the conservative perspective, and because of the profit incentives of crime stories in market-based media systems,.

Indeed, from 1991 to 1995, "citizen security" (defined in relation to common crime) was consolidated as a dominant theme in the mass media, an initiative led by *El Mercurio* owner Agustín Edwards Eastman and his newly created foundation Citizen Peace, but compatible with market-based media practices (Ramos A. and Guzmán de Luigi 2000, 52; discussed further in chapter 6). A study of TV news channels in 1996 found citizen security to be the second most reported news topic (Ramos A. and Guzmán de Luigi 2000, 51). By 2002, it was the most reported item on all open TV news channels (Spencer 2005, 131).

Certainly, as we will see, some newer alternative media have emerged, such as *The Clinic* (established 1998), *El Mostrador* (2000), *El Ciudadano* (2005), and *CIPER Chile* (2007), as well as some TV and radio programs, and the prolific use of social media. While these sources occasionally provide critical and important watchdog pieces, even on the police, they lack the audiences and agenda-setting power of the dominant two media companies. In 2016 El Mercurio owned three of the six largest national daily newspapers (*El Mercurio*, *La Segunda*, *Las* Últimas *Noticias*) and COPESA owned the other three (*La Tercera*, *La Cuarta*, *La Hora*).

Moreover, the market logic of neoliberal economic policies put in place during the dictatorship has shaped media democratization. In particular, public relations and public opinion companies played an important role in the 1988 plebiscite on the continuation of the Pinochet government. The opposition's sophisticated campaign drew on social scientists, media professionals, U.S. political marketing experts, as well as significant foreign funding for these efforts from the U.S. National Endowment for Democracy and other international funds (Crofts Wiley 2006, 672). Between 1987 and 1988 more than thirty institutions conducted approximately sixty public opinion surveys (Cordero 2009a, 77). While public opinion polls had been used in politics before, notably with the assistance of the sociologist Eduardo Hamuy from 1957 to 1973, their role in the 1988 campaign made the work more public than ever before (Cordero 2009a).

Both public relations and public opinion polls have flourished in Chile since 1990. The plebiscite showcased the work of public relations, whereas media privatization and electoral democracy further attracted many large and prestigious international public relations companies to the country. These companies encouraged both state and private organizations to adopt this new communicational management approach. In 1992 the Ministry of Education approved the issuing of public relations degrees (Aparecida Ferrari and França 2011, 64). The proliferation of public relations: is consistent with the market-based media logic of quick, cheap news; benefits from reduced watchdog journalism that might otherwise challenge the information; and has favored tough-on-crime voices in the media, over voices that promote human rights, owing to the better ability of the former to fund PR.

Similarly, polls offer a quick proxy for public opinion in market-based media systems as journalists have limited time to consult a wide array of sources. Indeed, a prolific increase in the production of public opinion polls emerged with the return of electoral democracy. While between 1957 and 1989 there were 153 published polls (82 in 1987–1988 alone), there were 845 from 1990 to 2006 (Cordero 2009a, 81). Since 1999 the mass media have become especially active in the production and dissemination of public opinion polls (Cordero 2009a, 79). However, foundations, research centers, and companies on the political right, especially Citizen Peace and Public Research Center (Centro de Estudios Públicos) on security issues, produce some of the most cited polls. The prominence of public opinion polls in the media in Chile has, in a somewhat circular manner, contributed to the growth of public relations in managing the image of institutions and public policies in these polls. Public opinion polls have also come to play an important role in public policy decision making in Chile (Cordero 2009a). This is particularly true in the areas of crime control, security, and policing.

In this manner, the media environment in Chile has embraced the structures of a (neo)liberal media system. This occurred before electoral democracy, making it more challenging for new media actors and practices to emerge. Moreover, the media have been "captured" by political interests (mostly but not exclusively opposition to the Concertación/Nueva Mayoría coalition) and by the economic interests of the owners of the dominant mass media companies. Thus, from the beginning of the current democratic period, media coverage of crime, security, and policing in democracy has followed a commercial (and associated political) logic that structures and limits public debates in a manner favorable to punitive populism and unfavorable to human rights. The following chapters examine more closely the changes in communicational practices that these reforms have produced.

Chapter 4

JOURNALISTS' PREFERENCE FOR TOUGH-ON-CRIME SOURCES

A dominant construction of (in)security emerges from the multiple, interacting, and routine practices of journalists, state actors, and civil society organizations. These practices and choices are shaped by the media system within which these actors work, and thus practices can change as the media system changes. Some practices favor certain actors over others, affecting whose voices and perspectives on (in)security come to dominate public discourse.

Chapters 4, 5, and 6 disentangle some of these routine and interacting practices in order to reveal the influence of media neoliberalization on punitive populism (see figure I.1). Among the notable ingredients that shape the way in which a news story is told are the sources journalists use to construct the story. Sources can determine the perspectives available to journalists when they choose how to frame a story. In an ideal democratic media system journalists use a wide variety of state and nonstate sources (Curran 1991, 30; Hallin and Mancini 2004, 189; Hughes 2003). For crime, policing, and security news stories this means that journalists do not rely solely on the police for information. As the comparison that follows reveals, journalists' sources for crime, policing, and security stories can also include the judiciary (defense lawyers, prosecutors, judges), civil society actors (e.g., security and human rights organizations), and citizens (e.g., victims, victims' families, witnesses).

In practice, market-based media systems, especially those most shaped by neoliberal economic policies, favor a restrictive number of sources. While ideally a market-based media system could increase competition for the production of quality news, in practice a deregulated media system has been shown to increase media ownership concentration. Even without this concentration, as Robert N. Entman (1989) argues, a market-based media system encourages competition to provide the most entertaining, cheapest, and fastest news stories, not the highest quality ones—as the former are more profitable. This type of competition has shaped journalists' practices by reducing the number of sources they use and increasing the tabloidization of news stories.

Regarding the number of sources, since speed and cost are priorities, journalists are more likely to rely on state sources and public relations (PR), as they are easy to access (speed) and inexpensive, and they provide valuable information

(Bennett 1996, 81; Entman 1989, 18–20; MacNamara 2014; Page 1996, 22). Many journalists face increased time constraints owing to cost-cutting layoffs and the emphasis on immediacy heightened by relatively or totally unregulated twenty-four-hour news (both TV and internet). Studies of the emergence of twenty-four-hour TV news, a format that exploded globally in the early 2000s, show that the medium's choice of emphasis on immediacy (especially in domestic contexts that lack regulations for promoting quality) has resulted in TV journalists' use of even fewer sources, more state sources, and less context than those working in other media formats (Gans 2003, 50–51; Lewis 2010, 86–90). State actors can organize scheduled events and provide prepackaged stories and material, both of which decrease media costs and increases the speed at which journalists can produce stories. State and civil society use of PR is discussed in more detail in chapters 5 and 6. This chapter focuses on shifts in journalists' choice of sources.

Deregulated market-based competition has also favored the tabloidization of mass media, even in quality newspapers (e.g., Cushion and Lewis 2010a; Garland 2001; Green 2008). Tabloidization refers to news media that use story frames emphasizing drama and emotion over context. Crime, along with entertainment and sports news, features prominently in such journalism. Deregulated commercial media gain far larger audiences at a lower cost than does watchdog journalism, by appealing to the emotions and drama provided by some sources over others, particularly the police and victims (Pratt 2007). The preference in such media (especially television) is for episodic frames (what is happening now) as opposed to more context-rich thematic frames. Shanto Iyengar, in his analysis of television framing of news in the United States, found that the use of episodic frames "breeds individualistic as opposed to societal attributions of responsibility; national issues are traced to private actions and motives rather than deep-seated socioeconomic or political conditions" (1996, 62). This allows state institutions to retain legitimacy by blaming wrongdoing on individual "bad apples"—a practice useful for diminishing the problem of police violence. It also favors a construction of insecurity focused on individual criminals rather than the socioeconomic context that exacerbates crime and feelings of insecurity. In this manner, journalists' use of episodic frames limits the discursive accountability media can provide.

In sum, the sources journalists use matter to the democratic role of the media. They affect whether or not the media hold punitive populists accountable for the consequences of their rhetoric and policies. They determine that which is understood as public opinion on crime and policing and the formation of public opinion. As a forum for public debate on security and policing issues, journalists' sources affect who participates in this debate. As the voice of public opinion in conversation with political elite, it matters which sources journalists use as proxies for the public as a whole. Finally, as a key source of information from which members of the public can form their own opinions, the sources journalists choose determine the information provided and the available or dominant explanatory frames.

In what follows I compare the influence of the implementation of neoliberal media policies on journalists' sources in Argentina and Chile. I find that the relatively late implementation of neoliberal media policies in Argentina initially contributed to a divergence in the array of sources used by journalists in the two countries after their respective returns to electoral democracy. However, once implemented, this has led to a convergence, where both media systems favor punitive populism. I focus on the shift in journalists' use of particular state and civil society sources.

This chapter is based primarily on 58 semistructured in-depth interviews conducted from 2009 to 2015 with police journalists (journalists who primarily cover crime stories), as well as their editors and producers, across formats and media groups in the two countries. It is also informed by interviews with over 130 state and civil society actors as well as by secondary materials. Journalists were asked what sources they rely on most to build their crime stories and, for more experienced journalists, how this has changed for them over time.

THE STATE AS A SOURCE: THE POLICE AND THE JUDICIARY

During authoritarian regimes, journalists rely on the state as a primary or sole source of information and mass media's role is to facilitate the state's communication with the people. This was the practice of police and crime reporting during the authoritarian regimes in both Argentina and Chile. Yet electoral democracy and neoliberal media policies had a different influence on journalists' use of the state as a source for crime stories in the two countries. In particular, they had an important but contrasting effect on the state sources journalists identified as their most important—the police and judiciary.

When journalists rely on the police as their only or primary source, crime stories tend to favor the law-and-order frame used by the police. That is, the problem is increased crime and the answer is tougher laws and greater police funds, power, and discretion. In some media contexts these frames are further reinforced by stories that celebrate the excellent work of police in this context, such as showcasing large seizures of drugs.

When covering crime, an alternative or supplementary authoritative state source identified by journalists is the judiciary (defined as prosecutors, judges, and defense lawyers). In both countries this source was relatively closed during their respective dictatorships. Journalists were expected to rely on the police for crime news, and military courts were closed to the public; judges spoke through their verdicts.

In democracy, the judiciary gradually became more accessible. In addition, both Argentina (in 1994) and Chile (in 2005) transitioned from a judicial system in which the judge leads the police investigation, to a system in which public prosecutors lead the police investigation. Thus in Argentina and Chile, the use of the judiciary as a source represents an expansion of journalistic sources (media democratization). Because it offers a diversity of perspectives, the judiciary could potentially provide frames that are less supportive of punitive populism. It can provide detailed information on crimes including the charges, the evidence and arguments provided by both the defense and the prosecution, and the judge's decision. It is also possible that cases of police wrongdoing might appear before the courts and therefore could be covered by journalists without media investigation or speculation. However, the preferential use of public prosecutors (found more commonly in Chile) reflects an extension of the police-as-source. Moreover, technical and drawn-out court cases do not provide the visible and dramatic stories that commercial media, and notably TV, use to attract large audiences and advertising. The police, especially at the moment of arrest, provide good images and drama. Thus it is interesting to note the differences and changes in journalists' use of the police and judiciary as sources in Argentina and Chile.

ARGENTINA

In Argentina, each province and the city of Buenos Aires has its own police force and at the national level (and until 2017, the city of Buenos Aires), the Argentine Federal Police (PFA). The PFA are more respected than the other police forces. Yet, regardless of the police force, people generally do not trust the police, and police are not authoritative journalistic sources. This is true for journalists and media outlets on the political right and political left. Of course, this has not always been the case. It emerged slowly and was most affected by experiences with media democratization prior to the full effect of neoliberal media reform. That is, journalists opened up to using a broader range of sources and this led journalists, and then the public, to question police legitimacy.

Prior to and during the dictatorship, most major media outlets had accredited police journalists who worked out of the PFA press office. At the time, this was the only police force for the city of Buenos Aires (as well as working nationally) and thus was a natural focus for national media based in the city. If other journalists needed information about crime or policing they could call their journalist at the police press office.[1] If you were not accredited, you either could not interview the police or the obstacles to arranging an interview were so time-consuming that, when received, the information was no longer newsworthy.[2]

While officially police journalists worked for their media outlet and received a salary from them, in practice they worked for the police and the government in power. As one journalist explained: "The journalist didn't know if [he or she] was a journalist or police."[3] For example, he explained that "they [the police] replaced police journalists' pensions with a Federal Police pension which pays much better. . . . So you can imagine the obligation [the journalist] has, a commitment that is almost economic as well as ideological."[4] The role of the police journalist was to report the official position; few media outlets questioned or edited what their police journalists sent them. Crime stories focused on political subversives and the success of the regime in stopping them (Fernández Roich 2017).

With the return of electoral democracy in 1983, many journalists continued to rely on either accredited police journalists or their close connections with local police chiefs. Police were a trusted source; journalists generally did not question the information police provided. However, police journalism was not well regarded by other journalists and their stories were commonly short and in the back of newspapers or broadcast segments; they rarely made headlines.[5] Gradually, both the use of police as sources and the relative importance of police journalism changed. Now there are almost no accredited police journalists.

Media democratization played an important part in this change. In 1987, *Página/12* was established as a left-of-center national daily newspaper committed to watchdog journalism, democracy, and human rights. A prominent *Página/12* journalist, Horacio Verbitsky, explained the newspaper's position that it "would never automatically accept the official police or government position, we would question it, investigate. And we published a lot of stories on police brutality."[6]

Following *Página/12*'s success with watchdog journalism, other mass media began to uncover cases of police wrongdoing. Media featured high-profile cases of arbitrary police killings (*gatillo fácil*) beginning in 1987 and throughout the 1990s. In 1996, Carlos Dútil and Ricardo Ragendorfer published an article in the news magazine *Noticias* titled "La Maldita Policía" (Damned police), which exposed the involvement of the Buenos Aires Provincial Police in crime. The article later became a best-selling book (1997) and popular film (2000).[7] In the late 1990s, Virginia Messi, a police journalist for *Clarín*, exposed the PFA's use of fraudulent and mediatized arrests to increase their arrests statistics. Thus once journalists began to question and investigate police reports they found that the police were not a reliable source of information. By the late 1990s very few journalists relied on police as their primary source of information. Uncovering police wrongdoing brought prestige to those journalists and their media outlets that exposed it.

Yet, at the same time that media democratization facilitated watchdog journalism and decreased reliance on the police, new neoliberal media policies encouraged a slow increase in the number and prestige of crime stories. In 1989 state-owned TV channels were privatized and twenty-four-hour cable TV news channels, such as Crónica TV (a twenty-four-hour tabloid news channel that focuses mainly on crime) and Clarín Group's TN Todo Noticias, began to air in 1994. Increased competition and decreased time and budgets made crime news attractive. Crime is a cheap way to fill all those hours, and gradually, spurred by the 2001–2002 political and economic crisis, it began to expand its presence in the print media as well.[8] As one journalist explained, during the economic crisis many journalists lost their jobs, media outlets closed, and those that remained "lost the resources and thus the interest in investigative journalism."[9] While some journalists argued that increased crime coverage reflected an increased crime rate, Guillermina Seri finds no explosive increase in crime at this time (2012, 31–33).

In addition to the neoliberalization of the media market and the ensuing economic crisis, some journalists argued that crime also began to be used politically as the media polarized those supporting the Cristina Fernández de Kirchner government and those against, most notably from 2008 to 2015. President Fernández de Kirchner identified crime as a key issue used by the mass media to discredit her government.[10] In an explicit example of the captured liberal media model, one journalist explained that when his media company was anti-Kirchner they had a "crime meter" on the cover of the newspaper to illustrate rising crime rates. This was eliminated once the company became pro-Kirchner.[11] Another journalist argued that the pro/anti-Kirchner battle in the media simply eclipsed or subordinated all other news stories, including police wrongdoing.[12]

Yet despite accusations of the political use of crime, the quantity and prestige of crime news stories remained high in most mass media whether they were pro-Kirchner (e.g., *Crónica* newspaper, C5N, Radio 10), anti-Kirchner (e.g., *Clarín*, TN, *La Nación*), or independent (e.g., América TV). For example, Argentina's two most widely circulated national newspapers, *Clarín* and *La Nación*, respectively introduced a "police" section in 2002 (before Néstor Kirchner's presidency) and a "security" section in 2011 (during Cristina Kirchner's presidency).[13] In 2007, C5N, a popular twenty-four-hour news TV channel, began broadcasting and it made policing and security one of its top news issues.[14] They continued this programming even after a change in ownership in 2012 that shifted the editorial line from anti- to pro-Kirchner. The difference between news media outlets supportive or not of the Kirchners came in the framing of crime as on the one hand, "the government is effectively combating crime" or "police are autonomous actors from the government," and on the other hand, "the government is unable to control crime" (interviews; Bonner 2016).

While police journalists continue to use the police as sources (usually through connections, not the press office), they generally do not rely on the police as the primary source. Even the producer of *Policías en Acción* (Police in action), a popular police reality-TV show (2004–2013) explained that it "show[s] what happens in greater Buenos Aires [not just the police]. So this gradually broke the prejudice people had against the program. To this day many people haven't seen the show because of the name."[15] That is, the police wrongdoing exposed by journalists in the 1990s, combined with a general distrust and fear of the police left over from the dictatorship, influenced a decrease in journalists' use of police as credible and sufficient sources, even for crime stories. While all interviewed journalists, editors, and producers said that their media outlet's editorial line continues to have no problem with reporting that is critical of police information and actions, since 2001/2002 journalists are less likely to search for such stories.[16]

Of course when covering crime, another authoritative state source journalists prioritize is the judiciary (defined as judges, lawyers, and public prosecutors). During the dictatorship, journalists had very limited access to the judiciary as a source. Today, for many but not all police journalists, the most important and reliable source for crime stories is the judiciary. Journalists who worked during the dictatorship emphasized how electoral democracy opened up this source as an important alternative to relying on the police.[17] Police journalists with connections to human rights organizations argued that with democracy many human rights organizations began to provide victims of police wrongdoing with lawyers.[18] These lawyers then became valuable official sources of information on the judicial proceedings. Indeed, lawyers often contact police journalists to help gain media coverage for their clients. In contrast, journalists at more conservative mass media outlets emphasized the importance of public prosecutors, since they lead the criminal investigation. Public prosecutors may provide a story that emphasizes a tough-on-crime frame similar to that of the police, but journalists argued that prosecutors are more reliable (although never completely so). Almost all police journalists mentioned that, with electoral democracy and extensive media coverage of police wrongdoing, the public and journalists began to view public prosecutors, judges, and judicial proceedings as more reliable sources than the police.[19] As one journalist put it: "You need to stick with the facts and it boils down to the court file. You can't fuck around with a court file."[20]

However, since the extensive implementation of neoliberal media policies and the subsequent rise in importance and number of crime stories, these judicial sources are often heavily supplemented with the voices of victims. Journalists can use the courtroom as a way to locate and capture statements from victims. This is especially the case for TV. The issue of victims as sources will be discussed in the next section.

CHILE

In contrast to Argentina, in Chile, police continue to be a central authoritative source and the police beat is very important for mass media outlets. Chile has two police forces, both of which are national: the Carabineros de Chile and the Investigative Police of Chile (Policía de Investigaciones de Chile, PDI). The Carabineros are the preferred source for journalists because they are the only uniformed police and, compared to the PDI, they are a much larger force that is responsible for a broader range of crimes. They are also one of the most respected institutions in Chile and they control their own media relations.[21] The Carabineros have played an important role in their public image through their disciplined and professional communications efforts (Bonner 2013). However, journalists' choice to cooperate and continue to rely on the police as a primary source has been shaped by the manner in which neoliberal media policies limited media democratization in the country.

As in Argentina, during the dictatorship only journalists accredited by the Carabineros (and supportive of the regime) had access to the police. Police journalists were expected to report what the police wanted them to report. This was generally restricted to selected isolated incidents and minimal follow-up was possible with police or the judiciary.[22] Near the end of the dictatorship and beginning of democracy, this limited access changed. Carabineros extended accreditation to journalists from opposition media outlets and thus became a source that most journalists could access, in the sense that they could ask for information or an interview.[23]

However, this opening of the police was still controlled, albeit differently from control during the dictatorship. The police developed a large communications department with a sophisticated proactive communications strategy that aims to manage journalists. No accredited journalists are completely excluded, they are just included differently.[24] The police response to journalists' requests for information and interviews varies (regarding timeliness and provision of information) among media outlets and in the potential impact of their news stories on police image. For example, one former police journalist for *La* Época (late 1990s) explained that he needed to be "symbolically" approved by the police before they would give him information; they tested him to make sure he wrote well about them and then gradually provided more information. Almost all police journalists (2009–2015) mentioned that police cut off (or delayed) access to information for a while in response to critical police stories.

Electoral democracy was also slow to bring a reduction in the number of laws that restrict journalists' coverage of the police. The Code of Military Justice still has a sedition clause (Articles 276 and 417) that criminalizes offensive language against the Carabineros and carries a punishment of up to ten years in prison (HRW 1998, 3, 53–54; 2001, 20). Libel and defamation laws also exist within the criminal code (Articles 263, 264, and 265), with a maximum sentence of three years (HRW 1998, 50). Finally, the 1980 Constitution (still in effect) emphasizes the special obligation (above others) to respect people's honor (León-Dermota 2003, 78). Some (but not all) of these laws were derogated in 2001 and, although one journalist reported that the police took him to court for his critical reporting on the police,[25] most journalists did not cite legal restrictions as limiting their work.

Yet, more than police public relations or laws, neoliberal media policies have contributed to media practices and editorial lines that encourage journalists to continue their deferential relationship with the police as a primary source. Neoliberal media policies were introduced in Chile during the Pinochet regime, which favored the concentration of mass media ownership in the hands of Pinochet supporters. With electoral democracy, political leaders accepted media market choice as equivalent to democracy. The media market in Chile remains dominated by a conservative duopoly of El Mercurio and COPESA media groups. The editorial lines of these media owners as well as market demands for cheap, quick, and entertaining news since the return of electoral democracy have contributed to an emphasis on crime stories and frames that generally portray police work positively and as the solution to insecurity.[26] Indeed, police journalists from both dominant media groups identified self-censorship based on editorial lines as the most important limit to their use of the police as a source.

Most mass media police journalists interviewed explained that they tend to work closely with the police, report stories selected from what the police offer them, and present issues and events from the perspective of the police. Police set the agenda and their information is cross-checked with information from public prosecutors or witnesses/victims/victims' families, or both, depending on time constraints. One TV assistant news director said that 80 percent of his outlet's crime stories came from the police. A radio police journalist said that he began his workday by meeting his editor at the Carabinero's communications department and, due to time pressures, additional sources were restricted to those people present at each crime scene, which were usually victims.[27] Most mass media police journalists noted time constraints as the reason for relying primarily on the Carabineros.

Critical journalism about the police is the exception, not the norm as it was in Argentina in the 1990s. Its presence in the mass media is limited and tends to focus on "bad apples" (e.g., Bonner 2018). Police wrongdoing is covered by mainstream mass media if it is stumbled upon and its evidence is indisputable, such as a judicial proceeding, mass media video images,[28] published photographs, or police admission to wrongdoing.[29] This was the case with the 2017 Carabineros corruption scandal, which was not covered in the mass media until the evidence was overwhelming. As a former journalist for *El Mercurio* explained, in *El Mercurio* "you need proof in your hand if you are going to criticize the Carabineros, proof which is not so often demanded for critiques of other institutions to be made."[30] Generally, police wrongdoing will not be sought through watchdog journalism.[31] Editors decide whether cases of police wrongdoing will be reported and if they appear they will most likely be in a small article in the back of a newspaper or a paragraph within an article, and follow-up will be limited.[32] All police journalists noted that, from about 2010 to 2013 onward, the proliferation of mobile video technology used by journalists and citizens has increased the amount of video footage of police wrongdoing. However, they explained that they generally use these images infrequently so as not to prejudice the image of police.

Most journalists and editors avoid stories that critique the police because of the alignment of this position with the editorial line and for market reasons. As one police journalist put it when asked about the legal limitations to covering the police: "[Legal limits are not an issue,] we have our editorial line, so we self-censor."[33] Many other mainstream media journalists said they agreed with their outlet's editorial line and that all institutions as large as the Carabineros have bad apples. Crime sells and critical reporting of the police can compromise journalists' access to the police as a key source of crime news.[34] Most police stories focus on the Carabineros' control of crime (through showcasing arrests) and maintenance of public order (through their control of protests). Reporting tends to frame the issue as a "war on crime" and a need for "citizen security" (defined as the protection of citizens from common crime). Indeed, one police journalist explained that many police journalists see themselves as playing an important role in this war on crime by supporting the Carabineros in their work and showcasing crime.[35] Another police journalist explained that he saw it as his duty to inform people about the dangers of crime and its proximity.[36] Thus the introduction of twenty-four-hour news channels in 2008 (CNN and TVN) as well as, in the same year, popular reality-TV police shows (*133* and *Policías en Acción*) reinforced, rather than spurred, extensive coverage of crime and limited critique of the police.

Of course, there is critical media coverage of the police and crime in Chile. For example, in the mass media, the TV program *Contacto* has included segments critical of the police. However, these stories have usually come to them rather than having been sought out.[37] Some TV media, whose audience is the lower socioeconomic groups, found that from approximately 2010 to 2015 their audiences began providing and asking for stories of police wrongdoing (especially noted by interviewees at Chilevisión and MEGA TV stations). Yet these stories tend to be given episodic coverage as is consistent with commercial TV's journalistic style.

In the mainstream print media, there are sometimes opportunities for journalists to seek out alternative sources or investigate the social context of crime or the actions of police. Yet most of these stories must either conform with the editorial line that crime is the problem and policing is the answer, or be relegated to small articles, paragraphs, or segments.[38] One journalist described the interest in watchdog journalism in the mass media as a cycle, not a commitment. He explained that there are cheaper ways to increase sales.[39] Thus most mass media police journalists continue to rely on the police as their primary source and generally report news that is favorable to the institution, whether this news reports crime or police actions.

Some alternative media emerged in the early 2000s and their stories are occasionally picked up by the mainstream mass media. Generally, these journalists do not rely on regular news from the police and thereby feel freer to be critical.[40] For example, CIPER Chile is an online award-winning investigative journalism site that uses access to information requests as the basis for many of its stories. This has uncovered cases of police wrongdoing. However, the site has a narrow audience and its stories on police wrongdoing are sporadic and few in number. Alternative media are also more likely to supplement or cross-check the information they collect from police sources against other sources, or even to prioritize these other sources.[41] However, those stories taken by mass media from alternative media are most likely to be stories that conform to their editorial line (support the police and expose crime) or provide unquestionable and unavoidable evidence of police wrongdoing (and even then it is likely the story will not be highlighted but only mentioned). It is thus not surprising that despite the explosive and extensive coverage of the 2017 Carabineros corruption scandal, public opinion polls still show them to be the institution in which Chileans had the second most confidence (down from first place) after the armed forces and in a tie with the PDI (CEP 2017).

Thus in Chile, journalists' continued preference for the police as the most important source of crime stories is maintained through the interacting dynamics of limited media democratization and the early application of neoliberal market principles to the media sector. Indeed it is these market principles that the Chilean Journalists Association (Colegio de Periodistas) views as having the most significant influence on freedom of expression in Chile.[42]

However, as in the Argentine case, the judiciary, which was predominantly closed to the media during the dictatorship (and into the 1990s in Chile), holds the potential to diversify or democratize journalists' sources. Yet, whereas in Argentina police journalists shifted to the judiciary due to the lack of public confidence in the police, in Chile, public confidence in the police is significantly higher than in the judiciary (see table 1.4).

Polls repeatedly show that Chilean citizens have more confidence in the police than in most other state institutions. For example, a 2014 poll conducted by Diego Portales University found that while 43 percent of Chileans had confidence in the police (higher than any other institution), only 8 percent had confidence in the judiciary.[43] One analysis of media coverage of crime stories in 2002 found that judicial actors constituted 7.6 percent of those actors that appeared in such stories in print media and 5.9 percent in TV crime stories; in contrast, the police constituted 20.5 percent and 21.7 percent, respectively (Dastres et al. 2005, 51, 158). Most police journalists interviewed noted the judiciary, and particularly public prosecutors, as a secondary source after the police. For more time-sensitive street journalism such as radio, public prosecutors were only used if they happened to be at the crime scene.

The inclusion of public prosecutors as a source is relatively new and could be described as part of the broader democratization process. The penal procedures reform (2000–2005) established a National Prosecutors Office, which now leads criminal investigations. This has sometimes made public prosecutors more knowledgeable than the police about crime stories. While expanding journalists' sources, this reform has not meant that police journalists have opened up to using the judiciary as a whole as a source on crime and policing. Instead, one journalist argued, the perspective of the public prosecutor is taken as the truth, even more so than the perspective of the judge presiding over the case.[44] Indeed, some police journalists explained that defense lawyers were too biased in favor of their clients.

One journalist from *La Nación* noted that even when trials are held against police for excessive violence, it can be difficult for journalists to cover them. He explained that he and his colleagues wrote an article that presented the types of trials taking place against Carabineros and the names of the officers on trial for excessive violence. However, they were not able to publish the article due to the pressure the Carabineros placed on the newspaper via the government.[45] Thus a combination of restricted media democratization, commercial preference for police action, and media owners' political preference for a law-and-order frame for crime stories, affects the use of the judiciary as a source in Chile.

In sum, the state is an important journalistic source in all countries. This is particularly true during authoritarian regimes. With electoral democracy comes the opportunity for journalists to expand the diversity of both their state and nonstate sources. In crime news, this involves an expansion of sources beyond the police to various judicial sources and the possibility to challenge the validity of these sources. Yet the comparison of Argentina and Chile reveals that neoliberal media reforms have played an important intervening role in this process of media democratization. Market pressures and editorial lines favor the proliferation of crime stories and, in the case of Chile, the primacy of police sources. Similar pressures affect the way journalists use civil society organizations and citizens as sources on crime stories.

CIVIL SOCIETY AND CITIZENS AS SOURCES

Under authoritarian regimes the media's role is to communicate what the state wants to say to the people. Thus the state, not the people, is the primary and often exclusive source of information. Media democratization involves expanding journalists' sources beyond the state to include the voices of the people (Hughes 2003). In its ideal, this inclusion facilitates the democratic role of the media as a forum for debate in which a public opinion can be formed and communicated to elected officials; in this way the media represent the voice of the people. Indeed, many studies show that when media use more civil society sources, their reporting tends to be less supportive of iron-fist policing and more supportive of civil rights (della Porta and Reiter 1998a, 19; Hughes 2003; Wisler and Giugni 1999). They are thus better able to provide discursive accountability.

Yet, after the implementation of neoliberal media policies, the public opinion that the media in Argentina and Chile appear to be presenting through the inclusion of citizen voices is one that largely supports punitive populism. The choices journalists make regarding which civil society organizations and citizens' voices are included and how play an important role in the construction of this public opinion. The comparison of Argentina and Chile highlights the importance of journalists' use of human rights organizations as authoritative sources for the development of police watchdog journalism (favoring media democratization) and the role of citizens' voices in building support for iron-fist policing (and encouraging the individualism and drama that is consistent with market-based media systems).

ARGENTINA

Media democratization in Argentina included journalists' expanded use of civil society organizations as authoritative sources. Human rights organizations have been important authoritative sources for journalists in Argentina since the end of the last dictatorship. The recognizable white headscarves of the Mothers of the Plaza de Mayo became media symbols of the struggle against the dictatorship and the trials and transitional justice projects that followed.

However, human rights organizations did not become important journalistic sources for those covering crime and policing until the 1990s. In particular, in

1991 the highly mediatized case of seventeen-year-old Walter Bulacio (who was beaten by police while in their custody and died of a resulting head injury) led to the formation of the Coordinator against Police and Institutional Repression (CORREPI) and, spurred the Center for Legal and Social Studies (CELS) to expand its work on current police violence. Lawyers from both organizations led the Bulacio trial.

New organizations of victims of police and criminal violence also began to form beginning in the 1990s, including the Commission of Family Members of Defenseless Victims of Social, Police, Judicial, and Institutional Violence (COFAVI, founded in 1991), Mothers of Pain (Madres del Dolor, founded in 2004), and the Network of Mothers and Family Members of Drug Victims (commonly known as Madres contra el Paco, founded in 2005). All these organizations have received significant media coverage at various times. Police journalists across the political spectrum now regularly use nongovernmental organizations (NGOs) as sources for their stories.

CORREPI and CELS are used most often in relation to cases of suspected police wrongdoing. Police journalists note that these organizations provide reliable statistics and background information on police violence. CORREPI's president, María del Carmen Verdú, is recognized by many journalists for her willingness to speak to the media and her familiarity to audiences (due to repeated appearances and as a lawyer on the Bulacio trial). Thus, despite CORREPI and María del Carmen Verdú's political position on the left, she receives media coverage for the work of CORREPI in a wide array of mainstream media. For example, she participated in a long interview on December 12, 2013, on the conservative TV channel América at prime time (10:30–11:00 p.m.) in regard to the ongoing police strike and looting at the time (fieldnotes, 2013).

While journalists in Argentina have commonly used citizens (people on the street, victims, criminals) as sources, with the extensive implementation of neoliberal economic and media policies, coverage of victims of crime and their families increased noticeably beginning in the early 2000s.[46] The stories are personalized and the perspective often focuses on the victim's pain or the loss of a loved one. There were other highly mediatized victims of crime, but Juan Carlos Blumberg was one of the first to use this attention to gain support for punitive policies. As explained in the introductory chapter, Blumberg led a number of large demonstrations demanding tougher penal laws and greater police discretion. Victims' discourses provide drama and make crime statistics appear cold and unfeeling. In turn, audience identification with victims also contributes to group formation, which political leaders can use to gain legitimacy (Samet 2013, 532). Indeed some victims' voices, such as Blumberg's, have reinforced a commonly heard slogan that "human rights organizations care more about the rights of criminals than those of 'citizens'" (Calzado 2015; Seri 2012). Thus, the "us" (citizens) versus "them" (criminals) rhetoric, emblematic of punitive populism, can be reinforced by the prominence of victims as sources.

The increased use of victims and victims' families as sources for police journalists emerged from the pressures of both media democratization and neoliberal media policies. In terms of media democratization, after the 1990s' watchdog journalism, crime stories could no longer center entirely on the police version of events.[47] These versions had to be verified and victims and their family members provided an avenue for confirmation. Moreover, by the end of the 1990s, media in Argentina had been extensively privatized and deregulated. In this context, victims' voices add drama and emotion to news stories that helps to expand commercial audiences. While many media rely primarily on state advertising for revenue, large audiences are particularly important for media that want to maintain political independence from the state or fill twenty-four-hour news spaces (TV and internet). Victims-as-sources also help meet time pressures. As one police journalist noted, victims' Facebook images and comments are easily and quickly accessed.[48] Some victims of crime, such as those associated with Madres del Dolor, emphasize police wrongdoing as part of the problem, but most victims do not. The more pervasive victims' voices then become a proxy for public opinion support for tough-on-crime policies.[49]

CHILE

In Chile, as in Argentina, NGOs were important sources for journalists in the anti-Pinochet media during the dictatorship.[50] In contrast, today in Chile, while human rights organizations are occasionally sources for journalists covering the trials of military leaders from the dictatorship and are important sources for some alternative media such as Radio Universidad de Chile and *El Ciudadano*, most of these NGOs do not work on current police wrongdoing. Even when they do, as one journalist explained, "I believe that the most important media we have today don't center their attention on social demands. It's very difficult to find an example of an article in a newspaper with national circulation where it's possible to know the demands of the Mapuche people or the specific demands of a medical office strike."[51]

For most mass media in Chile, NGO leaders are not considered authoritative sources or "leaders of opinion." They are seen as representing the views of a minority, "political" (not objective), and of little interest to the general public. If used, their views would appear in a small paragraph within an article. As one journalist notes, this is a vicious circle; without media coverage it is harder for these groups to build a large following or challenge the "objectivity" of state sources.[52] A former journalist for *El Mercurio* explained that the newspaper is not interested in interviews with protesters, and if they are included, as with the leaders of the 2006 student movement, these interviews are published as a small paragraph within an article.[53] Almost all mainstream mass media journalists and editors interviewed described NGOs as marginal or irrelevant sources, if used at all. Sometimes, when asked about their use of NGOs as sources the journalist responded by naming organizations that are private businesses such as private security firms or public opinion and marketing firms.[54] Indeed, a 2002 study of media coverage of crime in Chile found that NGOs and research centers were the least likely to be mentioned as an actor in crime news stories (0.5 percent of actors in print media and 0.3 percent on TV) (Dastres et al. 2005, 51, 158).

There are two exceptions to the general bias against NGOs as sources. First, in 1992 the owner of *El Mercurio*, Agustín Edwards Eastman, founded and funded, an NGO called Citizen Peace (Paz Ciudadana) that focuses its research on crime, victimization, and criminal policy. It is an accepted NGO source used by both media groups on issues of crime (Léon-Dermota 2003; Ramos and Guzmán de Luigi 2000; author interviews). Some journalists also mentioned Victims of Crime (Víctimas de la Delincuencia), an NGO founded in 2006 by former National Renovation (Renovación Nacional, a right-wing political party) congressman Gonzalo Fuenzalida. Thus connections to power or the state appear to make NGOs more authoritative as sources. Other NGOs occasionally mentioned were service providers such as Christ's Home (Hogar de Cristo) and various NGOs that offer rehabilitation programs for prisoners. In these cases the NGOs provide services that are consistent with most mainstream media's editorial line of tough on crime.

Second, social movement organizations occasionally use communications strategies that force media to cover them and their demands (see chapter 6). Students did this effectively during their 2006 and 2011–2012 protests, as did Andha Chile a Luchar in 2009 (Bonner 2014a). Yet most NGOs do not have a communication strategy and have limited professional communication assistance (Aparecida Ferrari 2003; author interviews). Indeed, many left-of-center NGOs do not reach out to the mainstream media in part because of a lack of confidence that they would receive coverage.[55] Thus NGOs are marginal sources for crime stories and when used are carefully selected in such a way that reinforces a tough-on-crime frame.

In contrast to NGOs, most mass media police journalists spoke of using witnesses, victims of crimes, or victims' families as one of three primary sources.[56] A 2002 media analysis of crime stories found that citizens constitute the largest group of actors found in such stories (26.8 percent in print media and 33.5 percent on television) (Dastres et al. 2005, 51, 158). The study notes that the concerns of these citizens are not always reported and there are disproportionate references across all types of crimes stories to businesspeople as being victims of crime or social conflict, or demanding new security policies, or taking someone to court (Dastres et al. 2005, 159).

Most journalists spoke of using victims, witnesses, and family of victims as sources because they are often at or near the scene of the crime. They are a convenient source that helps to cross-check police information, meet tight deadlines, and personalize the story. Other journalists mentioned investigative journalism TV shows, such as *En la Mira* and *Quien Vivo*, which examine crime as a social phenomenon generally (without questioning the role of the police).[57] These shows often document the lived experience with crime of people living in poorer neighborhoods (*poblaciones*). Similarly, the reality-TV show *Cárceles* (2007–2010) centers on stories told by prisoners, although the focus is on their humor or good storytelling more than their evaluation of the prison system or the social context of crime.[58] Some TV and radio stations mentioned that citizens call or email the news outlet to relate the crime stories these outlets should cover.[59] One police journalist explained that they occasionally like to do positive stories on criminals who have successfully been rehabilitated in jail.[60] Thus the selection of citizens as sources reinforces editorial lines.

Some journalists mentioned occasional opportunities to use citizens as more critical sources. One police journalist explained that when he was a police journalist for *La Tercera*, he and a colleague were able to focus a crime story on interviews done with individuals involved in crime. He said: "We did profiles, histories. We took, for example, say Juan Pérez is a new drug trafficker that has emerged in such and such *población*, and [we explained that] this guy came from here, and here, and here."[61] These sources, he argued, helped to give audiences a broader context within which to understand crime.[62] Another journalist, for an alternative newspaper, said that he has interviewed people affected by police violence, such as young protesters after a traditionally violent Day of the Young Combatant.[63] Yet these stories are the exception or they are limited to alternative media with smaller audiences. When asked how they use the proliferation of online images, websites, and social media that are exposing police wrongdoing, mainstream police journalists argued that they relied on these sources very little because they represent the views of a minority and are not reflective of public opinion at large.

Thus we see that in both countries, media democratization has opened up NGOs and citizens as potential sources, although Argentine journalists use NGO sources more often. In both countries market pressures (combined with editorial lines) have favored journalists' incorporation of NGOs and citizens as sources in selective ways that emphasize either NGOs' communicational abilities, their reinforcement of media outlets' editorial lines, or the drama and emotion of victims, or all three. The emphasis on victims' voices and law-and-order NGOs helps cultivate an environment (or as Bourdieu would call a "field") in which punitive populism becomes common sense and its rhetoric of "us" (citizens) versus "them" (criminals) is normalized.

CHOOSING TOUGH-ON-CRIME SOURCES

The most different cases of Argentina and Chile reveal neoliberal media policies to have shaped journalistic practices in a way that favors punitive populist discourses and undermines media democratization. In Argentina, initial media democratization encouraged a shift away from the police as the sole source for crime stories and facilitated a period of critical watchdog journalism. Journalists expanded their sources to include a diversity of actors from within the judiciary and civil society. Yet neoliberal media privatization and deregulation, combined with the 2001 economic crisis, led to reduced resources and time for watchdog journalism and limited the number of sources used. Journalists began to rely more heavily on the voices of victims and their families, who often reinforce and represent public support for tough-on-crime options.

The earlier adoption of neoliberal economic and media policies in Chile, and more limited media democratization, favored a continuation of journalists' reliance on the police for crime stories. In turn, to the extent that media democratization opened up sources to journalists, neoliberal market pressures and editorial lines favored journalists' use of selective NGO, citizen, and judicial sources. The exact sources that benefited most vary between the two countries (victims in Argentina and police in Chile), as they likely would elsewhere. However, in both cases it is tough on crime voices that emerge as dominant. Of course neoliberal media reforms have not just affected journalistic practices. The changes in journalistic practices have also influenced how the state engages with the media, the focus of chapter 5.

Chapter 5

THE RISE OF PUNITIVE VOICES FROM WITHIN THE STATE

In all countries, state actors actively participate in the media construction of particular definitions and solutions to insecurity. They do so from a privileged position. State actors are important authoritative sources for journalists. The more powerful the state actors, the more valuable they are as journalistic sources. State actors engage the media not only to maintain and build support for a specific government and its policies but also to maintain and grow the legitimacy of state institutions. That is, the mass media in a democracy ideally seek information for public debate and aim to hold state actors accountable, and state actors simultaneously attempt to control access to information, limit their accountability, and increase government and state legitimacy. This tension between accountability and legitimacy is central to media-state interactions on crime, security, and police violence, and is affected by media neoliberalization in particular ways. While democracy can open up an array of state actors to media scrutiny, I find that media neoliberalization and the journalistic practices it produces favor punitive voices through encouragement of particular state actors' use of public relations (PR), the mediatization of policymaking, and a showcasing of police work by state and media actors.

THE STATE AND THE MASS MEDIA

Ideally, democracy and authoritarianism attribute different roles to the media. Under most authoritarian regimes the state is an important, if not the only, journalistic source, often because it is the only permitted source or because the state and media consider it the role of journalists to communicate what the state wants to say to the people. The state may control the media through state censorship, restricted access to information, the closing of opposition media, and repression. The media are expected to support the regime in power and its policy goals, and thereby contribute to the construction and reinforcement of its legitimacy (Hughes 2003, 2006). In other words, in an authoritarian regime, the primary role of the media is to support regime legitimacy, not hold it to account.

In a democracy, the state is an important source for journalists because it is the center of public political power. In a democracy, the media are ideally expected to keep the public informed of state actions, omissions, and debates, as well as to hold the state accountable for perceived wrongdoing (by demanding answers and shaming) (Curran 2005; McNair 2003; Peruzzotti and Smulovitz 2006). Ideally, government and state actors gain legitimacy through their actions and omissions, and media communicate these choices to the broader public. To be legitimate, David Beetham argues, these actions and omissions should conform to established rules (or the law), which are based on shared beliefs and evidence of consent by the subordinate group in the power relationship established by these rules (1991, 15–16).

Consistent with this definition of legitimacy, in an ideal liberal democracy, public consent is expressed through regular, free, fair, and competitive elections. State actors are expected to be transparent, explain their actions or omissions (whether wrongdoing is suspected or not), and accept punishment by other state institutions (such as courts, elections, and oversight bodies) if wrongdoing is confirmed. When the public sees state actors involved in the criminal justice system, such as the courts and police, applying and accepting the weight of the rule of law equally and predictably to all, the institutions gain legitimacy (Beetham 1991; Holmes 2003; Maravall and Przeworski 2003).

Yet, in practice, this complicated relationship between accountability and legitimacy involves two important caveats. First, the *perception* of transparency and accountability is as important, or more so, than state actions (Edelman 1977; March and Olsen 1995; McNair 2003, 116; Tankebe 2010). Relations between the state and the mass media play an important role in the construction of *perceived* state legitimacy. Second, these relations play an important role in determining the actions or omissions the public perceives as necessary for transparency and accountability, and in constructing "public" consent itself. If the public is primed to view an act or omission as acceptable, it is unlikely that accountability will be demanded. This is what I have called elsewhere, discursive accountability (Bonner 2014a, ch. 2).

Discursive accountability, or its absence, is particularly important regarding issues pertaining to crime, security, and police violence, insofar as the police have a great deal of discretion in their methods of policing. While ideally police action is bounded by the law, as it applies to policing, the law rests heavily on police justification of their actions or omissions and the willingness of the public, political leaders, and the courts to accept these justifications. Public relations and mass media can facilitate the construction of acceptable justifications—usually by individualizing wrongdoing—that appear to the public as equal and predictable accountability, reinforcing institutional legitimacy, while doing little to ensure nonrepetition of police violence (Bonner 2018). As Richard V. Ericson puts it, "The rituals of expunging rotten apples offsets the possibility of a structural critique of the organization as a rotten barrel, thereby contributing to its continued legitimacy" (1991, 226). Thus, the stories we tell about accountability are as important as the institutions and laws established to govern it. Indeed, these stories can shape how we use these laws and institutions and whether or not steps are taken to reform or alter their practices or functions.

Media systems affect the type of stories told. (Neo)liberal media systems produce specific interactions between the mass media and the state that decrease the mass media's role in accountability and increase its role in reinforcing selective state legitimacy.[1] In particular, and as previously discussed, (neo)liberal media systems emphasize speed over quality news. This increases journalists' reliance on fewer, often state, sources (see chapter 4). It also favors state actors' use of prepackaged public relations material that fits journalists' preference for short, simple, and entertaining sound bites or images, and topics that can be "pegged" to top selling issues such as crime, scandal, sports, entertainment, or immediate events (Bennett 1996, ch. 3; Gans 2003, 49–54).[2] In turn this PR material aims to gain support for state actors' ideas and interests, often by deemphasizing facts and favoring emotions (Moloney 2006, 41).

Mass media openness to state public relations has also coincided with the adoption by many state bureaucracies of new public management. Applying neoliberal ideas to the civil service, new public management emerged, to varying degrees, in many countries beginning in the 1980s (Hood 1995). It advocates for state departments or ministries to compete with each other for funds. Those state institutions deemed most successful in terms of results and cost effectiveness receive more funds, ideally encouraging better state practices and economy through competition (Hood 1995; Mawby 2002).

However, again, public perception of effectiveness can be more important than institutions' actual practices. This has been particularly important for the police who have gained increased access to the media through the neoliberal media system's preference for crime stories. Thus, since the 1980s, countries such as the United Kingdom, United States, and Canada—as well as Chile and to a lesser extent Argentina—have seen significant growth in the establishment and expansion of police public relations offices as a response to both improving their image to attract state resources and to manage increased media demand (Fernandez 2008, ch. 6; Leishman and Mason 2003; Mawby 2002; Surette and Richard 1995). These public relations offices strategically control what is known and what people ask about the organization, draw on public emotions to build legitimacy, and enjoy an asymmetrical relationship with the media to their advantage (Chermak and Weiss 2005, 502; Ericson 1989, 217; Mawby 2010, 1061). Not all state agencies have the same access to the mass media nor the same available funds for public relations.[3]

In turn, media systems affect policymaking. Neoliberal media systems have encouraged what some scholars refer to as the "mediatization" of policymaking—policymaking decisions made primarily based on how issues or solutions will be portrayed in the media (Waisbord 2012, 438). Indeed, both British prime minister Tony Blair and U.S. president Barack Obama noted that the emphasis on speed and entertainment found in twenty-four-hour TV news (and since adopted by other media) encourages short-term policymaking (Cushion and Lewis 2010a, 3). As discussed in the introduction, this heightened importance of the media further strengthens its role in the creation of opportunities for new policies, communication between policy actors, the advantages and support it can provide to some policy actors over others, and influence and construction of public opinion.

In the Latin American–captured (neo)liberal media system, the mediatization of politics is high (Waisbord 2012, 438). State actors use media logic and public relations (in combination with clientelistic negotiations with media owners and selective distribution of advertising revenue) to attempt to control journalists' access to information and to shape the framing of stories. In many countries in the region, the mass media's increased focus on the image of leaders and their personalities has coincided with a hollowing out of political parties based on ideology (Boas 2005; Guerrero 2014; Waisbord 2012, 438). Public opinion polls drive political marketing, while elite-citizen dialogue and state accountability are reduced (Waisbord 2012, 438; 2013).

Thus, state actors have not passively accepted the changes in journalistic practices that came with neoliberal media policies. State actors' choices, while not always strategic or necessarily effective, have had an important influence on the saliency of crime news and its framing. This chapter examines three key issues that emerged as the most commonly referred to in interviews with state actors in both countries. State actors were selected based on their involvement in or communication of crime and security issues, and included members of the police, prosecutors, public defense lawyers, Ministry of Security/Interior, ombudsmen offices, and political parties across the ideological spectrum (57 interviews). Their perspectives were cross-checked with those of journalists and civil society organizations (approximately 132 interviews). The first issue pertains to state actors' use of public relations and the intrastate power dynamics it highlights. The second investigates state actors' choices of when and how they accept media frames (that is, the mediatization of public policymaking). The third involves assessing negotiations between the state and media in the development of entertainment-based reality-TV police programs.

THE STATE AND PUBLIC RELATIONS

Most states use professional public relations methods to communicate with the mass media. These can involve press releases, speech writing, press conferences, social media, staged events, prepared media material (news articles, photos, video, audio clips), and the selective use of exclusive interviews. Public relations is weak propaganda (Ellul 1965; Moloney 2006). The source of the information (e.g., a political leader or state institution) is usually but not always clear. The information presented is ideally true (although a selective truth), but not consistently true. Its purpose is always to make the political leader, government, or state institution look good and it thus aims to control information and accountability. In this way it reinforces the voices of dominant groups in public debate. For these and other reasons, many scholars critical of public relations do not consider it compatible with liberal democracy (Ellul 1965, 256; Moloney 2006, 3).

Public relations began in the United States in the late nineteenth century and in the United Kingdom in the early twentieth century. It gradually expanded but rose in importance most notably with the implementation of neoliberal economic policies in the 1980s onward and continues to enjoy strong growth today (MacNamara 2014, 73–74; Moloney 2006, 32). Public relations spread rapidly in Latin America in the 1990s, along with electoral democracy and neoliberal economic and media policies. According to one survey in the United Kingdom, news editors estimated that a quarter of all news stories are based on PR material; those working in PR believe the number is closer to 40 percent (Moloney 2006, 24).[4] Another study of media in Baltimore, Maryland, in 2009 found that 86 percent of stories could be attributed to PR, and 63 percent of stories came from government officials, mostly the police (MacNamara 2014, 125). Neoliberal media policies facilitate and encourage the use of PR because the market-based media environment makes it a quick and cheap news source for journalists and there is little watchdog journalism to hold PR to account. These dynamics place important limits on public debate on crime and security issues in particular.

Moreover, since professional public relations assistance and its corresponding products are expensive, not all state institutions have equal access. Indeed scholars of punitive populism in North America and Europe have argued that the new (neo)liberal media practices favor the voices of police and those using punitive populist rhetoric, over all other state actors, on criminal justice issues (Hall 1980, 15–17; Pratt 2007; Roberts et al. 2003). Consequently, they conclude that criminal justice experts in the judiciary and academia need to learn how to communicate better with the mass media (Pratt 2007, 176–179; Roberts et al. 2003, ch. 8 and conclusion). Yet unequal PR funding between state actors can impede such efforts.

Even in Latin America, where state capture of the (neo)liberal media market is significant, "the state" needs to be understood in terms of its multiplicity of actors. Indeed, in both Argentina and Chile a key question of debate regarding the communication of crime, security, and policing issues is: Who speaks to the media? Specifically: Are the police the primary state actors with the responsibility to respond to the media on security, public order, and crime control issues, or should this fall principally to political actors such as the minister of security, or a combination of these actors? The choice is fraught with issues of political power and concerns regarding police communicational autonomy.

In Argentina, political leaders emphatically argue that political actors should be the *only* ones to speak to the media. In Chile, the Carabineros assert themselves in this role. This debate is particularly interesting in the context of new democracies where civilian leaders are attempting to reclaim control over police previously led by the military. But it also provides reason for reflection on the significant growth of PR within police departments in more established democracies since the 1980s.

ARGENTINA: POLITICAL CONTROL OF SECURITY COMMUNICATIONS

Most state and nonstate actors in Argentina speak of police autonomy as one of the most important challenges to improving policing and crime control.[5] Similar to asserting civilian control over the military, this argument holds that police gained significant autonomy during the authoritarian regime, which they now use to maintain their involvement in criminal activities, avoid accountability for human rights abuses, and challenge political power that aims to reduce their autonomy. According to many interviewees and investigations by academics and journalists, governments favorable to maintaining police power receive money from the proceeds of police criminal activity and benefit from the selective use by the police of their criminal activity and violence (e.g., reducing the prevalence of some mediatized crime controlled by police, or the repression of opposition protests) (author interviews; Barbano 2015; Dutil and Ragendorfer 1997; Guerrero 2013; Saín 2008).

In this context interviewed state actors repeatedly argued it is essential that ministry or government actors be in control of media communication on policing, public order, and security issues. In Greater Buenos Aires this was the position of interviewees in the national, provincial, and municipal ministries of security. For example, a representative from the Ministry of Security for the Autonomous City of Buenos Aires explained, "Police have to preserve the crime scene, preserve the evidence of a crime. It is not their role to speak to the press."[6] Similarly an interviewee from the communications department for the Ministry of Security for the Province of Buenos Aires explained, "The police are subordinate to political control. They are not autonomous. . . . It is the political area of the ministry that communicates police action as well as institutional issues."[7]

Of the three police forces in Greater Buenos Aires (the Argentine Federal Police [PFA], Buenos Aires Provincial Police [BAPP], and the Metropolitan Police [2010–2017]), only the PFA has a substantial communications department. The PFA expanded its communication work after the return of electoral democracy and during the period of radical neoliberal economic reforms to include: an FM radio station (La Federal) in 1995; a website in 1996/1997; a TV show (*Prevenir*) in 1999; as well as preexisting magazines and ongoing school safety programs. Yet despite this investment in communications, at least under the Kirchner government (2003–2015), communication was centralized in the Ministry of Security (which in turn was tightly controlled by the executive branch). Officers in the PFA (as in the BAPP and Metropolitan Police under different governments) were prohibited from speaking to media without authorization (although journalists maintained their off-the-record sources). As the head of communications for the national Ministry of Security explained: "I strengthen the communications apparatus of the PFA, legitimate it, empower it, but they have to answer to me."[8]

Symbolically, the centralization of security communications in the ministry puts a civilian face on security policy in the media. As two interviewees explained, it also means that communications is focused on government security policy and not police public relations.[9] They explained that the latter can often undermine the security policy goals of the government by, for example, exaggerating the prevalence of certain crimes. Ministry control of communications is also a way to reduce "political problems." For example, the head of communications for the national Ministry of Security explained: "If I let something go, it means there is no political leadership. Because it means the leadership is not strong, that I don't really care. So if you don't really care today, tomorrow you will have a political problem you'll have to get rid of."[10] "Political problems" could include police use of iron-fist language, coverups of police wrongdoing, or other statements that challenge political leaders' goals, policies, or communicational strategy.

Thus, in Argentina, public relations is used most heavily by the various ministries of security. They use a wide range of public relations techniques, such as prepared multimedia material, selective exclusive interviews, staged events, social media, and (inconsistently) press conferences. Police public relations or (communications) departments are not well-funded (except for the PFA) and in most cases are no more than press offices (providing reactive relations with the press). This arrangement both reflects Argentina's relatively greater trust in political leaders than the police and reinforces this perception (see table 1.4). Yet despite this tight communicational control, political leaders in the Kirchner government still struggled to assume control over the security discourse in the mass media, and punitive populist voices dominated (discussed more in the next section).

CHILE: POLICE CONTROL OF COMMUNICATIONS

In Chile, police autonomy including, but not exclusively, in the realm of communications is also a common concern for state actors. However, rather than framed as an issue that political leaders have confronted by assuming control over media communications on crime, security, and public order, it is instead explained in terms of the inability (or undesirability) of political leaders to do so.

To some extent police autonomy in Chile is a legal legacy of the dictatorship. Unlike other public services in Chile that are subordinate to the minister and ministry they serve, the Carabineros are legally subordinate only to the Constitution (written under Pinochet in 1980) and the institution's Organic Laws (also written under Pinochet) (Candina Polomer 2005, 157–158). Regardless of where they are housed, they relate directly or indirectly to all the ministries (Candina Polomer 2005, 158). This reflects the idea in Chile that the police are meant to uphold the law, not respond to the orders of political leaders. Yet it also reflects effective police PR.

As part of its preparations for the transition to democracy and in response to a scandal that badly damaged the police force's public image, the Carabineros restructured and empowered its communications department with the goal of promoting an image of the police as part of the community.[11] Under the leadership of General Director Rodolfo Stange Oelckers, the Carabineros hired advisers, including the director of *La Tercera de la Hora* (now *La Tercera*), Alberto Guerrero Espinoza, to assess the public image of the police force and design an effective proactive communications department. In the last years of the 1980s they initiated a campaign with the slogan: "A friend on your path" (*Una amigo en su camino*) that later became "Always a friend" (*Un amigo siempre*). At the same time they launched a TV advertising campaign using a cartoon character named Pepe Grillo who explained preventive safety tips to citizens.[12]

The communications department grew substantially and included many civilians and journalists. As of 2015 approximately sixty people were working in the Carabineros' communications department (compared with seven in the communications department for the Investigative Police of Chile [PDI] the same year).[13] They moved away from simply providing lists of crimes and toward proactively preparing multimedia, ready-to-use media material for journalists. They provided media training for all Carabineros on how to speak to the media and on what issues they are permitted to speak at each rank. They launched their website in 1990 and their own AM radio station in 1997 (becoming FM in 2015) and have continued to have a clear communication strategy that comes from the top of the institution's command and aims, as one officer from the communications department described, to "maintain a good relationship with the community but above all with the media."[14]

These proactive and well-funded communications enhance the institution's ability to gain public support and to use this legitimacy to pursue its interests independently of less publicly supported state actors. For example, when seeking to reform the human rights training of its officers in 2011, rather than working with their civilian leaders in the Ministry of the Interior and Public Security (some of whom are leading experts in criminology), it chose to work with the International Red Cross. As Coronel Rodney L. Weber Orellana, the director of the institution's Department of Human Rights, explained:

> Carabineros is an institution that has a nature so special that, even though we are within the Ministry of the Interior, that is the government, we have our own authority. Politicians like to be close to the Carabineros because they are associating themselves with the institution in which people have the most confidence, [and which is] the most credible. So, we have to be very careful, for example, with whom we sign an agreement because we can give an advantage to those we choose to work with. And, of course, we have rejected many that have a political tint. But the International Red Cross Committee interested me, because we share the same principles and they have the same [level of] public confidence that we have.[15]

Communications officers and officials in the Ministry of the Interior and Public Security complained that the Carabineros often prioritize communications with the media over communications with them. One person in the ministry, who worked closely with the police, noted sometimes finding out about police initiatives through the media, instead of having been informed first.[16] A former communications office for the National Prosecutors office said the same occurred for many prosecutors who would receive a phone call from the media asking questions about a case they had not yet heard about from the police.[17]

Indeed sometimes Carabineros provide false information to the Ministry of the Interior and Public Security. This occurred when the Carabineros were accused of critically harming a protester, Rodrigo Avilés, in May 2015. Based on information provided to them by the Carabineros, the ministry publicly defended the institution. When it was revealed by a TV drone camera that at least one police officer had acted wrongly (firing a water cannon directly at Avilés), the ministry asked for a full report from the Carabineros within twenty-four hours, a request to which the Carabineros responded "no."[18]

Thus, ministry employees, as well as those working for the public prosecutors, PDI, and Gendarmería (prison guards), expressed concern that the Carabineros prioritize their image to the point that they do not see themselves as part of a larger criminal justice system. This has implications for policy and practices discussed in the next section. Ministry of the Interior and Public Security officials say that they work hard to coordinate both policy and communications with the police forces. Yet, one ministry communications officer surmised that the Carabineros "jump over institutional channels because in the end they have found that this strategy has borne valuable fruit for them."[19] The Carabineros' achievement has not been missed by the PDI, who in recent years have relatively successfully organized and asserted themselves in the mass media, albeit with far fewer resources. Among other efforts, the PDI's new communications strategy included a request that the Public Research Center (CEP) include their institution in those evaluated for public confidence in the yearly, and well-mediatized, polls.[20]

Thus in Chile, the Carabineros have a more effective public relations strategy than the ministry or other state institutions involved in criminal justice. This reinforces the confidence Chileans have in the Carabineros and takes advantage of market-based media practices and biases toward the police as a news source. This PR strength weakens the ability of the ministry to communicate its security policies and contributes to the spending of increased state resources on public relations as other criminal justice institutions (such as the PDI, Gendarmería, public prosecutor's office, judiciary—all of whom have recently expanded PR efforts) compete to have their voices heard and in turn their institutions valued and better funded. Indeed, new public management, which encourages state institutions to compete for funds, was introduced in Chile in the mid-1990s (Aninat et al. 2008, 192–193).[21] In sum, the increased importance of PR favors some state actors over others, which has important consequences for political power. In both Chile and Argentina, it also contributes to the mediatization of police reform and security policymaking.

STATE ACCEPTANCE OF MEDIA FRAMES: MEDIATIZATION OF POLICE REFORM AND SECURITY POLICYMAKING

In most democracies mass media play a role in policymaking and institutional reforms. Mass media can create political opportunities for change by drawing the public's attention to an event or problem, a policy or reform that could address this issue or make the political costs of pursuing some options too high. Mass media also provide a forum for communication between actors involved in policymaking or institutional reforms and thereby play a role in negotiations. Mass media might amplify the voice of a minority opinion, someone with less power at the negotiating table, or other actors with whom they have a good relationship for political or economic reasons. Of course, mediatization, or the ability of the mass media to shape the choices made by policymakers, is an option that can be accepted or not by political leaders. Political actors can choose to respond to the mass media, or not. More proactively, political actors are sometimes able to "index" news stories—that is, determine the news topic that is then followed by the mass media (Bennett 1990; Entman et al. 2010). Indeed, this is the goal of most public relations work.

The pressure for political leaders to use and respond to the dominant media logic is strong. As Robert M. Entman explains: "Demagoguery does feed on the biases of the news for the simple and symbolic, for the appearance of power and popularity and against any sign of ineffectiveness or public disfavor. . . . [The media discourage politicians] from telling the public complex or painful truths" (1989, 126). Thus, the mediatization of policymaking is especially high for populist (or punitive populist) governments, which place greater importance on media (Waisbord 2013). In both Argentina and Chile, media play a significant role in policy and reform choices.

ARGENTINA

In Argentina, media have affected policymaking and reform around policing and security by creating political opportunities for reform, fostering the perception that political leaders need short-term media-ready results, and favoring policy or political leaders whose ideas align with existing dominant media frames.

The majority of state actors agree that the most significant efforts at police reform in Argentina were able to occur as a result of a mediatized scandal in policing. The most sweeping and significant police reforms that have occurred in Argentina were led by León Arslanian in 1998–1999, after nearly a decade of mass media coverage of police wrongdoing, culminating in the 1997 police killing of photojournalist José Luis Cabezas. Many state actors identified the death of Cabezas as a key political opportunity to reform the Buenos Aires Provincial Police. Arslanian's second term as minister of security for the province (2004–2007), in which he reinstated many of the reforms undone by an intervening government, came on the heels of the 2002 police killing of two young protesters on Pueyrredón Bridge (Maximiliano Kosteki and Darío Santillán). Similarly, a widely mediatized case of cocaine drug trafficking at Ezeiza airport in 2005 in Buenos Aires provided the opportunity for the creation of a new Airport Security Police led by Marcelo Saín from 2005 to 2009. Finally, the death of Mariano Ferreya (with PFA complicity) in October 2010, followed by a PFA officer's killing of a protester in Indoamericano Park in December of that year, provided a political opportunity for reform of the PFA. However, this last incident reveals the limits media can place on police reform (Bonner 2016).

The protest in Indoamericano Park was a highly politicized battle between the national Kirchner government and the municipal Macri government, in terms of the protest issue itself and the police response from both the national PFA and the city's Metropolitan Police. Although an officer from the Metropolitan Police also killed someone at the protest, no reforms were pursued beyond individual accountability and calls for a better definition of the jurisdictional boundaries between the two police forces. Moreover, while the national government announced what it called significant reforms of the PFA, many critics, including some within the national government, said there was no presidential commitment to legal or structural police reforms.[22] The emphasis was on symbols and changes in protocols.

This leads to the second role of the media in security policy and police reform raised by state interviewees, the importance of providing the mass media, and thus the public, with short-term "results" of larger reform projects. One former vice-minister of security for the province of Buenos Aires explained that the public and media do not trust state institutions so political leaders cannot ask them to wait years for results.[23] The results need to be more immediate. For example, an interviewee from the communications department for the Ministry of Security (province of Buenos Aires) under Governor Daniel Scioli explained that Scioli's announcement of a "Security Emergency" for the province (April 2014–April 2015) allowed for the quick purchase of cars and other police equipment, the hiring of large numbers of new young police officers and getting them on the street quickly so people could see them.[24] Macri used a similar tactic upon assuming the presidency; he announced a security emergency for the entire country for December 2015–December 2016 (later extended to January 2018).[25]

While using different language and variations on the symbols, the Kirchner government, after announcing its creation of the national Ministry of Security and reform of the PFA in December 2010, also emphasized short-term accomplishments attractive to the mass media. Those involved in the reforms gave the following as successful examples: they renamed the police school from Ramón Falcón (a former police chief [1906–1909] symbolic of police violence) to Juan A. Pirkner (a former police chief [1987–1989] symbolic of democracy); they introduced new police technology;[26] and they called on the Gendarmería (national border police) and Prefectura (Coast Guard) to occupy shantytowns with a high crime rate (Operation Southern Belt).

As many of these examples suggest, short-term media-friendly results often favor choices consistent with punitive populism—especially increasing police presence. This is not surprising since punitive populism is based on appeasing immediate public opinion of an emotional nature. While short-term results can include actions that symbolize a commitment to reducing police violence, such as changing the name of the police school, in a somewhat circular manner the actions most likely to resonate in the mass media as "effective" are those that are consistent with existing "tough on crime" frames.

Thus the last point raised by state actors was that the mass media prefer policies and political leaders whose message corresponds to the dominant mass-media frames. In part, this is why mediatized events can create political opportunities for police reform. A spectacular event of police wrongdoing or an audience primed to be critical of the police provides media frames consistent with a political leader who seeks police reform, which benefited Arslanian. However, media frames change. Arslanian and those who worked closely with him argued that the media frame shifted during his mandate, thus challenging his reform. Indeed, his mandates (1998–1999, 2004–2007) coincide with a period of transition in the mass media environment away from watchdog journalism (see chapter 3). Ultimately, both his periods of reform were followed by the election of governors who favored punitive populism (Carlos Ruckauf and Daniel Scioli, respectively).

Similarly, those involved in various ways in the 2010–2013 reform of the PFA, including the head of communications for the Ministry of Security during the period, viewed the reforms initiated by Minister of Security Nilda Garré (2010–2013) as truncated in part by her relative weakness in engaging the mass media compared to the later appointed secretary of security, Sergio Berni (2012–2015). One member of her team explained that Garré had a strong media image as a defender of human rights and as someone who was able to assert civilian control over the military when she was minister of defense. She received extensive and positive coverage in *Página/12* (Bonner 2016).

However, in 2012 the president appointed Sergio Berni as Garré's secretary of security. Berni had a military background, prioritized crime control over police reform, and had a good relationship with the broader mass media. As one interviewee explained: "The problem was when Berni appeared and he 'took care of criminals' and he constructed a strong image in the media. . . . He started to appear in the more conservative media that played with a different logic like C5N, and from there he started to play with the image of the reform."[27] His frame alignment with the mass media further benefited from the conservative media outlets C5N and Radio10, which became supporters of the Kirchner government with a change of their ownership in 2012. Interviewees all noted this conflict between Garré and Berni as significant in Garré's ultimately stepping down as minister of security in 2013 and, most argued, the end of further human rights-based police reforms. Thus, in sum, in Argentina, mass media play an important role in political negotiations on police reforms and security policies, tipping the balance in favor of punitive voices and policies as the effects of neoliberal media reforms were felt.

CHILE

In Chile, one of the most important roles played by mass media in policymaking and reform around policing and security has been its influence on and repetitive publication of public opinion polls (see chapter 3). Unlike in Argentina, since the return of democracy in Chile, the mass media and state actors have used public opinion polls extensively as a proxy for democratic participation and to show the responsiveness of governments in power. Public opinion polls featured prominently in all interviewed state actors' explanations of the role of the mass media in public policymaking and reform related to policing and security. In particular, public opinion polls shape the relative power of some state institutions over others in defining the problems of and solutions to insecurity, the need for political leaders to prioritize security and particularly common crime (over other policies), and the creation (or not) of political opportunities for reform or policy action on police violence.

Of course, as discussed in chapter 2, public opinion polls have many important limitations. To review, mass media do not determine people's opinion (as in the hypodermic needle model) but instead play an important role in agenda setting (which issues are likely to appear important in public opinion polls) and framing (in our case, the solutions to the identified dominant problem of insecurity). Most people have little contact with the criminal justice system and most lack academic knowledge on the topic. In these cases, the mass media provide the most accessible information on which people base their opinions; that is, public opinion polls do not assess people's *informed* opinion but rather their impressions (usually gleaned from the mass media). Finally, by homogenizing public opinion, they also restrain opposition. Thus the significant role of public opinion polls in Chile raises some important concerns for security policymaking.

First, most interviewed state actors argued that the possibilities and limitations for policymaking and institutional reform were shaped in part by the power some state institutions derive from public opinion polls. That is, many Chilean and non-Chilean organizations (such as the CEP, Diego Portales University, and the Latin American Public Opinion Poll) conduct yearly public opinion polls that ask people to rank their confidence in various state institutions. These polls are then published widely in most mass media. The highly ranked institutions gain political power and often resources, and the less well-ranked are often motivated to dedicate more funds to better communications.

To illustrate, in most years, the institution that receives the greatest public confidence is the Carabineros. When asked about the possibilities for political leaders to initiate police reforms that might decrease human rights abuses and increase Carabineros' accountability, the answer was consistently, "It will never happen." The reason provided is that the Carabineros are the most highly ranked institution in public opinion polls. To quote one interviewee: "Obviously no political leader will want to be against an institution that is well evaluated by citizens."[28] Indeed, one communications officer for the Ministry of the Interior and Public Security explained that when police action is questioned by some members of the public, political leaders will "go with the polls, support the police."[29]

Another interviewee said that verbs other than "reform" might be used such as "consolidate," "strengthen," or "modernize" but any changes would be limited either to those that the Carabineros agree with or to those that they initiate themselves. For example, when public opinion polls showed a slight decline in public support for the police after their aggressive response to student protesters in 2011, the Carabineros, on their own initiative, created a human rights department within their institution (2011). The head of this department explained that "human rights have been present in our programs for more than eighty years. . . . This department was created to incorporate a more *modern* internal doctrine of human rights."[30] It was a "modernization," not a reform.

Other state institutions have seen the success of the Carabineros in gaining resources, prestige, and political power through effective communications. Interviewees with the PDI and Gendarmería (prison guards) explained that in recent years they have been investing significantly more in communications to improve public confidence in their institution and in turn, hope to increase the resources political leaders provide them.[31] Gendarmería in particular explained how their weak communications relative to the Carabineros have contributed to the focus of criminal justice policies in Chile on police actions and funding, and significantly to the underfunding of prisons (which, of course, house the growing number of people arrested by the police and provide rehabilitation programs) as well as the criminal justice system as a whole.[32]

Second, public opinion polls, and the media that promote and affect them, also contribute to setting the public agenda. All state actors interviewed recognized that, although security is an issue of the political Right, the fact that it has remained high on the list of top public policy concerns for citizens in public opinion polls has meant that political leaders on the left and the right have used security policies to help build confidence in their government. This has had policy implications, for example, in terms of the relative importance of crime statistics.

Unlike in Argentina, Chile has many widely available official and nonofficial statistics on crime. Yet many state actors, including the Carabineros, argue that crime statistics are often used in the mass media in a selective manner, and thus misrepresent the scope of the problem. Both the Ministry of the Interior and Public Security and the Carabineros maintain that crime is under control in Chile. Yet, as one communications officer explained, "We can't criticize the media because they are a part of the process."[33] Moreover, regardless of whether crime is increasing or not, or is at a significant level or not compared to other countries, state actors emphasized that the public's "fear of crime" must be taken seriously. One communications officer from the Ministry of the Interior and Public Security quoted the minister he was working for as saying: "We care about the numbers but we also care about the feelings of the people."[34] He continued, explaining that when people are afraid of crime you cannot tell them it is not increasing, the "feeling" is real. So in response to one such case of public demand for greater security, the government "invested $6 million in strengthening police stations by giving them more communications equipment, and computers, and professionals to help the police improve their relationship with neighborhood organizations. . . . There is a lot of strategic action."[35]

Finally, media and public opinion polls help shape the emergence (or lack) of political opportunities for policy change or reform. Unlike in Argentina, where mediatized cases of police wrongdoing have contributed to political opportunities for police reform, similar incidents in Chile have not produced such significant changes. For example, despite substantial public critique of police management of the student protests in 2011–2012, and most notably the police killing of Manuel Gutiérrez in 2011, political leaders did not initiate any significant police reforms (Bonner 2018). State communications (police and ministry) effectively framed the incidents as cases of bad apples (Bonner 2014a, ch. 10; 2018). Public opinion polls quickly returned the Carabineros to their relatively high level of confidence. In 2012, according to the CEP, 58 percent of Chileans had some or a lot of confidence in the Carabineros (compared to 50 percent in 2011) (CEP 2015, 9). That is, the Chilean public is primed to perceive the Carabineros positively. Combined with effective communications strategies on the part of the Carabineros, and comparatively low public confidence in political leaders, incidents of wrongdoing become aberrations. They do not change overall long-term support for the institution as a whole and thus limit the perceived receptiveness of the public to police reform.

Instead of political opportunities, state actors saw possibilities for change through a more long-term incremental process. Some mentioned that change was most likely to happen within the Carabineros as a result of gradual societal change, such as the way the institution has opened its doors to women recruits and its establishment of a human rights department. These arguments rest implicitly on the importance the Carabineros place on their image. The Carabineros want to be seen as "modern" and in touch with Chileans. This concern about image then encourages self-reform to maintain it, albeit in a selective manner.

For example, women Carabineros are used extensively in media presentations of the forces, yet the institution has done little to assist women Carabineros who face discrimination or (sexual) abuse within the forces, likely because the latter could lead to a negative image of the police in the mass media.[36] Thus, in Chile, as in Argentina, public relations and frame alignment with mass media prove important to policymaking on questions of crime, security, and police violence.

STATE AND MEDIA IN NEGOTIATING POLICE IMAGE: THE CASE OF REALITY TV

Thus far I have discussed the attempts of state actors to control their image in the mass media and the mass media's effects on security policymaking and reform. In this section I explore an important example of state and mass media interests when they are explicitly negotiated to portray a particular image of the police in democracy—reality-TV police shows.

Certainly, most police and security news emerges from a combination of state public relations and journalists' selection of sources. And, of course, fiction and nonfiction TV, movies, and books have long been studied in many countries as both reflecting and shaping the public's image of the appropriate role for the police in a defined struggle for security (Doyle 2003; Leishman and Mason 2003; Reiner 2000; Walsh 2015). Argentina and Chile are not exceptions. For example, in Argentina, Rodolfo Walsh is said to have established the genre of the nonfiction police novel with his 1957 publication of *Operación Masacre* (later made into a film), which questioned the official police investigation of a multiple murder (eight years before Truman Capote's *In Cold Blood* [1965] was written in the same style). More recently, similar semi- or fully fictionalized critiques of police competence and criminal activity include Pablo Trapero's film *El Bonaerense* (2001) and Miguel Cohan's *Betibú* (2014), both based on previously published and widely sold books.

In Chile, fictionalized critiques of the police have been less common. However, comedy has provided an outlet. In what started as a sketch on a popular Chilevisión TV program, a 2014 film *Fuerzas Especiales* (Special forces) presented parodies of the Carabineros. The police are portrayed as charming but not very bright, with some condescending class overtones. It was described in the national daily newspaper *Las* Últimas *Noticias* as "innocent humor that succeeds in providing a few laughs."[37]

Yet while these (semi)fictionalized portrayals of the police are interesting, they are produced independently of the state. In contrast, reality-TV police shows involve the state in the production of this media image. Media companies working in (neo)liberal media systems are motivated to produce such reality-TV shows because the costs are low and the ratings are high. The United States established the genre in 1989 with its long-running program, *Cops* (Doyle 2003), and many other countries adopted the format, such as the United Kingdom's *Traffic Cops*, Spain's *Policías en Acción*, Australia's *Gold Coast Cops*, and Canada's *To Serve and Protect*.[38] In all cases, they require media access to the police and thus negotiations with state actors. In turn state actors in both Argentina and Chile have considered reality-TV shows a unique public relations opportunity (at least for a period of time). Here I will discuss briefly the timing and negotiations of these shows, comparing the similarities and differences between the two countries.

ARGENTINA: *POLICÍAS EN ACCIÓN*

Argentina has had one significant reality-TV police show, *Policías en Acción* (Police in action). Produced by the Dutch company Endemol, it began airing in 2004 and ended in 2013. It was aired during prime time (10:00 p.m. to 11:00 p.m.) and received top ratings. It continues to run almost daily reruns on a couple of cable channels and many episodes are available on YouTube. While reality-TV police shows have been popular in many countries, their arrival in Argentina was possible due to a confluence of interests on the part of the media and the state.

On the one hand, the mass media were shifting in the early 2000s from an interest in police corruption and wrongdoing to insecurity. A former director of *Policías en Acción* explained that during the political and economic crisis of 2001, a TV program called *Chaos in the City* decided in one episode to spend twenty-four hours in a police station in the provincial suburbs of the city of Buenos Aires, filming events as they happened. This episode was so popular they decided to produce a whole program showing the "reality" of policing.[39] Of course, such a program requires the permission of the police and although they wanted to work with all the police forces, the PFA did not grant them permission. They did receive permission from the Buenos Aires Provincial Police, or rather from their political leaders.

A former journalist for the first season of *Policías en Acción* explained that in 2004 Carlos Ruckauf (an advocate of iron-fist policing) had just left the governorship of the province of Buenos Aires. The new governor, Felipe Solá, returned León Arslanian to the position of minister of security to again pursue police reforms. The new political leadership wanted to show that it was more open than the previous government and that the police were close to the community.[40] According to a police journalist from *Policías en Acción*, the show emerged after a police chief approached a police journalist with the idea. Arslanian confirmed, "I favored, facilitated, and authorized that they [*Policías en Acción*] work because it appeared to me that it was very important that the nature of police work and the reality of police action is known. I believe this program *Policías en Acción* was useful, helpful. My great worry was how to achieve, with a police force that was so discredited and so debased, a better relationship with the community."[41] The popularity of the show led political leaders from other provinces to invite the program to do episodes with their police forces. In 2009 the director of the show explained that about once a year they went to other provinces such as Mendoza, Cordoba, Rosario, and Salta. At times these invitations allowed the program to continue when political changes temporarily restricted their access to the Buenos Aires Provincial Police.[42]

The program itself very carefully managed citizens' distrust of the police, the media's desire to entertain in order to attract large audiences, and the political goals of the police and provincial governments. The journalists join police officers they are assigned to and when the police are called to respond to a problem they accompany them. As one regional police chief for the Buenos Aires Provincial Police, who liked the show, explained, most of the incidents the program shows are domestic issues (he said he would have preferred more coverage of police shoot-outs).[43] At the scene, the camera generally focuses on the strange behavior of the people the police encounter and, to the extent that the police appear, their patience in these situations. The audience is led to sympathize with the police and the difficult work they do.

For example, in one episode from 2007 the cameras focused on a mother who was very upset that police were taking her son to the police station for verification of his criminal record (*averiguacion de antecedents*). She cried that he had only just gotten out of jail. She and other women then went to the police station where they pleaded for his release. The audience is led to assume that her son probably did something wrong and she is just a hysterical mother. The coverage is episodic, providing no context or explanation. Yet human rights organizations have shown that when torture and abuse by police officers occurs, it is often when people are held in police custody, especially for verification of their police record. Of course, cameras do not go behind closed police doors.

The show also has an important class dimension. The director of the program explained that, in the end, working with the Buenos Aires Provincial Police was better than with the PFA because Greater Buenos Aires (the provincial outskirts of the city) has more poverty (than in the city of Buenos Aires where the PFA work): "Poor people who live in the more marginal zones have a different idea about television. . . . They like to be on TV. It's normal. They don't see it as something bad. So we focus more on poor neighborhoods. When we film in neighborhoods with more money it doesn't work as well because a lot of people don't want to be on TV, not even [for us to] show their houses."[44] While the director argued that *Policías en Acción* is a window for the middle class into the lives of people in these poorer neighborhoods, the show also reinforces the image of the police as protectors of the middle class from the apparently unruly lower classes.

A former journalist for the show explained that some episodes also serve political purposes. For example, he said that "the first cases they covered were in Lomas de Zamora, Lanús, Avellaneda, and were antidrug operations. It was to show that the police were cleaning up the outskirts of the City of Buenos Aires [*el cono urbano*]."[45] One critic of the show argued that it was very effective propaganda, much better than the TV show produced by the PFA, *Prevenir*, which showcases and celebrates police work but had much lower ratings.[46]

In sum, *Policías en Acción* has played an important role in Argentina in providing a (selective) window into what police do in a democracy. State and media negotiations helped produce a show that very carefully aimed to build public confidence in the police and reinforce their central role in crime control.

CHILE: *133, ALERTA MÁXIMA, BANDAS CRIMINALES, POLICÍAS EN ACCIÓN, BRIGADA POLICIAL*

In Chile reality-TV police shows arrived later but have proliferated to a greater extent, and in 2015, continued to run on multiple channels.[47] In Chile, the mass media came up with the idea to produce reality-TV police shows but the shows were created in careful collaboration with the police forces. The first police reality program, *133* (equivalent to the North American emergency police number 911) began to air in November 2007 on the TV channel MEGA (channel 9 on open TV). The producer of the program explained that they were watching the popularity of *Policías en Acción* in Argentina but were also inspired by the formats of such shows "in the United States, in Europe, in Spain, that are our principle references."[48]

MEGA was the ideal TV channel to approach the Carabineros with the proposal. MEGA was the first private TV channel in Chile and its owner at the time of initiating *133* was Ricardo Claro, a supporter of Pinochet and the military regime. Moreover, responding to pressure from the Carabineros, MEGA had since 2002 provided full live coverage of the institution's yearly anniversary ceremony.[49] Unlike in Argentina, producers did not need political permission but rather police permission. The Carabineros agreed to work with MEGA on the project because they trusted the channel and because the concept was to "draw attention to what we do in regard to the control and prevention of crime."[50] The producer explained that through this program they aimed "to show that a problem exists, like everywhere, crime, that we have danger in the streets. So others have to start to work to decrease these levels. So the intention is not to scare or create fear, but it is to let them know about the work of the Carabineros . . . and also the risks that they are ready to take on."[51] Despite its somewhat moralizing tone (the end of each episode often included a lesson for viewers about security), *133* was the most watched TV program in 2008. The producer attributed its success in large part to Chileans' curiosity, after such a long period of dictatorship, to see what the police do in democracy. The program ended after a second season in 2009 due to a change in the TV channel's ownership and orientation.

The Carabineros were very happy with the results of *133* for their image. They stressed that it enabled them to reach out to the community by being transparent and letting people know how and when to get in touch with them. They also claimed to watch the shows and follow the social media reactions in order to adjust their procedures to improve their officers' interactions with the community.[52] Given this success, it is not surprising that they were open to an offer by Chilevisión to participate in a new reality-TV police show called *Alerta Máxima* (Maximum alert) that began to air in 2014.

Chilevisión was a greater PR risk for the Carabineros, as the channel's news content has been more critical of the police, but it reaches the same popular classes, which was MEGA's traditional audience and a target audience for the Carabineros.[53] An editor from Chilevisión's news department felt that the alliance may also have been a way of pressuring their news department to decrease its critical coverage of the Carabineros, as they had heard the Carabineros expressing views inline with this argument.[54] From the perspective of the Carabineros, *133* and *Alerta Máxima* are "the same" in terms of content and the goals they achieved.[55] In 2015 the Carabineros began another reality-TV show with Canal 13 (whose audience is the upper and middle classes) called *Bandas Criminales* (Criminal gangs). It focuses on the more investigative work of their OS-9 group and includes general security advice aimed at these higher socioeconomic classes.

The PDI has also participated in reality-TV police shows initiated by TV channels, in the hopes of improving its institutional image. Chilevisión reached out to the Dutch company Endemol and its Argentine counterparts to determine whether they could bring Argentina's *Policías en Acción* to Chile. Since MEGA was already working with the Carabineros, the channel approached the PDI. The program ran from 2008 to 2009. The first season did not go very well from the PDI's perspective. It contended that the program showed too much police violence and too many "procedural irregularities" (e.g., police kicking down people's doors). The PDI felt it harmed their image. However, the show was popular with audiences, so it was decided to continue. The institution felt that it helped to "make the police visible."[56]

In 2009 the PDI dropped *Policias en Acción* and negotiated a new program with Chilevisión called *PDI: Brigada Policial* (PDI: Police brigade) that ran for two seasons. The PDI liked this program much better as it focused on the positive work of the PDI and the process of criminal investigation (similar to a reality version of *CSI*). The PDI ended this program, claiming that it interfered with the work of police officers and that their goals had been achieved. Chileans now knew how the PDI worked and public opinion polls conducted by Chilevisión before and after the show revealed that people now valued the work of the PDI more than they had in the past.[57] Indeed, in 2017 public confidence in the PDI was on par with the Carabineros (CEP 2017).

Thus in Chile, as in Argentina, reality-TV police shows, when managed carefully by the police or political leaders, have been an effective public relations tool to build public confidence in police work. Yet while positive for building police legitimacy, a significant concern in newer democracies, these shows simultaneously elevate the importance of the police perspective on crime, security, and police violence. As in most countries, the police perspective tends to emphasize a tough-on-crime approach, with police as the central protagonists.

In neoliberal media systems, state actors' communicational practices both respond to and shape journalistic practices in ways that favor punitive voices (such as the police). This occurs through: the state's regulation of the media system to favor market priorities; the degree to which and their use of public relations; the extent to which state actors prioritize (or not) mass media image and logic in policymaking and reforms; and, the decision to agree to participate in reality-TV police shows and negotiate the boundaries of that participation. This in turn contributes to a media environment in which political leaders who use punitive populist rhetoric find it resonates with the public as familiar and thus "true." While choice exists, the (neo)liberal media system favors journalistic and state practices that promote punitive populist ideas, leaders, and policies.

Chapter 6

THE RISE OF PUNITIVE VOICES FROM CIVIL SOCIETY

Punitive populism assumes that "the public," or at least the public that matters, is homogeneous. It is personified in public opinion polls, victims' voices, civil society organizations, or all three, which reveal "the public's" fear of crime and support for an iron-fist response. Yet many human rights organizations and other civil society groups argue that tough-on-crime policies exacerbate excessive police violence. For example, Cop Watch (in many North American and European cities), Black Lives Matter (United States and Canada), Killed by Police (United States), and international organizations such as Amnesty International and Human Rights Watch, all follow and advocate against police violence. These organizations generally contend that tough-on-crime policies undermine efforts at police reform and sustain or exacerbate police practices that may include arbitrary arrest, injury, sexual abuse, torture, disappearances, and random killings. Yet these civil society voices are often lost in mass media constructions of "public opinion" on crime and security.

As discussed in chapter 4, journalists can choose to represent "the public" in particular ways through their selection of sources. But, like state actors, most civil society organizations do not wait passively for journalists' attention. This chapter closely examines the communicational strategies of civil society organizations working on issues of police violence, crime, and/or security in Argentina and Chile. I find that the media system matters to whose voices are heard, about what, and how. In particular, neoliberal media systems and the journalistic practices they produce affect the ways in which civil society organizations engage the mass media and these practices benefit more punitive organizations.

CIVIL SOCIETY, DEMOCRACY, AND THE MASS MEDIA

In a democracy, mass media are meant to represent public opinion. Ideally this involves the inclusion of a wide variety of perspectives in news stories in order to provide a forum for debate from which a more unified public opinion can emerge. Yet, in practice, not all perspectives are included equally in mass media debates. In addition to the somewhat circular use of public opinion polls, media often choose proxies for public opinion from civil society. In turn, these sources can reinforce or shape the frames journalists use to tell news stories.

Civil society is the space of collective activity that exists between the state and the household. It is composed of an extensive range of organizations with equally varied goals, strategies, and engagements with the media. It includes nongovernmental organizations (NGOs), grassroots and social movement organizations, and research centers. NGOs have an office, paid staff, and (sometimes) substantial funding. In contrast, grassroots and social movement organizations may or may not have an office, paid staff, or any funding. Finally, research centers may be run as NGOs or housed in universities but they usually require an office, paid staff, and funding. Together these organizations play a number of important roles in democracy and democratic debate.

First, the civil society organizations analyzed in this chapter, like the media themselves, are widely recognized as actors of democratic accountability (Bonner 2014a, see also Diamond 1999, 239–240; Linz and Stepan 1996, 9; Peruzzotti and Smulovitz 2006). This includes: following state actions or omissions; shaming (or applauding) these actions or omissions; providing information that the state may not be able or willing to provide; and activating state institutions of accountability. This could include exposing police involvement in crime, critiquing a government security proposal, or initiating a court case against a police officer for excessive violence. In so doing, acts or omissions once deemed unfortunate but acceptable can be reframed as wrongdoing.

Civil society organizations also provide accountability through their participation in state policymaking. For example, they can offer alternative policies for crime reduction or criminal justice system reform, which, if not implemented, the opposition can use to question or probe government policy choices. The media play a significant role in the circulation of civil society ideas in such public policy debates and negotiations (Bennett 1996; Cook 2005; Kingdon 2003).

Civil society also contributes to a democratic political culture. The literature on democracy and democratization explains that citizens' participation in civil society organizations helps strengthen and legitimize democratic institutions, as citizens learn to use and trust them. Robert D. Putnam (2000) refers to this as building "social capital." It involves establishing trust between citizens, learning to compromise and resolve conflict peacefully (warding off political polarization), and building tolerance and respect for opposing viewpoints (Diamond 1999, 230–234; Schmitter and Karl 1991, 80). As Larry Diamond notes, social capital is "a critical resource for dealing with the seemingly intractable problems of poverty, alienation, and crime in the United States and other industrialized democracies" (Diamond 1999, 19). While Nancy Bermeo and Deborah J. Yashar do not use the term "social capital," they find that in newer democracies, the ability of social movements, working with political parties, to mobilize and coordinate people across various societal cleavage makes them "key to democratization's fate" (2016, 2).

Of course, this literature recognizes that not all ideas that emerge from and mobilize civil society are democratic. As Bermeo and Yashar contend, this uncertainty should encourage us to analyze further "if, where and why ideas take hold" (2016, 19). I argue that the media system, which shapes the principal public forum for debate between social movements, society, and political parties (as well as other state actors), plays an important role in the dominance of democratic or authoritarian ideas.

Yet even if the dominant ideas circulated by the mass media are democratic, civil society is also engaged in a public debate on the meaning, scope, and reach of democracy (Alvarez, Dagnino, and Escobar 1998b, 1). By attempting to redefine democracy and citizenship, civil society organizations can challenge persistent or reemergent authoritarian culture in both old and new democracies. Philip Oxhorn refers to this as the "social construction of citizenship"; civil society organizations struggle among themselves and with the state to determine "who is or is not included and the rights that citizenship entails" (2011, 5). This involves not only reforming political institutions but also producing cultural or symbolic changes in the public's behavior or attitudes (Alvarez, Dagnino, and Escobar 1998b; Melucci 1985; Offe 1987). For example, a civil society organization might aim to persuade the general public to view once acceptable police actions as wrongdoing or, alternatively, to see increased police presence as the answer to common crime. Again, the media play a central role in the circulation and relative dominance of competing civil society ideas. Different media systems vary in the frequency, scope, and manner in which civil society voices are heard.

Finally, neoliberal economic policies shape the boundaries of civil society participation in democracy. Political leaders supportive of neoliberal economic policies have celebrated the role of civil society in democracy, but confined it primarily to legitimizing a predetermined definition of democracy. In particular, civil society can increase state legitimacy by relieving the state of "the burden of expectations" by providing social services no longer supplied by the state and solving other social problems without the involvement of the state (Diamond 1999, 249–250). This is reflected in the popularity of community policing programs that include social service NGOs (Arias and Ungar 2009; Müller 2010). When civil society organizations conform to this role they are rewarded with access to power through connections to international funds, business support, media attention, or combinations of all three (Alvarez 1998; Bob 2005; Diamond 1999, 253). The organizations that benefit most are often closer to the state, international actors, or businesses through clientelism, geographic proximity, cultural or class connections, or because they provide legitimacy to government policies (Alvarez, Dagnino, and Escobar 1998b, 18; Davis 1999; Melucci 1998, 428–429).

However, many scholars of social movements have argued that the state downloading of responsibilities to civil society and emphasis on society's role in supporting state legitimacy, in fact places important limits on democratic debate. Such studies hold that when civil society organizations are perceived primarily as service providers, they assume a technical rather than political role, and this depoliticization then reduces their ability to engage in public debate that challenges the existing political system (Müller 2016; Paley 2001; Schild 1998). In this manner, as Alvarez, Dagnino, and Escobar contend, neoliberalism has significantly transformed "the conditions under which collective action may take place" (1998b, 23). This includes, I argue, the ways in which civil society organizations have access to and engage the mass media as well as which civil society voices benefit most.

Of course, civil society organizations use an abundance of strategies to achieve their goals, some but not all of which involve the mass media. Some civil society organizations are able to establish a direct relationship with policymakers, communicate via their own media channels (including social media), as well as use other strategies to achieve their desired change. Yet, for most organizations, accessing the mass media serves both internally and externally motivated purposes such as: mobilizing and communicating with the general public (beyond those already sympathetic or involved); expanding and encouraging membership; influencing public opinion and setting the public agenda; validating their organization's goals as worthy of attention from policymakers; increasing their power in policymaking negotiations; attracting the support of third parties whose alliance may be strategically important; attracting potential funders; and shifting the dominant frames used and reinforced in the mass media that contribute to the public's interpretation of events or issues (Gamson and Wolfsfeld 1993; Koopmans 2004; Waisbord 2011).

From the perspective of the democratic role of the media, when civil society organizations are included in media reports, ideally, the diversity and number of voices participating in this public forum of debate expands. For example, on the issue of crime, security, and police violence three dominant perspectives are found within the different civil society organizations analyzed in this chapter. First, there are those that favor a punitive approach and advocate for more policing, greater police discretion, and tougher criminal laws. Second, there are those organizations that argue in favor of institutional reforms within the existing system, such as police reform and socioeconomic reforms. Third, there are civil society organizations that favor rethinking the role of the police in society. This last set of organizations argue that reducing police violence and insecurity requires first recognizing the role of police and socioeconomic inequality in the current model of capitalism and from there reformulating or even rejecting capitalism.

The extent to which these different perspectives enter into the forum of public debate provided by the mass media is not as simple as right- and left-wing mass media and corresponding alignment of civil society organizations. Rather different organizations have different opportunities to enter the debate, different approaches to achieving frame alignment with the mass media in their particular media system, and different resources to sustain their inclusion (e.g., Carroll and Ratner 1999; Deacon 2003; Gamson and Wolfsfeld 1993; Koopmans 2004).

Certainly, hundreds of civil society organizations in Argentina and Chile are working on issues of police violence, crime, and security. Many other civil society organizations working on different issues, such as education, poverty, or housing, find they need to address police violence as it affects their members and their ability to advocate for their positions. Since I am particularly interested in the difficulty of hearing civil society voices on the topic of police violence, I chose the most well-known civil society organizations that work on or have been affected by police violence in each country. To facilitate some comparison and round out perspectives on policing, crime, and security, I also included the most prominent civil society organizations whose work focuses on security and crime control, but excludes police violence.[1] I have included NGOs (with offices and paid staff), as well as grassroots organizations (with primarily or exclusively volunteers and sometimes an office), and some prominent research centers. In total this chapter is based on 74 interviews with members of 38 different civil society organizations in Argentina and Chile between 2006 and 2015. In some relevant cases I interviewed members over time and recorded changes in perspectives or orientation. These interviews were cross-checked and analyzed in conversation with approximately 115 state and media interviews that I conducted for the book as whole, as well as secondary material. Drawing on these in-depth interviews, I compare two key communicational strategies identified as important by these civil society organizations in Argentina and Chile: frame alignment and discursive opportunities, and professional public relations (PR).

FRAME ALIGNMENT AND DISCURSIVE OPPORTUNITIES

The first and most common strategy used by the civil society organizations to have their views included in mass media discussions of policing, crime, and/or security is to develop or exploit frame alignment with the mass media and take advantage of related discursive opportunities for coverage.

Frames refer to the way we synthesize and condense complex issues or events in familiar ways so that they make sense given our understanding of history and current events (see chapter 2; Benford and Snow 2000; Goffman 1974). Frames resonate as true when they are familiar in some way (Benford and Snow 2000). Both media and social movements attempt to frame issues and events in particular ways that may or may not overlap. When they do not match we often call mass media frames "dominant frames," because they become the reference point from which most people unfamiliar with the issue will derive frames and because the mass media usually aim to use the most familiar frames possible to attract a broad audience that feels comfortable (familiar) with the story being told. Likewise, when in disagreement, social movements often provide counterframes. Counterframes offer a different way of understanding the same issue or event, both in terms of what happened and what the consequences or solution should be. Occasionally the counterframe will resonate with the public as more "true" than the dominant frame, allowing the counterframe to replace it as dominant. Counterframes may be included in mass media stories for balanced reporting or they may be excluded as a marginal frame that would not appeal to the media outlet's audience or because the dominant frame is so strong that journalists view the dominant frame as a neutral and uncontested description of reality.

Frame alignment occurs when the mass media frame and the social movement frame match. This can happen when civil society organizations conform to a mass media outlet's frame or when civil society organizations successfully shift the media frame. In both cases, frame alignment increases the chances that an organization will receive mass media coverage. In this section, I am interested in when and how civil society organizations perceive that they have achieved frame alignment and how this has shaped discursive opportunities.

Discursive opportunities are moments when the ongoing work or demands of a civil society organization gains resonance in the mass media because of its consistency with a new, current, and pressing issue of concern (Koopmans 2004, 370; Tarrow 1998, 76–80).[2] These can also be events that act as a founding moment that brings people together around an issue and leads to the formation of a new civil society organization. These discursive opportunities can bestow momentary mass media attention or can be used by organizations to launch their sustained authority as a journalistic source. In what follows, I compare within and between Argentina and Chile the changes in frame alignment and types of discursive opportunities that have brought authority to the voices of civil society organizations working on police violence, crime, and security.

ARGENTINA

In Argentina, media democratization played an important role in reorganizing the relationship between the mass media and civil society organizations before neoliberal media reforms were extensively implemented. I trace how this affected frame alignment between organizations working on police violence and the media and the emergence of key discursive opportunities for these organizations to have their voices heard.

Unlike in Chile, the return to electoral democracy in Argentina in 1983 came with a near societal rejection of the last dictatorship (1976–1983) and a celebration of the role human rights organizations played in confronting the regime. Most of the well-known human rights organizations have continued their work and derive authority as journalistic sources from this experience. Those working on police violence include: the Center for Legal and Social Studies (CELS), the Permanent Assembly for Human Rights (APDH), the Ecumenical Movement for Human Rights (MEDH), and the Argentine League for the Rights of Man (La Liga). In addition, the Provincial Commission for Memory, established in 1999 by judges and public prosecutors working on cases from the dictatorship, has similarly gained mass media attention for its work on this period of gross human rights abuses and its work in solidarity with the historical human rights organizations.

Yet, while these organizations have name recognition due to this long and prominent human rights struggle, it is not obvious that this media attention can be sustained over time. Indeed, the MEDH preferred not to maintain a high mass media profile, which it felt did not benefit (but rather exploited) the people with whom they work in the poor communities.[3] Moreover, these organizations' status as authoritative sources on the dictatorship did not obviously translate into becoming authoritative sources on police violence, crime, and security; the APDH did not establish a committee addressing security issues until 2002.[4] Furthermore, while these organizations agree in their condemnation of the military regime, their perspectives on police violence, crime, and security are not unified. All these organizations view insecurity in Argentina as stemming primarily from socioeconomic inequality and police violence. Yet they disagree (both between and within their organizations) on whether police violence is part of the structure of the capitalist model that produces and reinforces socioeconomic inequality (MEDH, La Liga, APDH) or whether police can be reformed to be less violent and more effective at controlling crime within the existing system (CELS, APDH). These disagreements reduce the authority that could be derived from a more unified alliance between organizations (Gamson and Wolfsfeld 1993). Thus while the dictatorship has provided these organizations authority as sources, the challenge has been to sustain and transfer this authority to the issues of police violence, crime, and security.[5]

In this regard, the opening up of the mass media to watchdog journalism with the establishment of *Página/12* in 1987 facilitated frame alignment between the mass media and civil society organizations working on or affected by police violence. This began most notably in 1990 with the case of María Soledad Morales. One longtime police journalist, who reported on the case for *Clarín*, said this was a turning point in media methods of covering policing in Argentina.[6] The sons of people with power in the province of Catamarca killed seventeen-year-old Morales, a young girl from a humble background. Police were suspected of covering up evidence. Nationwide "marches of silence" drew public and mass media attention to the case and the semifeudal politics of the province that facilitated impunity for months. The case drew such attention that a film dramatizing the events was released in 1993.

With this new dominant mass media frame—"police are violent and corrupt"—civil society organizations were then able to take key events and convert them into discursive opportunities to give their previous or new work on police violence a voice in the mass media. Most notably, CELS and the Coordinator against Police and Institutional Repression (CORREPI), civil society organizations with the longest history of working on issues of police violence in democracy, both provided lawyers who assisted in the court case that tried police officers for the death of Walter Bulacio. In 1991, a year after the death of María Soledad Morales, seventeen-year-old Bulacio went to a rock concert. The police raided the event and Bulacio and many other attendees were taken to a police station and beaten. In the morning, Bulacio was moved to a hospital where he died five days later from his injuries. The high-profile case went through the national and later the Inter-American Courts, all of which was covered extensively in the mass media up to the Inter-American Court decision in 2003. One interviewee from CELS notes that it was the combination of the media attention on the María Soledad Morales case and the organization's leadership role in the Bulacio case that helped CELS to emerge as an authoritative source for the media on police violence, despite years of having tried to put the issue in the media before these incidents.[7]

The case also led to the founding of CORREPI and the public profile of its president, María del Carmen Verdú, who was a lawyer on the Bulacio case. The Antirepressive Coordinator for People's Rights (CADeP, a group that splintered from CORREPI in 2009) also has two members who were lawyers on the Bulacio case. Other organizations formed and benefited from media attention on the issue of police violence during this period, such as the Commission of Family Members of Defenseless Victims of Social, Police, Judicial, and Institutional Violence (COFAVI), founded by the mother of a victim of police violence in 1991, and Relatives and Friends of the Victims of the AMIA Attack, who formed after the 1994 attack on the Jewish community center in Buenos Aires in which police were complicit.

Many journalists, who were police journalists throughout the 1990s, spoke of how this critical coverage shaped their vision of what good journalism is and heightened their interest in cases of police wrongdoing. However, with the extensive implementation of neoliberal media policies throughout the 1990s, which included the privatization and deregulation of the media discussed in chapter 3, combined with the economic crisis of 2001, few media outlets had the resources to continue pursuing expensive watchdog journalism or an interest in doing so. Beginning in the late 1990s, but especially by the early 2000s, editorial pressure shifted in favor of stories of insecurity defined as common crime.

To be sure, the issue of police violence in the mass media did not disappear. Dramatic cases pursued in the courts continue to provide discursive opportunities for some civil society organizations to become authoritative journalistic sources. For example, the Professional Center for Human Rights (CeProDH) worked on the court case against police for the disappearance of Julio López in 2006, and the APDH was involved in a case against police for the torture and disappearance of Luciano Arruga in 2009. Organizations whose members were victims of police repression of large protests, such as Frente Santillán or Frente Tierra y Vivienda (Land and Housing Front, FTV), have also attracted media attention. Yet these opportunities have become fewer and less sustained compared to the 1990s, when there was greater frame alignment between mass media and civil society organizations working on and affected by police violence.

The most notable shift in ways in which civil society organizations are used by journalists as authoritative sources was seen in the emergence of Juan Carlos Blumberg and his Axel Blumberg Foundation in 2004, discussed at the beginning of the introduction. To review, on March 22, 2004, Blumberg's son Axel was kidnapped and murdered. He went to the media to denounce "insecurity" and used his victim status and the media attention on his situation to mobilize large protests and successfully advocate for tougher laws to punish crime. Similarly, the Network of Mothers and Relatives of Drug Victims (commonly referred to in the media as Madres contra el Paco), formed in 2005, gained media attention for their advocacy for a better government response to the growing problem of crack cocaine (*paco*) and police incompetence in resolving the problem. The organization members emphasize their victimhood and loss of their children (to drugs) and call for greater police presence and broader police powers. Finally, the Mothers of Pain (Madres del Dolor), formed in 2004, brought together a group of women whose children were killed as a result of crime, police incompetence, police violence, or a combination of all three. Their vision of insecurity emphasizes the interconnection between police incompetence, police violence, and crime, and thus, unlike some of the civil society organizations focused on police violence alone, they are able to use frame alignment with the mass media on the concern about crime to draw attention to issues of police violence.

In an attempt to reachieve frame alignment, in the early 2000s CELS began to reframe its work on police violence as an issue of "security." This culminated in a 2009 campaign, led by CELS, to organize a wide range of civil society organizations and public figures in support of an Agreement on Democratic Security. The goal was to redefine security and mainstream media discussions of security in terms of democracy, rather than "tough on crime."[8] This shifted the conversation from simply denouncing police violence toward advocating for police reforms that would both reduce crime and make the police less violent.[9] Civil society organizations such as CORREPI, CeProDH, and MEDH criticize the approach of CELS for achieving frame alignment with the mass media and government at the expense of resolving the issue, which for the former civil society organizations is the structural issue of the current model of capitalism and the role it assigns the police.[10]

Other organizations have used media politicization along pro- or anti-Kirchner government lines as a way to achieve frame alignment. This division became particularly acute beginning in 2008 (see chapter 3). In this media environment political divisions often superseded simple "human rights" versus "tough on crime" frames, allowing for frame alignment between civil society organizations critical of the Kirchner government, such as CORREPI and Frente Santillán, which view insecurity and police violence as rooted in the current capitalist model, and anti-Kirchner media that prefer a "tough on crime" frame. Since these civil society organizations were willing to criticize the Kirchner government's handling of policing, they found a platform from which they could offer to the mass public their more critical views of the socioeconomic role of policing and police violence.[11] Thus, in these cases, media politicization increased opportunities for frame alignment but did not ultimately alter the dominant mass media frame of "insecurity" and the need for a tough-on-crime response.

CHILE

In Chile, the ability of civil society organizations working on or affected by police violence to achieve frame alignment with the mass media and take advantage of corresponding discursive opportunities has been much more limited, and consistently so, than that experienced in Argentina. This media environment has been shaped by the implementation of neoliberal media policies (including the privatization and deregulation of the media discussed in chapter 3) prior to electoral democracy.

As in Argentina, some human rights organizations in Chile came out of the dictatorship as well-known public actors. While many human rights organizations folded with the return of democracy, some organizations, such as the Corporation for the Promotion and Defense of People's Rights (CODEPU) and Social Assistance Foundation of the Christian Churches (FASIC), continued their struggle for truth, justice, and memory. In 2001, a group of ex-political prisoners formed the Ethical Commission against Torture (CECT). Together these organizations have used their connection to the dictatorship to help gain mass media attention primarily in their struggle for a truth commission, trials, and reparations.

However, given the connection between most mass media companies in Chile and the military regime (1973–1990), as well as the manner in which the dictatorship implemented neoliberal media policies to the advantage of these dominant media groups (discussed in chapter 3), and significant support for the dictatorship by an important portion of the population,[12] even gaining mass media attention to issues of past human rights abuses has been a significant challenge. As one member of CODEPU explained, mass media paid attention to them when they met with President Aylwin and he held the first truth commission (Rettig report published in 1991). Afterward, however, they were largely ignored until Pinochet was arrested in London in 1998.[13] Thus while the dictatorship and its legacy provided these organizations' authority as journalistic sources, this was more often limited to their coverage in alternative or smaller media outlets, except in dramatic and brief cases of reconciliation with the past that could not be ignored by the mass media.[14]

Despite the significant task of seeking truth, justice, and memory of the past, these organizations, to varying degrees, also took on the issue of police violence in democracy. Both CODEPU and FASIC mentioned that people (often youth) approached them consistently since 1990 with cases of police violence in democracy, including torture. A lawyer from FASIC spoke of trying to gain mass media coverage for cases of police violence as a form of "reparation" to the affected families. Media coverage, he argued, contributes to public recognition of police violence as a problem and challenges the mass media's framing of victims of police violence as criminals.[15]

Initially, the CECT focused almost entirely on achieving a truth commission on torture, justice in the courts, and reparations. They achieved all three but in forms far from what they had hoped.[16] Frustrated with the results, the organization shifted its attention to torture in democracy, highlighting the continuities from the past.[17] However, the CECT, while gaining a national and international profile for its advocacy for the Valech Report (2004) on torture during the dictatorship, has otherwise remained a source for primarily alternative or smaller media. Thus, while the dictatorship provided some prestige to some human rights organizations, it did not do so to the degree that occurred in Argentina, nor was there frame alignment between the mass media and these organizations on the issue of the dictatorship, thus further limiting their ability to transfer authority to the issue of police violence.

Instead a key event (discursive opportunity) in 1991 found significant frame alignment with the media: the kidnapping of Cristián Edwards. In 1991, Cristián, the son of Agustín Edwards (owner of the El Mercurio media group) was kidnapped. While the crime was politically motivated, Edwards and his media framed the event in terms of a broader crime threat (Ramos and Guzmán de Luigi 2000, ch. 2). Cristián was kidnapped by the Manuel Rodríguez Patriotic Front, which was dissatisfied with the compromises made in the transition to democracy. This event led to the creation of one of the most journalistically cited civil society organizations on crime and security, Citizen Peace (Paz Ciudadana). As the organization's communications director put it: "Citizen Peace has always been an important civil society source for the media."[18]

Citizen Peace was created through an endowment from Agustín Edwards and retains close relations with his media group (El Mercurio). The organization was formed to produce studies and polls on crime and security in order to contribute to public policy decisions. Certainly other factors have contributed to the strong reputation of Citizen Peace as an authoritative journalist source (such as the quality of its research). Yet, Cristián's kidnapping provided a significant opportunity from which to begin to shift the agenda-setting mass media conversation and dominant frames from human rights (particularly the 1991 Rettig Commission) to crime and insecurity.

However, over time the positions of Citizen Peace, mass media, and conservative political parties have diverged slightly, leading some members of civil society organizations to note a decline in mass media coverage of Citizen Peace (albeit a decline not recognized by the organization itself). One explanation for this shift may be one of Citizen Peace's founding projects, the penal procedures reform. The reform moved Chile from a colonial legal system centered on a judge to a more diffuse system involving a public prosecutor's office, defense councils, and judges (who were then independent from the criminal investigation process). This reform was initiated by lawyers and law students at the Diego Portales University, Citizen Peace, and University Promotion (Corporación de Promoción Universitaria) in the early 1990s and was implemented throughout Chile from 2000 to 2005.

Lawyers involved in the reform explained that one of the most significant challenges was to convince political party members on the political right and members of institutions most resistant to change (notably the police and judiciary) to support the reform. To achieve this, one of the key pillars of the process involved frame alignment with the mass media, particularly with El Mercurio Group. This was achieved through constant outreach to the media and training of journalists regarding problems with the old system and the solutions offered in the proposed reform. The frame used for the reform by Citizen Peace emphasized that the planned system was more "efficient" and would therefore better ensure punishment of those guilty of crimes. This was consistent with the security frame used in the mass media. Many lawyers from Diego Portales University preferred to view the reforms in terms of the expected improvements to human rights, as the reforms aimed to increase oversight of police actions. However, they recognized the efficiency frame as an acceptable compromise in order to achieve their goal of reform. All interviewees involved in the reform described attaining frame alignment with the media as "fundamental" to the reform's success.[19]

However, Citizen Peace's involvement in the reform and its emphasis on quality and technical research have influenced its policy recommendations in ways that, by the late 1990s, began to diverge with the more populist iron-fist positions of some leaders on the political right, most notably beginning with Joaquín Lavín (mayor of Las Condes 1993–1999). As the political Right gradually splintered between those more supportive of iron-fist policing and those supportive of less populist institutional approaches, so did the mass media. This provided opportunities for other civil society organizations on the political right to provide less technical and more emotional contributions to discussions on security and crime in the conservative mass media.

For example, drawing on their previous experience in President Sebastián Piñera's government (2010–2014) and in conservative municipal governments, civil society organizations such as Victims of Crime (Víctimas de la Delincuencia, established in 2006) and Safe Citizen (Ciudadano Seguro, established in 2014) gained considerable mass media attention for relatively small and new organizations. Interviewees from Safe Citizen, an organization that advocates for increasing the numbers and powers of police, described having little problem accessing mass media, particularly television.[20] One member explained: "There was this junction where the media found they were missing something and we were there, so in truth, this part [gaining mass media coverage] has been very easy."[21]

That said, civil society organizations working on or affected by police violence have found a few strategies to achieve frame alignment and create discursive opportunities. The most important were the 2006 and 2011 student protests. In both cases large numbers of students held protests advocating for the improved quality and accessibility of education. The quantity of students and their supporters at these protests, combined with their skillful handling of media relations, contributed to gaining considerable public support for their cause (Domedel and Peña y Lillo 2008).[22] Thus when police responded to the protests with violence, the mass media and public were watching and generally primed to sympathize with the students. That is, while police tactics had not changed significantly since the dictatorship, the public's perception of acceptable levels of police repression in managing large protests had (see Bonner 2014a, ch. 10).

The first time since the return of democracy in 1990 that this accepted frame on protest policing was so publicly challenged occurred during the 2006 high school student protests. This contributed to President Michelle Bachelet's unprecedented condemnation of police actions. It not only raised the profile of high school student groups as authoritative sources but motivated some civil society organizations that had long worked on issues of police violence in democracy to initiate a campaign with the slogan: "Stop there! Enough Police Violence" (*Alto ahí! Basta de violencia policial*).[23] One member of Citizen Observatory, an organization that works with indigenous communities in Chile, explained that the mass media attention on the students opened the door for them to show the similarities with police violence against indigenous communities, workers, and other marginalized people in the country.[24] However, mass media attention on the campaign and the civil society organizations involved remained low, with greater coverage in alternative and smaller media. Members of the organizations involved explained that the campaign's importance was about initiating a conversation as much among themselves as with the broader public.[25]

The university student protests that began in 2011 produced an even more significant change in civil society organizations' resistance to restrictive laws on protests, the mobilization of old and new organizations around issues of police repression of protests, and media attention on these organizations. Indeed, in 2011, for the first time, the conservative and prestigious Public Research Center (CEP) included students among the institutions evaluated in its regular, widely covered opinion polls on public confidence.[26]

Some civil society organizations used the mass media attention on the protests and police reaction to gain mass media attention for their organizations in order to pressure the police and government to change their tactics. For example, the CECT documented and followed up with arrested students regarding their treatment by security forces on the street, in police vehicles, and in prison. New organizations such as August 4th Coordinator (Coordinadora 4 de agosto) and Popular Defense (Defensoría Popular) formed to assist students with their legal situations and push for changes in police and political practices around protest policing. Popular Defense gained some mass media attention for its legal assistance to protesters. However, it received more extensive, positive, and ongoing coverage in alternative or smaller media for the cases it defended.[27]

Certainly many civil society organizations rely on protests to gain mass media attention and thereby have their voices included in public debates on issues of importance to them. These debates can provide discursive opportunities to become authoritative sources in the mass media. Yet many organizations working on police violence lamented that this was in fact the only way to have their voices included in such debates.

Another strategy used by civil society organizations working on or affected by police violence to have their voices heard in the mass media is to align their message with the position of international organizations and agreements. For example, the 2009 Amnesty International annual report criticized Chilean police actions and argued for increased political control of the police. Given the organization's international stature, the minister of the interior and public security responded to the report in the mass media denying that the government has a policy of repression. This provided a platform that Amnesty International–Chile used to have its position and response to the minister disseminated in all the major mass media.[28] The CECT has similarly benefited from its contributions to United Nations human rights reports.[29] While human rights organizations generally perceive that they receive very little coverage in Chilean mass media, especially television, some noted that CNN Chile (a twenty-four-hour news channel that began broadcasting in 2008) was an exception. Although it is a cable channel, and therefore not available to many Chileans, CNN Chile has international ownership (jointly owned by Turner Broadcasting System Latin America and VTR Chile), and a number of civil society organizations perceive that its approach to news is different compared to other mass media in the country.[30]

Finally, and similar to Argentina, some civil organizations were able to find frame alignment with certain mass media based on mutual disagreement with the government. One member of the student organization Chilean Student Federation (FECH) explained that the FECH often received positive coverage in *El Mercurio* when it criticized the government (*La Nueva Mayoría*), as opposed to coverage in *La Tercera*, which they described as more supportive of the government and more likely to focus on divisions within the student movement.[31] A member of Andha Chile a Luchar, a group from the popular classes that was protesting housing issues in 2009, explained that they often received positive coverage on Chilevisión, a TV channel then owned by Sebastián Piñera (president of Chile 2010–2014), because their organization was critical of the Bachelet government.[32] The interviewee from the Teachers' Association (Colegio de Profesores) explained that such frame alignment comes and goes. In 2008 they received a lot of media coverage in the right-wing mass media that wanted to criticize the Concertación, but in 2009, with a national election approaching, their issues were not the ones the political Right wanted to focus on and the mass media coverage declined.[33] As in Argentina, discursive opportunities for civil society organizations working on or affected by police violence occur occasionally (albeit less often than in Argentina), but do not ultimately displace the dominant mass media frame of insecurity and the need for a tough-on-crime response.

PROFESSIONAL PUBLIC RELATIONS

Although not essential, professional public relations assistance can help civil society organizations to find frame alignment with the mass media and effectively exploit discursive opportunities to become authoritative journalistic sources. Professional public relations officers can establish a communications strategy that conforms to the mass media logic and can follow media twenty-four hours a day and seven days a week. Moreover, they know how and when to intervene. They can also train members in how to speak to the media, thereby controlling the organization's message. The argument in favor of public relations is that the practice could improve democratic debate by facilitating better communication between actors (Moloney 2006, 2).

However, critics raise two important points. First, professional public relations is expensive, which favors NGOs that have substantial funding over NGOs or grassroots organizations that have limited or no funding (Deacon 2003; Fenton 2010; Moloney 2006). Second, mediatization is a potential problem. This occurs when civil society organizations change or choose their position, policies, and actions based primarily on media considerations (Waisbord 2011). Together these drawbacks reinforce and legitimize the ideas and interests of powerful political and economic actors by priming audiences to view the PR information they provide as "common sense" (Moloney 2006, 94). From this perspective, public relations reduces rather than enhances pluralistic democratic debate.

Professional public relations has existed in Latin America since the late 1950s (initially limited to private businesses) but expanded significantly in the 1990s, along with the adoption of neoliberal economic policies (Aparecida Ferrari and França 2011, 49–50). As discussed in chapter 5, a market-based media system with reduced regulations has increased pressure on state and civil society organizations to conform to the mass media logic in order to have their voices heard. Mass media have focused on cost cutting in order to increase profits, and journalists have thus reduced the number of sources they use as well as expensive and time-consuming watchdog journalism. Relatively unregulated twenty-four-hour-TV and internet news have further increased pressure for quantity and speed over quality of news. In this context, professional public relations material is attractive to journalists because it is cheap (usually free) and easy to access. Comparing Argentina and Chile, I find that public relations has a longer history and greater importance for civil society organizations in Chile than in Argentina. This is in part due to the earlier adoption of neoliberal economic and media policies in Chile and the different way in which the mass media have been "captured" in each country.

ARGENTINA

Civil society organizations can certainly engage the mass media without professional public relations services. In Argentina the most common tactics used by civil society organizations to attract mass media attention are protests, which may also include the dissemination of pamphlets that explain the organization's demands. They also almost all use websites, press releases, contacts with supportive journalists (who may even be members of their organization), alternative media, email lists, and social media. Some interviewees described alternative and social media primarily as a means to speak to supporters or those already sympathetic to the organization. Others maintained that mass media journalists sometimes take information from these social media sites, alternative publications, and news agencies, and are thus a means to access the mass media. Indeed, some police journalists said that they followed the Twitter feeds of alternative news agencies such as Cosecha Roja and La Garganta Poderosa. Yet professional public relations can raise an organization's profile, increasing the likelihood that it is considered an authoritative journalistic source.

Of the eighteen civil society organizations interviewed in Argentina, two had professional paid public relations staff, CELS and the Provincial Commission for Memory. Both organizations receive substantial funding that pays for a large comfortable office as well as other paid staff and other resources. CELS receives funding from many international organizations such as the Ford Foundation, Tinker Foundation, and the Open Society Foundations. The Provincial Commission for Memory receives substantial funding from the Buenos Aires provincial government, although the commission is independent of the state itself. That is, both organizations are NGOs.

However, CELS has a long history, beginning in 1979 during the last dictatorship, that has led them gradually to their current professionalization. It was not until 2005 that they acquired a professional communications department, whose directors have included former journalists and public relations experts.[34] The Provincial Commission for Memory was founded in 1999 with professional communications staff but only began to work with focused attention on police violence and prison torture in 2005.

Some key issues distinguish the communications strategies of these organizations from the others. First, they have a carefully designed communications strategy. They are clear about who in their organization should speak to the media and on which issues, and they understand the mode of communication needed for the type of issue. For example, one communications director for CELS explained that they use Twitter for smaller issues or if they primarily want to communicate an idea or critique to political leaders (many of whom follow CELS on Twitter). For larger issues they might write an opinion piece (which, due to their reputation, newspapers will often publish) or write a pre-prepared article that could be used by a journalist or editor. For an even larger issue they might hold a press conference with the president or director of CELS present, as this will provide visuals for television.[35]

They also have the resources to develop a wide array of pre-prepared material. For example, CELS's website includes blogs and detailed entries about ongoing trials for human rights abuses that journalists might be following but do not have time to do the background work or attend the trials. The Provincial Commission for Memory runs its own news agency, andar (www.andaragencia.org), from which journalists can take stories. Both organizations said that while their organization's name does not always appear in the mass media, their stories often do and sometimes word for word as they wrote them. In sum, these NGOs proactively engage the media using media logic, seeking out political opportunities (small and large), and finding frame alignment. However, whether by choice, due to funding concerns, or the constraints of public relations, these organizations aim to reform the criminal justice system within the existing dominant institutional structures and language—a perspective not shared by many less well-funded civil society organizations.

Yet public relations is not limited to professional paid staff. Most of the civil society organizations interviewed have dedicated volunteers, some with journalism or communications training, who assist in communicating the goals and work of the organization. In the Argentine media system, these organizations benefit most from journalists' (and all citizens') restrictive access to information. That is, some information is not collected because it is not in the political interest of state actors to collect it and other information is provided selectively in clientelist exchanges. In this environment, information becomes an important resource used by civil society organizations to gain access to or influence the content of mass media news.

Statistics are particularly hard to acquire in Argentina, especially as they relate to police violence (the latter is a problem in many countries). CORREPI and CELS both provide rigorous and comprehensive statistics on police violence that no one else can provide. Lacking a cumbersome communications department,

CORREPI is often faster than CELS at providing these statistics.[36] The Provincial Commission for Memory provides similar statistics on prison conditions and torture in the province of Buenos Aires. All three organizations release annual reports that synthesize this information for the year and are sometimes used by journalists.

Civil society organizations can also use access to people as a resource. For example, both CORREPI and Frente Santillán have extensive memberships and networks in the shantytowns on the outskirts of the city of Buenos Aires (as well as elsewhere). When violence, crime, or other forms of institutional or noninstitutional wrongdoing occurs in these communities these organizations provide journalists with connections for interviews or information on what is happening or both.[37] For example, during the protest in Indoamericano Park in 2010, in which police killed three people, Frente Santillán was a primary source for journalists about what was happening and the names of those killed.[38]

However, it was a challenge for all civil society organizations to provide visuals. As one interviewee from the organization Relatives and Friends of Victims of AMIA lamented, the written word, even as used in social media, is "cold." He argued that people have to see and hear the passion of their members in order to "awaken" their interest.[39] Yet, high-resolution visuals (especially TV-ready video) is expensive to produce and to do well. Organizations can and do post pictures and some videos on YouTube, but they are not always usable for the mass media, and journalists do not always trust such images. Public protests are another tactic used to provide the visuals needed particularly for television, but some organizations explained that even when protests were held in the Plaza de Mayo, journalists did not always attend. Moreover, if journalists attend a protest, the images often make protesters appear threatening or violent and ignore or downplay their demands.[40] Press conferences were only deemed effective by the two NGOs with professional public relations. Most organizations said that few journalists attend if they organize a press conference.

In sum, professional public relations assists with more consistent media coverage in Argentina, especially since the extensive implementation of neoliberal media policies. The use of professional PR benefits civil society organizations that can afford it and, as a consequence, promotes some ideas over others. However, professional PR does not determine media coverage. Civil society organizations can use volunteers to mobilize potentially inexpensive PR strategies, notably information (such as statistics) and access to people, to have their voices included in the mass media. However, the problem of visuals is a greater challenge for all interviewed civil society organizations than for the state (see chapter 5). Thus PR not only favors some civil society organizations over others but also reinforces journalists' preference for state over civil society actors as news sources.

CHILE

Unlike in Argentina, most civil society organizations interviewed in Chile have the legal status equivalent to that of an NGO, or are striving to obtain it (the terms used in Chile are "corporación" and "fundación"). This legal status requires organizations to have an office, a board of directors, and internal governing regulations. One student organization that was working to obtain the legal status of "corporación" explained that it was seeking the status in order to gain "social worth" (*valorización social*), to organize "correctly," and to be able to attract funding to pay for full-time staff salaries.[41]

The sources from which organizations receive funding include varying amounts from state institutions, universities, international organizations, and private companies. The more focused the interviewed NGO is on security and crime (as opposed to human rights or police violence), generally the greater the amount of private funding that was received in the form of both donations and contracts. In 2014, Citizen Peace received Ch$474,911,395 (approximately US$839,146.61) in donations from twenty-three businesses, including some of Chile's largest companies such as Banco de Chile, Banco Santander, Falabella, and El Mercurio Group.[42]

Certainly the NGO-ization of civil society in Chile facilitates, in theory, the availability of funds for professional public relations staff. However, many organizations still rely on volunteer journalists to help them develop and implement a communications plan. The reliance on funding and emphasis on public relations to obtain and retain it may also contribute to a narrowing of the range of issues and the ways they are discussed in the public sphere. This is in part because some NGOs have more funds available for public relations than others but also because some issues more easily attract media attention than others (contributing to the mediatization of NGOs' issue selection). As discussed in the previous section, civil society alignment with media frames is more easily found on crime and security topics than police violence, and NGOs that work on these issues also have better funding.

Some of the most well-funded NGOs interviewed that work on issues of policing, crime, and/or security, have paid communications staff, and receive mass media attention in Chile are: Citizen Peace, Safe Citizen, Amnesty International–Chile, and FECH. The first two organizations work on crime and security, the latter two work on or are affected by police violence. CEP and CED are also well-funded and have access to some of the same media relations techniques, but they work more tangentially on issues of policing, crime, and security.

In addition to a clear communications strategy, most of these organizations have access to resources that allowed them to provide particular products that are attractive to the mass media. For example, when asked about how they attract mass media attention, one of the first things Citizen Peace mentioned was their yearly, widely covered crime victimization surveys.[43] Indeed, CEP, which also receives significant mass media coverage for its public opinion polls, noted that it generally does not survey people about security issues anymore because Citizen Peace does this.[44] Public opinion polls, such as the victimization surveys, are very costly to do well and are therefore beyond the financial capabilities of most civil society organizations.[45]

All these organizations (with the exception of FECH) also have access to people who have power within (or formerly within) the state or internationally. These public figures can then be used to attract mass media attention. For example, Citizen Peace holds a yearly forum (*consejo consultivo*) to which they invite ministers, congress members, the president, and other high-ranked public officials to meet to discuss security issues.[46] They also hold presidential debates on security issues in election years.[47] Similarly, the executive director of Safe Citizen was previously the coordinator of public security for the Santiago Metropolitan Area (2013–2014). In that position he was frequently consulted by the media on daily crime news and, upon creating the NGO in 2015, has maintained his position as a regular media contact on both daily crime and issues of security more generally.[48] The CED mentioned receiving little media coverage except when it invites public figures to give talks at its institution.[49] Amnesty International–Chile benefits (albeit to a lesser extent) from its connection with its London office.

Arguably, alternative media, the internet, and social media in particular could offer a more level playing field for NGOs. Human rights organizations and organizations working on or affected by police violence make wide use of alternative media, and they often receive good coverage (in quality and quantity) especially from radio and some written and online alternative media such as *El Ciudadano*, *El Siglo*, and *El Mostrador*. Television, which reaches the largest audiences,[50] was consistently noted by human rights organizations as the most challenging to access. As one interviewee stated, "Television for human rights news is practically nonexistent."[51] Indeed, one study of TV news coverage found that in 2007, 0.8 percent was related to human rights compared to 20.1 percent on police and security (the latter exceeded only by sports and social issues) (Marín and Cordero 2009, 263). Most interviewees argue that while the alternative media are important, these media do not help them to communicate with the broad audience they hope to reach.

In this respect, internet-based media appear at first glance to be better than alternative media. Indeed, many interviewees noted the student movements' effective use of social media to mobilize people to attend their protests and the explosion of effective social media use generally during the first Piñera government (2010–2014), especially by students. Yet with time and reflection, most civil society organizations also observed important limits to the use of the internet and social media. The most common response from civil society organizations was that they use digital media (websites, social media, email) primarily to communicate to their members, supporters, and those who might want more information on their organization and its activities (including but not exclusively journalists). Email lists were one of the most cited means of connecting with this base of supporters, and for some organizations email is their primary means of communication.[52]

Websites were also important to organizations for posting basic information about their organization and cross-referencing material from civil society organizations with whom they work in solidarity. Many organizations saw Twitter and Facebook as reaching a narrower demographic. Others described Facebook as equivalent to a webpage but with a more defined audience, whereas Twitter reached an amorphous audience that was hard to target. One member from Amnesty International–Chile noted that since the 2011 student protests, social media have become so widely used that they no longer provide consistently reliable information and "there is an explosion of use of social media that in the end makes any one voice invisible."[53]

In contrast, organizations with better communicational resources were able to use social media in a more targeted manner. For example, Amnesty International–Chile offers a "public information service," similar to a news agency, in which it sends human rights-related articles from the media to key decision makers such as "the minister of the interior, the cardinal, the chief of police." It offers a second email list to subscribers (approximately 7,000), journalists, and "leaders of opinion" through which it sends Amnesty International's own human rights material.[54] Even more refined, Citizen Peace is able to capitalize on its reputation and connections with power holders to use Twitter as a way to communicate news and the results of its studies with state actors, such as public prosecutors and defense lawyers, who follow them.[55] Thus professional public relations assists with the effective use of social media in ways similar to its use of the mass media. It favors some civil society organizations and some voices over others, to the more consistent benefit of those with greater financial resources.

MEDIA AND THE RISE OF PUNITIVE CIVIL SOCIETY VOICES

To summarize, in Argentina, electoral democracy and media democratization preceded the introduction of neoliberal economic reforms to the media. Media democratization, particularly with the expansion of watchdog journalism in the late 1980s and 1990s, opened up discursive opportunities for civil society organizations working on police violence to become authoritative journalistic sources and achieve frame alignment with the mass media on this issue for an extended period of time (most of the 1990s). In turn, this facilitated the access of civil society organizations, especially those with limited funds for public relations, to the mass media through the provision of related information, such as statistics on police violence and contacts in shantytowns. However, with the advancement of neoliberal economic and media policies (notably by the late 1990s/early 2000s), discursive opportunities and frame alignment decreased on police violence and increased on the topics of crime and insecurity. Public relations (and the associated need for funding) became more important for civil society organizations working on police violence, except when media politicization has been effectively exploited.

In contrast, in Chile neoliberal economic and media reform predates electoral democracy. This has decreased discursive opportunities for organizations working on police violence to become authoritative journalistic sources or achieve frame alignment with the mass media. In large part this is due to the dominance of the two largest, and conservative, media groups, El Mercurio Group and COPESA, which benefited from the ways in which neoliberal media policies were implemented under the dictatorship (discussed in chapter 3). In this context, public relations has become more important to civil society organizations, and the types of resources used to attract media attention are more costly (such as public opinion polls and access to people in positions of political power). However, civil society organizations concerned with police violence have found some possibilities for having their voices heard in the mass media through more limited discursive opportunities, social media, connections to international organizations, and disagreements with the government.

Clearly, not all civil society voices are heard equally in the mass media coverage of insecurity and common crime. While all civil society organizations can find moments of frame alignment or discursive opportunities, neoliberal media systems favor organizations that can find frame alignment with the dominant tough-on-crime discourse established by the practices of journalists and state actors, and can afford professional public relations assistance. These practices in turn narrow the range of civil society voices heard in mass media debates on crime, security, and police violence. Most notably they marginalize sustained public discussion on police violence, reducing accountability. The resulting, more homogeneous, "public" (as represented by those civil society organizations found most often in the mass media) appears predominantly punitive. This neoliberal media environment then encourages political leaders to use punitive populist rhetoric and policies to win this public's support.

Conclusion

The "silent majority" is not necessarily punitive. Indeed, we can imagine Juan Carlos Blumberg's story, which began this book, unfolding in a very different manner with a change in communicational practices. For example, when Blumberg's son was kidnapped and murdered he went to the mass media to plead for greater security. He did this because the mass media were receptive; kidnappings and their victims provide good drama and were capturing news media attention at the time. The mass media coverage gave Blumberg a public platform as a victim of crime, which enabled him to mobilize large protests and advocate for a tough-on-crime response. The media attention led companies, individuals, and organizations interested in tough-on-crime solutions to reach out to Blumberg with assistance (financial and otherwise).[1] Blumberg explained that people who worked in public relations (PR) for "important companies" helped with his Axel Blumberg Foundation's PR strategy, including training him in how to speak to the media.[2]

Had the media not been receptive to his story or subsequent PR material, Blumberg's perspectives on crime control would not have featured as a proxy for public opinion. Had human rights organizations been the primary source for journalists covering extortive kidnappings, or had mass media companies given greater priority to watchdog journalism, perhaps this crime concern would have been framed differently. For example, interviewees for this book and less prominent media reports note that the police were involved in Axel Blumberg's kidnapping as well as in many similar extortive kidnappings.[3] Indeed, three Argentine Federal Police (PFA) officers were eventually charged with involvement in Axel's kidnapping (Guerrero 2013, 89) and this included the former head of the PFA's Anti-Kidnapping Brigade.[4] A frame of police wrongdoing, if it had been emphasized as agenda-setting news, might have mobilized protests in favor of police reforms that aimed to decrease police violence and increase civilian oversight, rather than advocate for more police on the streets with greater discretion. Thus, the stories the mass media tell about crime, insecurity, and police violence are important to both crime control and police reform. The construction of the problems and solutions will be shaped by those who are telling the stories.

Hence, if punitive populism is to be challenged, we must ask, as this book has: How do some voices come to dominate public debate on these issues? Rather than analyzing the resulting discourses, this question requires us to examine the everyday and interacting practices of those involved in the production of public discourses from within the mass media, state, and civil society, and the conditions that favor some choices (and some voices) over others.

The question this book has posed is relevant not only to the cases of Argentina and Chile but also to the wide range of countries around the world confronting the rise of tough-on-crime rhetoric and policies, from the United States and the United Kingdom to South Africa and the Philippines. Further studies could refine the way in which the introduction of neoliberal media policies (and the extent of its implementation) has combined with different preexisting media systems to favor similar or slightly different punitive rhetoric. The cases of Argentina and Chile have allowed us to turn a critical eye on assumptions made about punitive populism in the Euro-American literature (through a most different comparison with Latin America), as well as to compare the influence of neoliberal media policies in two very different settings (a most different comparison of Argentina and Chile and a most similar within case comparison of Argentina over time). This analysis has found three key answers to the research question. First, neoliberal media systems reduce the ability of journalists and civil society to hold punitive voices to account. Second, neoliberal media systems tend to homogenize public opinion as punitive by favoring punitive voices. Third, media, state, and civil society communicational practices in neoliberal media systems encourage the mediatization of policymaking to the benefit of punitive policies. In what follows, I draw together the lessons learned on each of these points.

DECREASED ACCOUNTABILITY

Punitive populism is not necessarily a problem for democracy as long as the ideas, emotions, policies, and their consequences are held to account. Neoliberal media systems decrease the ability of the mass media to do this. Ideally, in a democracy, the mass media can expose and redefine wrongdoing, shame wrongdoers, demand answers for that wrongdoing, and activate institutions of accountability that can apply punishments (Bonner 2014a; Peruzzotti and Smulovitz 2006). While the literature on democracy and democratization assumes that this role is achieved when the media are free and independent of the state, this book has shown that the market also limits the ability of the mass media to hold powerful actors to account. This finding is important to many areas of study on democracy, including environmental protection, economic policymaking, and social service provision. However, it is particularly important to the rise of punitive populism and the protection of human rights. This book has revealed that a neoliberalized media system decreases the mass media's role in accountability in two key ways: it reduces watchdog journalism and it increases use of public relations (PR) material.

REDUCED WATCHDOG JOURNALISM

Watchdog journalism acts as an important check on punitive populism. By spending time on a story and collecting a wide range of sources, journalists are in a better position to present a strong, context-based, analysis of the problem, to offer a wide array of solutions, and to explain and follow up on the consequences of each solution. In this manner, if punitive policies produce human rights abuses, including police violence, journalists are more likely to expose them and demand answers. Certainly *Página/12*'s commitment to democracy allowed it to spur a flourishing of watchdog journalism in Argentina in the 1990s that encouraged some of the most important police reforms since the return democracy (see chapter 3; Waisbord 2000). Yet the newspaper's precarious financial situation in an increasingly neoliberalized media system left it vulnerable to clientelism. In contrast, in other media systems, the state (through an independent governing body) provides supports, regulations, and subsidies that offer a more consistently favorable media environment for watchdog journalism and for journalists' prioritization of democratic goals over the pressures of the market or clientelism (see chapter 2).

Certainly, watchdog journalism is expensive. It requires journalists to spend an extended period of time on one story, rather than on many stories, and it may require additional funds to pay for the investigation itself. Neoliberal media systems prioritize profit over democratic goals. To increase profit, media outlets cut the number of journalists on staff and require that they produce more stories more often. Watchdog journalism can attract audiences (increasing revenue) but so can drama, and the latter is less expensive. As discussed in chapters 2, 3, and 4, the increased demands on journalists to produce stories leads to their reliance on fewer sources and increases the media outlet's preference for sensationalist front-page crime stories. Such stories are plentiful, cheap, and dramatic. As seen in chapters 4 and 5, a preference for crime stories favors the police as a source, and a resulting reticence on the part of the mass media to criticize or hold them accountable. This reduces the likelihood of critical reporting on police violence and the punitive populist rhetoric and policies that encourage it.

INCREASED PUBLIC RELATIONS

The neoliberal media system's pressure on fewer journalists to write more stories more often, makes journalists open to using PR material uncritically. As some scholars of PR have noted, PR is not necessarily bad for democracy. It could enhance communication between different actors (Moloney 2006). However, for PR to contribute positively to democracy, media need to hold it to account. Journalists need to use other sources to verify whether the information is true or whether other issues or perspectives have to be considered. Yet journalists in neoliberal media systems often lack the time to cross-check PR material. This makes the mass media vulnerable to reinforcing the views, ideas, and interests of powerful political, economic, and civil society voices, as these are the actors most able to produce regular, high-quality, professional PR material. As discussed in chapters 5 and 6, the aim of PR material is to promote the legitimacy of producers of the PR, thus priming audiences to consider their views, ideas, and interests as "common sense," and thus not in need of accountability.

As shown in chapters 5 and 6, the state and civil society actors most able to produce professional PR material are those most likely to favor punitive approaches to crime control, notably the police and security/crime-oriented civil society organizations. These sources and their PR material also reinforce the neoliberalized mass media's existing preference for dramatic and episodic (what is happening now, not context) crime stories. PR material that offers human rights stories of police violence resulting from punitive policies, while potentially dramatic, risks alienating the police as a primary source of information on crime. In this manner, PR material, uncritically reproduced, reduces the role of the mass media in holding to account powerful actors with punitive ideas for the consequences of those ideas.

HOMOGENIZATION OF PUBLIC OPINION

Neoliberal media systems also tend to decrease the pluralism of public opinion. Ideally, in a democracy, the mass media provide a forum for public debate where a wide range of ideas, emotions, policies, and perspectives are discussed and a more unified public opinion can emerge, particularly on contentious issues. In this manner, the media become the voice of the people, reflecting public opinion to political leaders who can then make choices based on a better understanding of what the public wants. As discussed in the introduction, the literature on democracy and democratization assumes that media that are uncensored by the state will produce this plurality of ideas. Yet this perspective neglects the role of the market in restraining whose voices participate in media-based public debates and how public opinion is presented. The needs of mass media profit making are not necessarily those of democracy.

Journalists working in neoliberal media systems face pressures to homogenize public opinion and this contributes to the rise of punitive populism. For punitive populists, public opinion is central. It is what gives their policies legitimacy. Yet when public opinion is presented as heterogeneous, not homogeneous, it is more likely that voices critical of punitive populism will be heard and will hold it to account. While not necessarily the model for all countries, the democratic corporatist media system (see chapter 2) provides an example of how regulations and subsidies can be used to ensure that voices, not commercially viable but important to democracy, are heard in public debates. In contrast, neoliberal media systems let the market decide which views participate in and dominate media-based public debate. As this book reveals, journalistic practices in this system favor the more cost-effective use of proxies for public opinion (which tend to homogenize) instead of using a diverse array of sources that build a heterogeneous understanding of public opinion. Most notably, journalists in neoliberal media systems rely heavily on public opinion polls and selective citizen/civil society organizations as proxies for public opinion. These choices often favor punitive voices.

PUBLIC OPINION POLLS

As shown in chapters 2 and 3, public opinion polls grew in popularity with the spread of neoliberal media policies. While public opinion polls vary in quality, most have a circular relationship with the media. That is, unless the individual responding has firsthand knowledge or experience, most people respond to polls based on impressions gleaned from the mass media. Neoliberalized mass media encourage journalistic practices that favor punitive state and civil society voices, and these perspectives are reflected and reinforced in public opinion polls. These polls then confirm that "the public" (in the singular) desire punitive crime policies and legitimize punitive populist leaders' policy choices.

CITIZENS/CIVIL SOCIETY PROXIES

In addition to public opinion polls, journalists sometimes use individual citizens and civil society organizations as proxies for public opinion. In neoliberal media systems, journalists are encouraged to use proxies over an array of sources to help increase the number and speed of stories they produce. As revealed in chapters 4 and 6, the citizens and civil society organizations preferred as proxies are those that are readily available and, ideally, add to the drama of the story. Victims of crime are easy to locate and they provide drama. Civil society organizations whose ideas confirm, rather then challenge, the perspective of the police (a valuable source for crime stories) can also be used as proxies for public opinion without the risk of alienating a primary news source. Owing to their consistency with the police, the views of victims and these organizations are familiar to journalists and audiences and are therefore more likely to resonate as "true" or even as "common sense." Moreover, punitive populist leaders can use their own and audiences' self-identification with victims as an empty signifier that unites "citizens" against "criminals" (Laclau 2007; Samet 2013, 532).

Certainly, clientelism (Argentina) and political alignment (Chile), as well as additional social movement strategies discussed in chapter 6, can create political opportunities for human rights organizations to oppose punitive populism and reveal its implications for police violence. Yet, in a neoliberal media system, these opportunities are not consistently available and thus limit the ability of these organizations to shift dominant media frames.

MEDIATIZATION OF POLICYMAKING

Media play an important role in policymaking. As discussed in the introduction, the rise of punitive populism can be explained by the negotiations and influence of an array of political and economic actors at the local, state/provincial, national, and international levels. Yet the media play an often overlooked role in these negotiations and the ideas that emerge as dominant. Neoliberal media systems favor some ideas over others in these debates. This finding is as important to punitive populism as it is to other policy debates in democracy.

Mass media can create political opportunities for the introduction of new policies, facilitate communication between policy actors, favor the ideas of some actors over others in policy negotiations, and influence and construct public opinion more favorable to some proposed policies than others. While political actors can ignore the media in policymaking—or remove some policy areas from public debate—the mass media are increasingly important to political leaders' decision making, especially those using populist strategies (see the introduction and chapter 2). Both political leaders and civil society organizations engaged in policy debates may choose to mediatize policymaking by selecting and advocating for particular policies based on how well they are likely to be covered in the mass media. While this can occur in all democratic media systems, a neoliberalized media system favors more punitive policy choices over others. This is the result of two key issues related to the salience of crime and the prominence given to the voices of victims and the police.

SALIENCE OF CRIME

In democracy, political actors address a wide array of policy issues. As discussed in the introduction and chapter 4, crime has not always been a central area of policy concern. Indeed, David Garland (2001) and many other scholars of punitive populism emphasize that the transition from penal welfare crime control approaches (a policy area dominated by criminal justice experts) to punitive populism involved increased public interest in crime as a policy area. As examined in the introduction and chapter 1, neoliberal economic policies opened up a large array of policy concerns related to insecurity, which include but are not limited to crime. They also involve precarious employment, decreased access to quality social services, and financial insecurity (loss of savings and property). Neoliberal media systems encourage journalistic practices that favor extensive, prominent, and regular coverage of crime to increase audience size and thus revenue. Story frames tend to be episodic to emphasize drama and emotion. The repetition of these stories as agenda-setting news and their selective use of available statistics on common crime (defined as robbery, theft, and homicide) prime audiences to view this issue as the most important facing their country and the basis upon which to evaluate political leaders' performance (see chapters 1 and 2). These practices then increase the salience of crime as a policy issue.

VICTIMS AND THE POLICE

For reasons discussed above and throughout the book, neoliberal media systems favor crime stories and rely heavily on victims and the police as sources. This strengthens these actors' views, ideas, and interests in policy debates. Political and civil society actors whose perspectives align with the views of victims and the police will find their policy frames resonate as familiar with the public. Human rights organizations or those concerned with police violence are more likely to find their views marginalized or even presented as disrespectful to the police, victims of crime, or both.

Media systems that favor watchdog journalism and the use of a wide array of sources are more likely to emphasize other policy issues and the ideas of both punitive and nonpunitive policy actors (e.g., Green 2008). As discussed in chapter 3, crime was an issue in Argentina in the 1990s. However, media attention on police violence and corruption meant that crime and punitive responses were not necessarily the most important policy issues. These ideas had to compete with pressures on political leaders to address human rights and police violence. The neoliberalization of media in Argentina significantly reduced this policy competition in favor of crime and punitivism. Thus, media systems matter to policymaking.

Media play an important, even a defining, role in democracy. This is widely accepted in the literature on democracy and democratization. Yet, democratic media, uncensored by the state, can produce undemocratic outcomes. In part, this is because some democratic media systems are more supportive of the democratic role of the media than are others. The priority in a neoliberal market-based media system is profit, not democracy. Thus comprehending democratic media systems (in the plural), and the journalistic, state, and civil society practices each produces, is important to our understanding of when and how media strengthen democracy and when they weaken it. This is particularly important to our understanding of the rise of punitive populism and its implications for human rights, especially police violence. As this book has shown, neoliberal media systems encourage communicational practices that favor punitive voices, which results in a mass media construction of (in)security that supports the rise of punitive populism (see figure I.1).

Media reform thus becomes an integral part of building a stronger democracy, more successful crime control, and increased accountability for police violence. Criminal justice experts who learn to communicate better, deliberative polls, or heroic journalists are not sufficient (see chapters 2 and 3; Green 2008; Roberts et al. 2003; UNDP 2013a, 2013b). Indeed, journalists in many countries have been mobilizing for media reforms, such as the Coalition for Democratic Broadcasting in Argentina, the Journalists Association (Colegio de Periodistas) in Chile, the Media Reform Coalition in the United Kingdom, and Free Press in the United States. The best types of reforms will depend on the local context. Yet, through understanding the details of the types of communicational practices used by journalists, state actors, and civil society organizations that encourage punitive populism, we can begin to identify the types of changes that might reduce it.

In particular, the practices explored in this book reveal the need for media systems that support and encourage more diverse journalistic sources, more heterogeneous depictions of public opinion, more watchdog journalism, and regulations on the use of PR as well as on criminal justice reality shows and certain news formats. Such reforms reassert democracy (over profit) as the purpose of mass media news and reimagine the state's role not as a threat to democracy, but as a facilitator. What these reforms look like in practice in diverse local contexts is beyond the scope of this book, but it is an area of much needed research.

APPENDIX

This book is based on 194 semistructured interviews (1 to 4 hours each) with people working on issues pertaining to crime, security, and police violence—particularly but not exclusively with those working as communications officers, directors of communications, journalists, or volunteers in communications. Most interviews were one-on-one, but some were with two or more interviewees at the initiative of the interviewees.

Media actors I interviewed included journalists, editors, directors, and producers who covered crime and policing from a cross-section of both mass media and alternative news media including newspapers, magazines, radio, TV, and internet. Many journalists had worked for more than one company, and sometimes more than one medium, and could speak about the similarities and differences across media outlets and formats as well as over time. I also interviewed relevant journalists' unions or organizations.

State actors included policymakers and communications officers from the ministries responsible for security policy at the national, provincial, and (capital) city levels, as well as the most important police forces. Also included were interviewees from the prosecutor's office and public defense lawyers. I spoke to people responsible for security topics or the communication of these topics for most major political parties. I also spoke to people responsible for portraying the history of security and human rights issues in police and human rights museums.

Civil society actors included communications officers/volunteers and those working on policing or security issues from within human rights organizations and organizations of victims (or supporting victims) of police violence and/or crime. They also included those working on security issues or organizations affected by police violence. Sometimes multiple people were interviewed from the same organization to capture different perspectives, different capacities, and differences over time.

The bulk of the interviews were conducted in 2009 and 2015 in Argentina and Chile. However, additional interviews were carried out in 2006 (Chile, Argentina), 2007 and 2013 (Argentina), and in various years between 2009 and 2015 at conferences and via Skype. The interview breakdown is as follows:

ARGENTINA

STATE ACTORS INTERVIEWED: 31

Ministry of Justice and Human Rights (federal government, 2009), Ministry of Security (federal government, 2013, 2015), Ministry of Security (Buenos Aires Provincial Government, 2009, 2013, 2015), National Senate (UCR, secretary for the Commission on Rights and Guarantees, 2009), Defensoría del Pueblo (similar to ombudsman's office, Autonomous City of Buenos Aires, 2009), Procuración General de la Nación (national public judiciary, 2009), Metropolitan Police and public relations company that worked with the Metropolitan Police (Autonomous City of Buenos Aires, 2009, 2013, 2015), Buenos Aires Provincial Police (2009), Airport Security Police (federal, 2009), Argentine Federal Police (2009, 2015), Ministry of Justice and Security (Autonomous City of Buenos Aires, 2009, 2013, 2015), Buenos Aires Provincial Congress member (2013), Federal Police Museum (2015), Memory and Human Rights Space, Ex-Esma (2015).

MEDIA ACTORS INTERVIEWED: 27

La Nación (newspaper, 2009, 2015), *Clarín* (newspaper, 2009, 2013, 2015), *Página/12* (newspaper, 2009, 2013), *Díario Crónica* (newspaper, 2013, 2015), *Crítica* (newspaper, 2009), *Miradas al Sur* (alternative newspaper, 2009), TN (TV, 2015) Canal 13 (TV, 2015), América 2 (TV, 2009, 2015), C5N (TV, 2013), Crónica TV (TV, 2015), Director of and journalist for *Policías en Acción* (2009), Infobae (Online, 2015), Informe Reservado (online and TV, alternative, 2009), Radio 10 (radio, 2013), Radio Mitre (radio, 2015), *Noticias* (magazine, 2015), Communications professor (Universidad Austral, 2009), FATPREN (journalists' union, 2009), FOPEA (journalists' organization, 2015).

CIVIL SOCIETY ACTORS INTERVIEWED: 39

CELS (Center for Legal and Social Studies, 2006, 2009, 2013, 2015), CORREPI (Coordinator against Police and Institutional Repression, 2009, 2013), APDH (Permanent Assembly for Human Rights, 2009), MEDH (Ecumenical Movement for Human Rights, 2009), Argentine League for the Rights of Man (La Liga Argentina por los derechos del hombre, 2009), CADeP (Antipressive Coordinator for People's Rights, 2009), Mothers of Pain (Madres del Dolor, 2009), COFAVI (Commission of Family Members of Defenseless Victims of Social, Police, Judicial, and Institutional Violence, 2009), Axel Blumberg Foundation (2009), Relatives and Friends of Victims of the AMIA Attack (2009), FTV (Land and Housing Front, 2009), Darío Santillan Popular Front (Frente Popular Darío Santillan 2009, 2013), "La Alameda" Assembly (Asamblea "La Alameda", 2006, 2007), Revolutionary Workers' Movement "Mario Roberto

Santucho" (Movimiento de Trabajadores Revolucionarios "Mario Roberto Santucho," 2006, 2007), Network of Mothers and Relatives of Drug Victims (2009), CeProDH (Professionals for Human Rights Center, 2015), Provincial Commission for Memory (Comisión Provincial por la Memoria, 2015).

CHILE

STATE ACTORS INTERVIEWED: 26

Ministry of the Interior (national government, 2009), Ministry of Interior and Public Security (national government, 2015), Public Ministry (National Prosecutors, 2009), Municipality of Santiago (2009), Judicial Assistance Corporation (2009), CONADI (Indigenous Development Corporation, national government, 2009), Chilean Christian Democratic Party (2009), National Renovation Party (2009), Chilean Socialist Party (2009), Chilean Communist Party (2009), Carabineros (2009, 2015), PDI (Investigative Police of Chile, 2009, 2015), Prison Guards (Gendarmería, 2015), Museum of Memory and Human Rights (2015), INDH (National Institute of Human Rights, 2015), Historical Museum of the Carabineros (2015)

MEDIA ACTORS INTERVIEWED: 31

El Mercurio (newspaper, 2009, 2015), *La Tercera* (newspaper, 2009, 2015), *La Nación* (newspaper, 2009), *The Clinic* (newspaper, 2009), *La Cuarta* (newspaper, 2015), *El Ciudadano* (alternative newspaper, 2009), El Mostrador (Online, 2009), CIPER Chile (Online, 2009), Megavisión (TV, 2009, 2015), Chilevisión (TV, 2009, 2015), Canal 13 (TV, 2015), TVN (TV, 2015), Radio Bío-Bío (radio, 2015), Radio Universidad de Chile (radio, 2015), Radio Cooperativa (radio, 2015), Asuntos Públicos (Online, 2009), Agencia EFE (Spanish news agency, 2009), Journalism professor (Universidad Alberto Hurtado, 2009), Independent journalist (2009), journalist author of *El Diario de Agustín* (2009), journalist author of *El Libro Negra de la Justicia Chilena* (2015), Chilean Journalists Association (Colegio de Periodistas, 2009, 2015), as well as journalists who had previously worked at Últimas *Noticias* (2009), *La* Época (2009), and *El Mercurio* (2009) among other publications.

CIVIL SOCIETY ACTORS INTERVIEWED: 35

CODEPU (Corporation for the Promotion and Defense of People's Rights, 2009), FASIC (Social Assistance Foundation of the Christian Churches, 2009), FECH (Chilean Student Federation, 2009, 2015), Amnesty International–Chile Section (2009, 2015), CED (Center for Development Studies, 2009), Center for Justice Studies of the Americas (2009), Ford Foundation (2006), Security and

Citizenship Program (FLACSO-Chile, 2006, 2009), Human Rights Center (Diego Portales University, 2009, 2011), CESC (Center for Studies in Citizen Security, 2006, 2009, 2015), Teachers' Association (Colegio de Profesores, 2009), Human Corporation (Corporación Humana, 2009), Option Corporation (Corporación Opción, 2009), Participate Corporation (Corporación Participa, 2009), National Association of Housing Debtors (Andha Chile a Luchar 2009), Ethical Commission against Torture (Comisión Ética contra la Tortura, 2015), Citizen Observatory (Observatorio Ciudadano, 2009), Citizen Peace (Paz Ciudadana, 2009, 2015), Safe Citizen Foundation (Fundación Ciudadano Seguro, 2015) 4th of August Coordinator (Coordinadora 4 de agosto, 2015), CEP (Public Research Center, 2015).

INTERNATIONAL ACTORS: 5

International Development Research Council (2014), Interpeace (2014), ICPC (International Centre for the Prevention of Crime, 2014), WOLA (Washington Office on Latin America, 2015).

Total: 194

NOTES

INTRODUCTION: MEDIA AND THE RISE OF PUNITIVE POPULISM

1. *La Nación*, "La verdadera voz de la mayoría silenciosa," April 2, 2004, accessed May 12, 2016, http://www.lanacion.com.ar/588740-la-verdadera-voz-de-la-mayoria-silenciosa.

2. The "Blumberg Laws" (laws 25.886 and later 25.882 and 25.891) modified the penal code in various ways including: increasing the maximum prison sentence from twenty-five to fifty years; increasing the punishment for crimes committed with a firearm; and reducing the possibility of parole.

3. Cathy Lisa Schneider (2014) provides a thorough examination of the blurred line between anti-"immigrant" and anticrime rhetoric in France, with both disproportionately affecting those considered Arab or black. See also James P. Walsh (2015) for examples from Australia.

4. The social movement literature is often critical of journalists' practices that can lead to unflattering portrayals of social movements' goals and ideas (Oxhorn 2011, 20; Tarrow 1994). Yet the literature assumes that media systems function in a uniform manner across time and space.

5. Carlos E. Cué, "Argentina endurecerá la ley para proteger la mano dura de los policías," *El País*, February 7, 2018. accessed July 18, 2018, https://elpais.com/internacional/2018/02/06/argentina/1517949204_193684.html.

6. One exception is Lisa Miller (2016). However, she argues that increased violent crime (defined as homicide) increases the saliency of crime as a political issue for the public, but does not necessarily lead to a rise in punitive populism.

7. Igarapé Institute, "Homicide Monitor," accessed September 22, 2018. https://igarape.org.br/en/homicide-monitor/.

8. Loïc Wacquant explains that the classic text used by the Manhattan Institute to support its theory of crime control, "Broken Windows" (*Atlantic Monthly*, March 1982), was peer reviewed but not empirically verified; its statistical conclusions have been rejected due to errors and missing data, and no studies have confirmed the theory (others have disproved it) (2009, 264–265). Yet, despite the lack of academic rigor, in many countries these policy prescriptions are so accepted in public discourse that they appear to be the commonsense response to crime.

9. Mary Anastasia O'Grady, "Peronist Argentina's Other Hallmark: Rampant Crime," *Wall Street Journal,* June 18, 2004.

10. Robert Reiner (2012) refers to this as a shift away from "social democratic criminology," which he describes as an emphasis on the structural socioeconomic and cultural causes of crime; criminal rehabilitation; limited use of the judiciary; and a downplaying of the significance of crime relative to other issues.

11. Similarly, in their study of a child sex scandal in Australia, Claire Konkes and Libby Lester conclude that when assessing journalistic coverage of crime and social problems it is essential that "both journalistic practices *and* the communications strategies of sources be taken into account" (2016, 32).

12. Mass media democratization can be measured in terms of more or less, rather than presence or absence. How many sources and how much watchdog journalism is needed to reduce punitive populism likely depends on the scope and quantity of sources and investigations pursued.

CHAPTER 1: INTERPRETING STATISTICS ON CRIME, INSECURITY, AND POLICE VIOLENCE

1. IGARAPÉ Institute, "Homicide Monitor," accessed May 20, 2016, http://homicide.igarape.org.br/.

2. World Values Survey, accessed September 22, 2018, www.worldvaluessurvey.org.

3. *El Tribuno*, "Ricardo Barrera: el femicida perdonado por la sociedad," November 12, 2012, accessed April 12, 2016, http://www.eltribuno.info/ricardo-barrera-el-femicida-perdonado-la-sociedad-n222118.

4. For example, Gisele Sousa Dias, "'Contá la violencia': 12 mujeres por minuto describen las agresiones que sufrieron," *Clarín*, June 3, 2016, accessed June 15, 2016, http://www.clarin.com/sociedad/Conta-violencia-describen-agresiones-sufrieron_0_1588641295.html.

5. María Helena Ripetta (police journalist, *Diario Crónica*, Buenos Aires), interview by author, July 29, 2015, Buenos Aires.

6. Ripetta, interview July 29, 2015. Sergio Dima (police journalist, *Clarín*), interview by author, July 30, 2015, Buenos Aires.

7. *El Mercurio* On-Line (*EMOL*), "Las protestas ciudadanas con las que el sector oriente de Santiago pide más seguridad," June 30, 2015, accessed June 15, 2016, http://www.emol.com/noticias/Nacional/2015/06/30/723754/Vecinos-de-la-zona-oriente-de-Santiago-se-organizan-y-llaman-a-cacerolazo-contra-la-delincuencia.html.

8. One common reason given by many journalists for greater coverage of crime in these neighborhoods was that their primary audiences live in these communities and thus these stories respond to their audience's interest.

9. World Bank, GINI index, accessed June 14, 2016, http://data.worldbank.org/indicator/SI.POV.GINI.

10. Anonymous, International Development Research Centre, interview by author, May 21, 2014, Chicago; Isabel Aguilar Umaña (coordinator, Central American Youth Programme, Interpeace), interview by author, May 23, 2014, Chicago; Anonymous (International Centre for the Prevention of Crime), interview by author, July 21, 2014, Montreal; Adriana Beltrán (senior associate for Citizen Security, Washington Office on Latin America), interview by author, June 12, 2015, Washington, DC/Victoria, BC (via Skype).

11. James Hohmann, "Trump, in Tennessee, Downplays Police Brutality, Promises to Get Rid of Gangs," *Washington Post*, August 29, 2015, accessed June 9, 2016, https://www.washingtonpost.com/news/post-politics/wp/2015/08/29/trump-in-tennessee-downplays-police-brutality-promises-to-get-rid-of-gangs/.

12. Carlito Pablo, "Vancouver Cop Watch Patrols Downtown Eastside." *Georgia Straight*, March 14, 2012, accessed June 9, 2016, http://www.straight.com/news/vancouver-cop-watch-patrols-downtown-eastside.

13. CORREPI is a social movement organization in Argentina well-known for its work on police violence in democracy.

14. Killed by Police, accessed June 9, 2016, www.killedbypolice.net. If we adjust the numbers for population we find that the rate of police killings in Argentina is 0.35/100,000/year and in the United States it is 0.32/100,000/year. In contrast, according to the Australian government, 105 people were fatally shot by police from 1989 to 2011, giving it a rate of 0.02/100,000/year (Australian Institute of Criminology 2013). However, all these statistics have significant limitations. For example, while CORREPI's database includes cases from 1983 onward, its numbers are more accurate since the 1990s, when it began to systematically collect and document cases.

15. The RNTS derives its numbers from face-to-face interviews conducted by members of the Provincial Commission for Memory, mostly with prisoners but also with those who approach them or the commission's Committee against Torture or those with whom the committee works. Interviewees are asked if they have experienced torture or mistreatment in the past sixty days.

16. CELS, "Estatísticas," blog, accessed June 14, 2016, http://www.cels.org.ar/blogs/estadisticas/.

17. *La Nación*, "Daniel Scioli decretó la emergencia en seguridad en la provincial de Buenos Aires," April 5, 2014, accessed June 15, 2016, http://www.lanacion.com.ar/1678413-daniel-scioli-decreto-la-emergencia-en-seguridad-en-la-provincia-de-buenos-aires; *La Nación*, "Oficializan la declaración de emergencia en seguridad," January 22, 2016, accessed June 15, 2016, http://www.lanacion.com.ar/1864382-oficializan-la-declaracion-de-emergencia-en-seguridad.

18. *El Ciudadano*, "Chile: Estudiantes marcharán 'tuertos' contra la violencia de Carabineros y los balines de pintura," April 18, 2013, accessed April 22, 2016, http://www.pressenza.com/es/2013/04/chile-estudiantes-marcharan-tuertos-contra-la-violencia-de-carabineros-y-los-balines-de-pintura/.

19. Juana Aguilera (president and founding member of the Comisión Ética contra la Tortura), interview by author, June 30, 2015, Santiago.

20. *Diario Octubre*, "Polémica en Chile por homenaje a Chile," November 23, 2015, accessed April 22, 2016, https://diario-octubre.com/?p=26165.

21. *La Tercera*, "Lucía Hiriart sobre asistentes a homenaje a Pinochet: 'Me hace pensar que aún quedan chilenos que son fieles y leales,'" November 25, 2015, accessed April 22, 2016, http://www.latercera.com/noticia/politica/2015/11/674-657543-9-lucia-hiriart-sobre-asistentes-a-homenaje-a-pinochet-me-hace-pensar-que-aun.shtml.

22. In 1985, Carabinero officers were found to have decapitated three communists (one human rights lawyer and two teachers) and left the bodies on the side of the road. This incident sullied the reputation of the Carabineros so badly that even the military government sought to distance itself from them. The Carabineros responded with a substantial overhaul of their communications department and, using this strategy, entered electoral democracy in 1990 as the institution in which Chileans have the most confidence (Bonner 2013, 684–687).

23. *ADN*, "Senadores RN pidieron que INDH retire texto donde critica actuar de Carabineros en marchas," April 6, 2015, accessed April 22, 2016, http://www.adnradio.cl/noticias/politica/senadores-rn-pidieron-que-indh-retire-texto-donde-critica-actuar-de-carabineros-en-marchas/20150406/nota/2705654.aspx; on response of Carabineros, see *EMOL*, "General director de Carabineros critica a INDH: Presenta a policías como 'victimarios,'" April 5, 2015, accessed April 22, 2016, http://www.emol.com/noticias/nacional/2015/04/05/711287/general-director-de-carabineros-critica-accionar-de-instituto-nacional-de-ddhh.html.

24. *El Mostrador*, "General Director de Carabineros apunta al INDH y dice que 'denuncias infundadas de las organizaciones' limitan su actuar," May 23, 2016, accessed June 15, 2016, http://www.elmostrador.cl/noticias/pais/2016/05/23/general-director-de-carabineros-apunta-al-indh-y-dice-que-denuncias-infundadas-de-las-organizaciones-limitan-su-actuar/.

25. While a 2017 corruption scandal in the Carabineros decreased public confidence in the police, both forces remained tied in second place, after the armed forces, as the institution in which citizens had the most confidence (CEP 2017).

CHAPTER 2: THE MASS MEDIA'S ROLE IN EMOTIONS AND PUBLIC OPINION

1. *El Mostrador*, "Encuesta de INDH," October 19, 2015, accessed October 19, 2015, http://www.elmostrador.cl/noticias/pais/2015/10/17/encuesta-del-indh-un-504-cree-que-proteger-los-dd-hh-dificulta-el-combate-contra-la-delincuencia/. See also National Institute of Human Rights (INDH), *Informe Final de Resultados: Encuesta Nacional de Derechos Humanos*, 2015, 41, accessed October 19, 2015, http://bibliotecadigital.indh.cl/bitstream/handle/123456789/864/Informe.pdf?sequence=8.

2. Thrift (2004) does recognize that it is possible to use television or video images in alternative ways but he does not discuss what types of media systems would encourage or discourage such alternative techniques.

CHAPTER 3: COMPARING MEDIA SYSTEMS

1. When sound films emerged, 90 percent of those shown in Buenos Aires were from Hollywood (Caimari 2017, 55).

2. The Argentine truth commission report *Nunca* Más (Never Again) documents eighty-four journalists as having disappeared, but not all disappearances were reported to the commission (CONADEP 1984, 374). Silvio Waisbord cites the number of disappeared journalists to be as high as ninety-three (2000, 23). Most journalists disappeared in 1976, the first year of the dictatorship (CONADEP 1984, 369).

3. State advertising increased 60 percent under the military regime (Fox 1988a, 26).

4. Martín Sivak (2013) explains that while *Clarín* was relatively quiet on the human rights abuses of the military regime, it strongly disagreed with the neoliberal economic policies led by the minister of economy, José Alfredo Martínez de Hoz (1976–1981). Instead, *Clarín* promoted military leaders who were more supportive of state-led development.

5. Juliet Pinto (2008) argues, drawing on a content analysis of the three major national Argentine newspapers, that neoliberal economic and media policies played an important role in changing the political and economic environment within which journalists work in a way that contributed to the ultimate decline of watchdog journalism by the early to mid-2000s.

6. In response to the economic crisis, President Néstor Kirchner (2003–2007) passed the Law for the Protection of Cultural Heritage and Property (25.750). The law stipulated that media ownership must be national. Foreign shareholder equity as well as foreign voting rights could not exceed 30 percent. However, the law was not retroactively applied to existing companies (Blanco and Germano 2005, 201–203).

7. In Argentina, 80 percent of households access TV through cable (Becerra 2015, 106).

8. Eighty percent of TV programming is now produced in Buenos Aires, and the city is home to all three national newspapers.

9. Ricardo Canaletti (police journalist, TN and Canal 13, formerly *Clarín*), interview by author, August 3, 2015, Buenos Aires. It is also interesting to note Lila Caimari's finding that the expanded use of photographs in the 1920s and 1930s contributed to the increased sensationalization of crime in that late liberal media environment (2017, 45–46)

10. Werner Pertot, "Para que los medios queden en pocas manos," *Página/12*, January 5, 2016, accessed June 21, 2016, http://www.pagina12.com.ar/diario/elpais/1-289603-2016-01-05.html.

11. See, for example, *Clarín*, "Qué significa la Emergencia de Seguridad Pública que decretó el Gobierno?" January 19, 2016, accessed September 23, 2018, https://www.clarin.com/politica/emergencia-seguridad-publica-decreto-gobierno_0_41gBpdoOg.html.

12. Adrónico Luksic is one of Chile's wealthiest businessmen. For reflections on his desire to expand his holdings in the mass media in order to "defend business ideas," see *El Mostrador*, "A Adrónico Luksic se le abrió el apetito: dice que quiere compar más medios para defender ideas del empresariado," April 29, 2017, accessed May 1, 2017, http://www.elmostrador.cl/noticias/pais/2017/04/29/a-andronico-luksic-se-le-abrio-el-apetito-dice-que-quiere-comprar-mas-medios-para-defender-ideas-del-empresariado/.

13. "The Chicago Boys" is a term used to refer to Chilean economists trained in neoliberal economics by Milton Friedman at the University of Chicago.

14. For this and other roles the newspaper played during the dictatorship, the Chilean Journalists Association expelled Agustín Edwards Eastman from its membership on April 21, 2015. See Colegio de Periodistas, "COMUNICADO OFICIAL: Histórico: Colegio de Periodistas explusa a Agustín Edwards por graves faltas de éticas," April 21, 2015, accessed June 22, 2016, http://www.colegiodeperiodistas.cl/2015/04/comunicado-oficial-historico-colegio-de.html.

15. There were forty-six daily newspapers in Chile under Allende (Léon-Dermota 2003, 6). In 1972, ten of these were national newspapers (Salinas 1986, 232). *La Tercera* was tied to the Radical Party until 1965 when it became politically and denominationally independent.

16. *La Época* was established in 1986 by progressive Christian Democrats with financial support from Western Europe (Polumbaum 2002, 69).

17. Of the ten daily newspapers with a national circulation in Chile in 1972, there were only five by 1984, three of which were owned by the El Mercurio group (Salinas 1986, 232).

18. See Law 19.132 passed March 30, 1992. Also, *La Tercera*, "El Modelo de Financiamiento de Televisión Nacional," January 30, 2016, accessed May 2, 2017, http://www.latercera.com/noticia/el-modelo-de-financiamiento-de-television-nacional/. Due to financial difficulties in 2016, the government provided TVN funding.

CHAPTER 4: JOURNALISTS' PREFERENCE FOR TOUGH-ON-CRIME SOURCES

1. Horacio Verbitsky (journalist at *Página/12*), interview by author, November 30, 2009, Buenos Aires; Carlos Rodríguez (journalist at *Página/12*), interview by author, December 1, 2009, Buenos Aires; Ricardo Canaletti (police journalist at TN, Canal 13, and former editor of policing for *Clarín*), interview by author, August 3, 2015, Buenos Aires.

2. Verbitsky, interview, November 30, 2009; C. Rodríguez, interview, December 1, 2009; Canaletti, interview, August 3, 2015.

3. C. Rodríguez, interview, December 1, 2009.

4. C. Rodríguez, interview, December 1, 2009.

5. Emilio Balcarce (editor of police section, *Diario Crónica*), interview by author, December 11, 2013, Buenos Aires; Paulo Kablan (police journalist, C5N [TV]), interview by author, December 13, 2013, Buenos Aires.

6. Verbitsky, interview, November 30, 2009.

7. See the bibliography for book details. The film, *El Bonaerense*, was directed by Pablo Trapero.

8. Carlos Rodríguez (journalist at *Página/12*), interview by author, December 11, 2013, Buenos Aires; Fernando Rodríguez (editor of Buenos Aires and Seguridad section, *La Nación*), interview by author, July 28, 2015, Buenos Aires; Canaletti, interview, August 3, 2015.

9. Gabriel Michi (vice president and founder of the Argentine Press Forum), interview by author, August 7, 2015, Buenos Aires.

10. *La Nación*, "Cristina Kirchner responsibilizó a los medios por la 'sensación de inseguridad,'" March 27, 2009, accessed August 11, 2016, http://www.lanacion.com.ar/1112667-cristina-kirchner-responsabilizo-a-los-medios-por-la-sensacion-de-inseguridad.

11. Balcarce, interview, December 11, 2013.

12. Michi, interview, August 7, 2015.

13. Rolando Barbano (editor of police section, *Clarín*), interview by author, December 17, 2013, Buenos Aires; Gabriel Di Nicola (police journalist, *La Nación*), interview by author, December 3, 2009, Buenos Aires; F. Rodríguez, interview, July 28, 2015.

14. Kablan, interview, December 13, 2013.

15. Gustavo Hazán (director of *Policías en Acción* and *Cárceles*), interview by author, November 11, 2009, Buenos Aires.

16. Virginia Messi (police journalist, *Clarín*), interview by author, November 24, 2009, Buenos Aires; Barbano, interview, December 17, 2013; F. Rodríguez, interview, July 28, 2015; Federic Fahsbender (police journalist, INFOBAE, formerly at *Noticias*), interview by author, August 5, 2015, Buenos Aires.

17. Balcarce, interview, December 11, 2013; C. Rodríguez, interview, December 1, 2009.

18. C. Rodríguez, interview, December 1, 2009.

19. This agreement among journalists contrasts with public opinion poll data shown in table 1.4 that reveals higher public confidence in the police (25 percent) than the courts (18.5 percent). This may reflect journalists' *informed* opinion (compared to polls), or a difference between the public's perception of the reliability of the police and courts as media sources and the level of confidence they have in the institutions in their other roles, or both.

20. Fahsbender, interview, August 5, 2015.

21. There have been dips in public confidence in the Carabineros, notably after their management of student protests in 2011–2012 and a 2017 corruption scandal, but even in

these cases it retained much stronger support than police in most other countries in Latin America (Bonner 2013, 669; CEP 2015, 2017).

22. Mario A. Gálvez (police journalist, justice and security section, *El Mercurio*), interview by author, July 21, 2015, Santiago.

23. Jorge Molina (journalist, *El Mostrador*), interview by author, July 3, 2009, Santiago; Anonymous (journalist, *The Clinic*), interview by author, July 3, 2009, Santiago; José Ch. Mora Quevedo (Carabinero and journalist, Carabinero's Communication Department), interview by author, June 30, 2009, Santiago.

24. Molina, interview, July 3, 2009; Anonymous (*The Clinic*), interview, July 3, 2009; Anonymous (*El Mercurio*), interview by author, July 2, 2009, Santiago; Anonymous (Chilevisión), interview by author, July 9, 2015, Santiago; Anonymous (Canal 13), interview by author, July 7, 2015, Santiago; Anonymous (*La Cuarta*), interview by author, July 14, 2009, Santiago.

25. Gustavo Villarrubia (police journalist, MEGA, formerly CIPER and *Contacto* on Canal 13), interview by author, July 24, 2015, Santiago. The report in question was on a child-sex ring that involved members of the Investigative Police (PDI). The reporter was taken to court for not having completed a degree in journalism.

26. That said, some media outlets do criticize the police for not doing enough to combat crime For example, Gálvez, interview, July 21, 2015; Anonymous (editor at *El Mercurio*), interview by author, July 17, 2015, Santiago; Felipe Cornejo (police journalist, Radio Bío-Bío), interview by author, July 22, 2015, Santiago.

27. Cristóbal Valenzuela Maulme (subdirector of Prensa, MEGA), interview by author, July 21, 2015, Santiago; Cornejo, interview, July 22, 2015.

28. An example cited widely by journalists interviewed in 2015 mentioned a TVN drone that captured video footage of police spraying a water cannon at student protester, Rodrigo Avilés, causing him to be critically injured in May of that year. The video footage disproved the position of the Carabineros that they were not involved in his injuries, and all media covered the incident.

29. Pedro Ramírez Pinto (journalist, CIPER Chile, formerly editor at *Las* Últimas *Noticias*, El Mercurio Group), interview by author, July 14, 2009, Santiago; Anonymous (former journalist for *El Mercurio*), interview by author, July 2, 2009, Santiago; Victor Salas (photojournalist for Agencia EFE), interview by author, July 2, 2009, Santiago; Anonymous (TVN), interview by author, July 9, 2015, Santiago.

30. Anonymous (former journalist for *El Mercurio*), interview, July 2, 2009.

31. Anonymous (former journalist for *El Mercurio*), interview, July 2, 2009; Salas, interview, July 2, 2009.

32. Anonymous (former journalist for *El Mercurio*), interview, July 2, 2009; Salas, interview, July 2, 2009.

33. Eduardo Urtubia (editor of police section, *La Cuarta*), interview by author, July 14, 2015, Santiago.

34. Anonymous (former journalist for *El Mercurio*), interview, July 2, 2009; Molina, interview, July 3, 2009; Salas, interview, July 2, 2009.

35. Anonymous (*The Clinic*), interview, July 3, 2009.

36. Cornejo, interview, July 22, 2015.

37. The most notable example was a 2009 *Contacto* story that exposed a PDI-run child-sex ring in Valparaíso. One of the journalists involved said that it began when an officer from the PDI approached them with the story (Villarrubia, interview by author, July 24, 2015).

38. Anonymous (*The Clinic*), interview, July 3, 2009.

39. Ramírez Pinto, interview, July 14, 2009.

40. Mauricio Becerral (*El Ciudadano*, formerly at *El Mercurio*), interview by author, June 26, 2009, Santiago; Two Anonymous (journalists at Radio Universidad de Chile), interview by author, July 23, 2015, Santiago; Ramírez Pinto, interview, July 14, 2009; Anonymous (*The Clinic*), interview, July 3, 2009.

41. Becerral, interview, June 26, 2009; Two Anonymous (journalists at Radio Universidad de Chile), interview, July 23, 2015.

42. Javiera Olivares Mardones (national president, Chilean Journalists Association), interview by author, July 13, 2015, Santiago; Colegio de Periodistas, "Libertad de expresión y de información y sistema público de medios propugnan como base de nueva Carta Fundamental," June 13, 2016, accessed August 12, 2016, http://www.colegiodeperiodistas.cl/2016/06/libertad-de-expresion-y-de-informacion.html.

43. Instituto de Investigaciones de Ciencias Sociales, Universidad Diego Portales, "Encuesta Nacional: udp 2014," accessed February 2, 2016, http://encuesta.udp.cl/descargas/publicaciones/2014/Resultados%20Encuesta%20UDP%202014.pdf.

44. Anonymous (*The Clinic*), interview, July 3, 2009.

45. Jorge Escalante (*La Nación*), interview by author, June 15, 2009, Santiago.

46. Gabriel Di Nicola (*La Nación*), interview by author, December 3, 2009, Buenos Aires; María (Helena) Ripetta (*Crítica*), interview by author, December 1, 2009, Buenos Aires; Canaletti, interview, August 3, 2015; Sergio Dima (police journalist, *Clarín*), interview by author, July 30, 2015, Buenos Aires; Liliana Caruso (police journalist, América TV, formerly *Clarín* and Radio Mitre), interview by author, August 5, 2015, Buenos Aires.

47. For example, Messi, interview, November 24, 2009; Fahsbender, interview, August 5, 2015; Kablan, interview, December 13, 2013.

48. Dima, interview, July 30, 2015.

49. Sarah Wright (2016) identifies the rise of the victim-hero in crime news in New Zealand to have occurred in the late 1990s, which coincides with the implementation of neoliberal economic policies in that country. She provided a media narrative analysis of two cases that show how the victim-hero is constructed to provide drama and encourage a tough-on-crime response.

50. Ramírez Pinto, interview, July 14, 2009.

51. Ramírez Pinto, interview, July 14, 2009.

52. Ramírez Pinto, interview, July 14, 2009.

53. Anonymous (former journalist for *El Mercurio*), interview, July 2, 2009. See also Bonner (2014a) for supporting evidence.

54. Victor Durán (editor, *La Cuarta*), interview by author, July 14, 2015, Santiago; Cornejo, interview, July 22, 2015.

55. Juan Manuel Barrera (editor of police section, TVN), interview by author, July 9, 2015, Santiago; Juana Aguilera (president and founding member of the Comité Ética contra la Tortura), interview by author, June 30, 2015, Santiago.

56. In order of importance: police, public prosecutors, witnesses/victims/victims families. Radio tends to omit public prosecutors unless they happen to be at the scene of the crime.

57. Anonymous (former journalist for *El Mercurio*), interview, July 2, 2009; Anonymous (TV news editor, Chilevisión), interview by author, July 9, 2015, Santiago.

58. Angela Poblete (journalist with *Policías en Acción* and *Cárceles*, Chilevisión, TV), interview by author, June 11, 2009, Santiago.

59. Anonymous (news editor, Chilevisión), interview, July 9, 3015; Cornejo, interview, July 22, 2015.

60. Gálvez, interview, July 21, 2015.

61. Anonymous (*The Clinic*), interview, July 3, 2009.

62. Anonymous (*The Clinic*), interview, July 3, 2009.

63. Becerral, interview, June 26, 2009. Protest participants are also used as primary sources by Radio Universidad de Chile (Two Anonymous [Radio Universidad de Chile], interview, July 23, 2015).

CHAPTER 5: THE RISE OF PUNITIVE VOICES FROM WITHIN THE STATE

1. As seen in chapter 4, not all state institutions and actors receive the same degree of reinforced legitimacy from the mass media.

2. As James Curran (2005, 121) notes, media attention to scandal in a market-based media system is not the same as watchdog journalism aimed to hold state actors to account. Given the emphasis on speed and few sources, news stories involving scandal are more often given to journalists by state actors as part of an intrastate conflict. Scandals thus depend on the emergence of such conflict and are bounded by the parameters set by state actors.

3. For example, social workers and mental health professionals might have a very different story to tell about crime and insecurity, but in most countries they do not have the same access to the mass media.

4. Studies of Australian and U.S. media have found similar or higher journalistic use of PR material (MacNamara 2014, 123–127).

5. Whether police are autonomous in Argentina and what this means in practice is beyond the scope of this book. What is important here is that state actors believe police autonomy to be an issue and that they view control of communications as an important avenue to reduce it. This is true even for governments, such as Mauricio Macri's, that have implemented laws aimed at increasing police discretion and thus their autonomy.

6. Horacio J. Garcia (subsecretary in charge of the Metropolitan Police), interview by author, August 13, 2015, Buenos Aires.

7. Anonymous (Communications Department, Ministry of Security, province of Buenos Aires), interview by author, August 11, 2015, Buenos Aires.

8. Diego Lluma (director of communications, Ministry of Security, National Government), interview by author, December 18, 2013, Buenos Aires.

9. Diego Gorgal (security expert, former vice-minister of security, province of Buenos Aires, under Solá, and former secretary of security, City of Buenos Aires, under Telerman), interview by author, December 19, 2013, Buenos Aires–Washington, DC, via Skype; Lluma, interview, December 18, 2013.

10. Lluma, interview, December 18, 2013.

11. In 1985 Carabinero officers killed three human rights activists and left their bodies, with their throats cut, on the side of the road. The incident, known as the Slit Throat Case (*Caso de Degollados*), led even the military government to distance itself from the police force (Policzer 2009, 120).

12. José Ch. Mora Quevedo (Carabinero [R] and journalist, Communications Department, Carabineros de Chile), interview by author, June 19, 2009, Santiago.

13. Coronel Mario Alberto Rozas Córdova (head of the Department of Social Communications, Carabineros de Chile), interview by author, July 8, 2015, Santiago; Subprefecto Rodrigo Fuentes Azócar (national head of public affairs, PDI), interview by author, July 7, 2015, Santiago. There were only four people in PDI communications in 2005.

14. Mora Quevedo, interview, June 19, 2009.

15. Coronel Rodney L. Weber Orellana (director of the Department of Human Rights, Carabineros), interview by author, July 8, 3015, Santiago.

16. Anonymous (Ministry of the Interior and Public Security), interview by author, July 2, 2015, Santiago.

17. Anonymous (formerly of the National Prosecutors office), interview by author, July 15, 2015, Santiago.

18. Anonymous (subsecretary of the interior), interview by author, July 15, 2015, Santiago. For a similar example, in the 2011 case of Manuel Gutiérrez, see Bonner (2018).

19. Anonymous (subsecretary of the interior), interview, July 15, 2015.

20. Ricardo González Toro (coordinator of the Public Opinion Program, Centro de Estudios Públicos), interview by author, July 22, 2015, Santiago.

21. Pinochet reduced the size of the state through the privatization of public companies and the social security system. Later democratic governments applied new public management principles to what was left (Aninat et al. 2008, 191–192).

22. Author interviews. For a detailed discourse analysis of the politicized newspaper coverage of this incident and the role of the media in the attempted police reform, see Bonner (2016).

23. Gorgal, interview, December 19, 2013.

24. Anonymous (Communications Department, province of Buenos Aires), interview, August 11, 2015.

25. Télam, "El Gobierno extendió un año la declaración de la Emergencia de Seguridad Públic." January 20, 2017, accessed May 18, 2017, http://www.telam.com.ar/notas/201701/177257-gobierno-extiende-emergencia-seguridad-publica.html.

26. Lila Caimari (2017) argues that the acquisition and mass media visibility of new technology for police was key in improving police image in 1930s Buenos Aires.

27. Anonymous (Ministry of Security), interview by author, August 4, 2015, Buenos Aires.

28. Anonymous (employee of the Chilean state working in the area of security issues), interview by author, June 23, 2015, Victoria, BC–Santiago, via Skype.

29. Anonymous (Ministry of the Interior and Public Security), interview by author, July 3, 2015, Santiago.

30. Coronel Weber Orellana, interview, July 8, 2015; emphasis added.

31. Subprefecto Fuentes Azócar, interview, July 7, 2015; Joe González (president of the Association of Subofficials and Gendarmería), interview by author, June 30, 2015, Santiago; Ariella Olivares (head of communications, Gendarmería), interview by author, July 15, 2015, Santiago.

32. González, interview, June 30, 2015; Olivares, interview, July 15, 2015.

33. Anonymous (communications officer, Ministry of the Interior and Public Security), interview by author, July 3, 2015, Santiago.

34. Anonymous (communications officer, Ministry of the Interior and Public Security), interview, July 3, 2015.

35. Anonymous (communications officer, Ministry of the Interior and Public Security), interview, July 3, 2015.

36. Helena Olea (Corporación Humana), interview by author, June 19, 2009, Santiago.

37. Enrique Niño, "No muy buenos días: 'Fuerzas Especiales,'" *Las* Últimas *Noticias*, October 2, 2014.

38. James P. Walsh (2015) analyzes Australia's reality-TV show *Border Security: Australia's Frontline*, which provides an example of punitive populism's blurred line between the policing of migrants and criminals.

39. Gustavo Hazán (director of reality-television shows *Policías en Acción* and *Cárceles* [Prisons]), interview by author, November 11, 2009, Buenos Aires.

40. Daniel Parcero (Argentine Federation of Press Workers and former journalist for *Policías en Acción*), interview by author, November 19, 2009, Buenos Aires.

41. León Arslanian (former minister of security for the province of Buenos Aires), interview by author, November 11, 2009, Buenos Aires.

42. Hazán, interview, November 11, 2009.

43. (Rubén) Fabián Perroni (district chief of Lomas de Zamora, Buenos Aires Provincial Police), interview by author, November 25, 2009, Lomas de Zamora, province of Buenos Aires.

44. Hazán, interview, November 11, 2009.

45. Parcero, interview , November 19, 2009.

46. Gerardo Echeverri (lawyer, Argentine League for the Rights of Men and the Antirepressive Coordinator for People's Rights), interview by author, November 24, 2009, Buenos Aires.

47. Interestingly, police reality TV arrived in Chile in almost the same year as twenty-four-hour TV news (2007 and 2008, respectively).

48. Manuel Cotapos (editor of the program *133*, Megavisión TV), interview by author, June 12, 2009, Santiago.

49. Mora Quevedo, interview, June 19, 2009; Cotapos, interview, June 12, 2009.

50. Coronel Rozas Córdova, interview, July 8, 2015.

51. Cotapos, interview, June 12, 2009.

52. Coronel Rozas Córdova, interview, July 8, 2015.

53. Owned by conservative businessman Sebastián Piñera until he became president of Chile in 2010. It was then sold to the U.S.-based Turner Broadcasting System.

54. Anonymous (press editor, Chilevisión), interview by author, July 9, 2015, Santiago.

55. Coronel Rozas Córdova, interview, July 8, 2015.

56. Patricio Tudela (Citizen Security, Chilean Investigative Police, PDI), telephone interview by author, July 21, 2009, Victoria, BC–Santiago; Subprefecto Fuentes Azócar, interview, July 7, 2015.

57. Tudela, telephone interview, July 21, 2009. Subprefecto Fuentes Azócar, interview, July 7, 2015; Angela Poblete (journalist, *Policías en Acción* and *Cárceles*, Chilevisión TV), interview by author, June 11, 2009, Santiago.

CHAPTER 6: THE RISE OF PUNITIVE VOICES FROM CIVIL SOCIETY

1. An organization was considered well-known or prominent if it was cited often in the mass media, mentioned by journalists I interviewed, or recommended to me by interviewed civil society, state actors, or local academics.

2. I borrow the term "discursive opportunity" from Koopmans (2004). It is similar to Kingdon's (2003) concept of "policy windows" but focuses on inclusion in media debates rather than policymaking. Of course, the former may lead to the latter.

3. Anonymous (MEDH), interview by author, November 6, 2009, Buenos Aires.

4. Ernesto Moreau (APDH), interview by author, December 14, 2009, Buenos Aires.

5. I discuss this issue in more detail in Bonner (2014b).

6. Ricardo Canaletti (police journalist, TN, and Canal 13, formerly editor of police section of *Clarín*), interview by author, August 3, 2015, Buenos Aires.

7. Sofía Tiscornia (CELS), interview by author, December 10, 2009, Buenos Aires.

8. Marcela Perelman (director of research, CELS), interview by author, August 6, 2015, Buenos Aires.

9. Perelman, interview, August 6, 2015.

10. Nine members of CORREPI, interview by author, December 18, 2013, Buenos Aires; Alejandrina Barry (CeProDH), interview by author, August 14, 2015, Buenos Aires.

11. Nine members of CORREPI, interview, December 18, 2013; Two members of Frente Darío Santillán, interview by author, December 18, 2013, Buenos Aires.

12. A 1991 poll found that 57.9 percent of Chileans viewed the Pinochet government as both good and bad, 20 percent described it as good or very good (Stern 2010, 90). This support has declined in recent years.

13. Anonymous (CODEPU), interview by author, June 10, 2009, Santiago.

14. Anonymous (CODEPU), interview, June 10, 2009; Luis Cortés (FASIC), interview by author, June 9, 2009, Santiago; Juana Aguilera (president and founding member, CECT), interview by author, June 30, 2015, Santiago.

15. Cortés, interview, June 9, 2009.

16. The Valech Report on torture (published in 2004 and updated in 2005 and 2010) included only those cases of torture that occurred in prisons (not, as often took place, in homes, public spaces, vehicles, student centers, or factories), where the victims were Chileans tortured in Chile (not foreigners tortured in Chile or Chileans tortured outside Chile under the Condor Plan), and did not include third parties affected (such as babies born to mothers who were tortured while pregnant or family members whose loved ones were tortured to death). Reparations included a small monthly pension and access to medical treatment in public hospitals (similar to that offered to the poor). They did not include assistance with education or transition to the workforce, as victims had hoped. Finally, those charged for torture in courts were far fewer than the numbers CECT had identified as involved (Aguilera, interview, June 30, 2015).

17. Aguilera, interview, June 30, 2015.

18. Claudio Soto Corondado (communications officer, Paz Ciudadana), interview by author, July 3, 2015, Santiago.

19. This paragraph is based on interviews with Anonymous (lawyer, Law Faculty, Diego Portales University), interview by author, June 16, 2009, Santiago; Anonymous (Center for Justice Studies of the Americas), interview by author, June 30, 2009, Santiago; and Soto Corondado (Paz Cuidadana), interview, July 3, 2015. All three were involved in various ways with the penal procedures reform.

20. David Rozowski G. (executive director) and Alexandre Hernández A. (communications director, Fundación Ciudadano Seguro), interview by author, July 3, 2015, Santiago.

21. Rozowski and Hernández, interview, July 3, 2015.

22. This was repeated in many interviews. In 2015, the CEP provided me a PowerPoint with the results of their first poll done on Chileans' confidence in the student movement during November–December 2011. In this poll, people's confidence was placed at 35 percent, which was higher than the courts (13 percent) or public prosecutors (17 percent).

23. The organizations involved included: Citizen Observatory (Observatorio Ciudadano), Amnesty International–Chile, CODEPU, FASIC, Corporación Opción, the CECT, the Diego Portales University Human Rights Center, American Association of Jurists, the Center for Mental Health and Human Rights, the Chilean NGO Network on Children and Youth, and the Professional College of Chile.

24. Paulina Acevedo (Citizen Observatory), interview by author, June 15, 2009, Santiago

25. Sergio Laurenti (Amnesty International–Chile), interview by author, June 16, 2009, Santiago; Anonymous (CODEPU), interview by author, June 10, 2009, Santiago; Cortés, interview, June 9, 2009; Acevedo, interview, June 15, 2009; Osvaldo Vásquez Rossoni (Corporación Opción), interview by author, July 1, 2009, Santiago; Aguilera, interview, June 30, 2015.

26. Ricardo González Toro (Public Opinion Program coordinator, CEP), interview by author, July 22, 2015. Santiago.

27. See, for example, this article in El Mercurio Group's afternoon paper *La Segunda*: Viviana Candia, "Defensoría Popular, la ONG que representa a los encapuchados: 'Protestar no es un delito,'" *La Segunda*, October 21, 2011, accessed September 26, 2018, http://www.lasegunda.com/Noticias/Nacional/2011/10/691062/defensoria-popular-la-ong-que-representa-a-los-encapuchados-protestar-no-es-un-delito.

28. Laurenti, interview, June 16, 2009.

29. Aguilera, interview, June 30, 2015.

30. Valentina Saavedra (president, FECH), interview by author, July 15, 2015, Santiago; Roberto Morales (president, Amnesty International–Chile), interview by author, July 1, 2015, Santiago; and Vásquez Rossoni, interview, July 1, 2009.

31. Saavedra, interview, July 15, 2015.

32. César Zagal (Andha Chile a Luchar), interview by author, June 25, 2009, Santiago.

33. Danae Prado (Teachers' College), interview by author, July 15, 2009, Santiago.

34. Verónica Torres (director of communications, CELS), interview by author, December 14, 2009, Buenos Aires; Diego de Charras (director of communications, CELS), interview by author, December 16, 2013, Buenos Aires.

35. De Charras, interview, December 16, 2013. The president of CELS, Horacio Verbitsky, is a prominent journalist who worked for *Página/12* from 1987 to 2017.

36. María del Carmen Verdú (president, CORREPI), interview by author, November 6, 2009, Buenos Aires. While I am not a journalist, in 2011, I emailed both CELS and CORREPI for a statistic on police violence that was not available on their websites or annual reports. I received an email reply from the president of CORREPI within a couple of hours but I never heard back from CELS.

37. María del Carmen Verdú (president, CORREPI), interview by author, November 6, 2009, and December 18, 2013, Buenos Aires; and Federico (spokesperson) and Luca (member) (Frente Darío Santillán), interview by author, December 18, 2013, Buenos Aires.

38. Federico and Luca (Frente Darío Santillán), interview, December 18, 2013. Their organization was named repeatedly in the extensive news reports on the protest in *Clarín* and *Página/12*, which I analyzed for a separate study (Bonner 2016).

39. Sergio Burnstein (Relatives and Friends of Victims of the AMIA Attack), interview by author, November 25, 2009, Buenos Aires.

40. Verdú, interview, November 6, 2009, and December 18, 2013; Federico and Luca, interview, December 18, 2013; Carina López (communications director, Frente Darío Santillán), interview by author, November 18, 2009, Buenos Aires; and Alejandrina Barry (CeProDH), interview by author, August 14, 2015, Buenos Aires.

41. Luis Guerro Paredes (Coordinadora 4 de agosto), interview by author, July 8, 2015, Santiago.

42. See the website of Paz Ciudadana, accessed March 23, 2016, http://www.pazciudadana.cl/quienes-somos/financiamiento/. In 2015 Safe Citizen received almost all its funding from contract work with private companies (Rozowski, interview, July 3, 2015).

43. Soto Corondado, interview, July 3, 2015.

44. González Toro, interview, July 22, 2015.

45. For more on changes in the use of public opinion polls in Chile, see chapters 3 and 5 as well as Cordero (2009a).

46. Soto Corondado, interview, July 3, 2015.

47. Isabel Retamal (Paz Ciudadana), interview by author, June 12, 2009, Santiago.

48. Rozowski, interview, July 3, 2015.

49. Two Anonymous members (CED), interview, June 18, 2009.

50. Consejo Nacional de Televisión, "Chilenos consumen más TV," August 25, 2011, accessed September 27, 2016, http://www.cntv.cl/chilenos-consumen-mas-tv/prontus_cntv/2011-08-25/132533.html.

51. Laurenti, interview, June 16, 2009.

52. This was particularly true of the Comisión Ética Contra la Tortura and Coordinadora 4 de agosto, neither of which had "corporación" (official NGO) status when interviewed in 2015.

53. Morales, interview, July 1, 2015.

54. Laurenti, interview, June 16, 2009.

55. Soto Corondado, interview, July 3, 2015.

CONCLUSION

1. Blumberg's supporters (financial and political) included, but were not limited to, Carlos Ruckauf (quoted in the introduction to this book), the Chilean neoliberal think tank Fundación Libertad, and the U.S.-based Manhattan Institute (Guerrero 2013, 85–86).

2. Juan Carlos Blumberg (Axel Blumberg Foundation), interview by author, November 17, 2009, Buenos Aires.

3. Anonymous (MEDH), interview by author, November 6, 2009, Buenos Aires; *La Nación*, "Detienen a dos policías por un secuestro," March 18, 2009, accessed June 5, 2017, http://www.lanacion.com.ar/582857-detienen-a-dos-policias-por-un-secuestro; Barbano 2015, 349–354.

4. *Página/12*, "Caso Axel, el encubrimiento," September 22, 2014, accessed June 5, 2017, https://www.pagina12.com.ar/diario/sociedad/3-41347-2004-09-22.html.

REFERENCES

Abrahamsen, Rita, and Michael C. Williams. 2011. *Security beyond the State: Private Security in International Politics.* New York: Cambridge University Press.

Achen, Christopher, and Larry Bartels. 2016. *Democracy for Realists: Why Elections Do Not Produce Responsive Government.* Princeton, NJ: Princeton University Press.

Agamben, Giorgio. 2005. *State of Exception.* Chicago: University of Chicago Press.

Aguiar, César. 2009. "Apuntes para una historia de los estudios de opinión pública en América Latina." In Cordero, *La Sociedad de la opinión*, 29–44.

Alvarez, Sonia E. 1998. "Latin American Feminisms 'Go Global': Trends of the 1990s and Challenges for the New Millennium." In Alvarez, Dagnino, and Escobar, *Cultures of Politics*, 293–324.

Alvarez, Sonia, E. Dagnino, and Arturo Escobar. 1998a. *Cultures of Politics/Politics of Cultures: Re-Visioning Latin American Social Movements.* Boulder, CO: Westview.

Alvarez, Sonia, E. Dagnino, and Arturo Escobar. 1998b. "Introduction: The Cultural and Political in Latin American Social Movements." In Alvarez, Dagnino, and Escobar, *Cultures of Politics*, 1–29.

Amnesty International. 2007. *Amnesty International Report 2007: The State of the World's Human Rights.* London: Amnesty International. www.amnesty.org.

Amnesty International. 2009. *Amnesty International Report 2009: The State of the World's Human Rights.* London: Amnesty International. www.amnesty.org.

Amnesty International. 2012. *Amnesty International Report 2012: The State of the World's Human Rights.* London: Amnesty International. www.amnesty.org.

Andersen, Martin Edwin. 2002. *La Policía: Pasado, presente y propuestas para el futuro.* Buenos Aires: Editorial Sudamericana.

Aninat, Cristóbal, John Londregan, Patricio Navia, and Joaquín Vial. 2008. "Political Institutions, Policymaking Processes, and Policy Outcomes in Chile." In *Policymaking in Latin America: How Politics Shapes Policies*, edited by Ernesto Stein and Mariano Tommasi,155–198. Washington, DC: Inter-American Development Bank.

Aparecida Ferrari, María. 2003. "Public Relations in Chile: Searching for Identity amid Imported Models." In *The Global Public Relations Handbook: Theory, Research, and Practice*, edited by Krishnamurthy Sriramesh and Dejan Verčič, 378–395. Mahwah, NJ: Lawrence Erlbaum.

Aparecida Ferrari, María, and Fabio França. 2011. *Relaciones públicas: Naturaleza, function y gestión en las organizaciones contemporáneas.* Buenos Aires: La Crujía.

Arias, Enrique Desmond, and Daniel M. Goldstein, eds. 2010a. *Violent Democracies in Latin America.* Durham, NC: Duke University Press.

Arias, Enrique Desmond, and Daniel M. Goldstein. 2010b. "Violent Pluralism: Understanding the New Democracies of Latin America." In Arias and Goldstein,*Violent Democracies*, 1–34.

Arias, Enrique Desmond, and Mark Ungar. 2009. "Community Policing and Latin America's Citizen Security Crisis." *Comparative Politics* 41, no. 4: 409–429.

Australian Institute of Criminology. 2013. "Police Shootings of People with a Mental Illness." *Research in Practice* 34 (May). Canberra: Australian Government. http://www.aic.gov.au/publications/current%20series/rip/21-40/rip34.html.

Bakker, K. 2013. "Neoliberalism versus Postneoliberal Water: Geographies of Privatization and Resistance." *Annals of the Association of American Geographers* 100, no. 2: 253–260.

Bal, Mieke. 1988. *Death and Dissymmetry: The Politics of Coherence in the Book of Judges.* Chicago: University of Chicago Press.

Barbano, Rolando. 2015. *Sangre Azul: Historia Criminal de la Policía Federal Argentina.* Buenos Aires: Planeta.

Becerra, Martín. 2015. "Transgresión, propaganda, convergencia y concentración. El sistema de medios en el kirchnerismo." In *¿Década Ganada? Evaluando el legado del kirchnerismo*, edited by Carlos Gervasoni and Enriquie Peruzzotti, 89–111. Buenos Aires: Random House Mondadori.

Beetham, David. 1991. *The Legitimation of Power.* Atlantic Highlands, NJ: Humanities Press.

Benford, Robert, and David Snow. 2000. "Framing Processes and Social Movements: An Overview and Assessment." *Annual Review of Sociology* 26: 611–639.

Bennett, Lance. 1990. "Toward a Theory of Press-State Relations." *Journal of Communication* 2: 103–125.

Bennett, W. Lance. 1996. *News: The Politics of Illusion.* 3rd ed. New York: Pearson.

Bennett, W. Lance. 2005. *News: The Politics of Illusion.* 6th ed. New York: Pearson/Longman.

Bergman, Marcelo S. 2006. "Crime and Citizen Security in Latin America." *Latin American Research Review* 41, no. 2: 213–227.

Bermeo, Nancy, and Deborah J. Yashar. 2016. "Parties, Movements, and the Making of Democracy." In *Parties, Movements, and Democracy in the Developing World*, edited by Nancy Bermeo and Deborah J. Yashar, 1–27. New York: Cambridge University Press.

Blanco, Daniela, and Carlos Germano. 2005. *20 años de medios y democracia en la Argentina.* Buenos Aires: La Crujía.

Boas, Taylor C. 2005. "Television and Neopopulism in Latin America: Media Effects in Brazil and Peru." *Latin American Research Review* 40, no. 2: 27–49.

Bob, Clifford. 2005. *The Marketing of Rebellion.* New York: Cambridge University Press.

Bonner, Michelle D. 2009a. "Media as Social Accountability: The Case of Police Violence in Argentina." *International Journal of Press/Politics* 14, no. 3: 296–312.

Bonner, Michelle D. 2009b. "State Discourses, Police Violence and Democratisation in Argentina." *Bulletin of Latin American Research* 28, no. 2: 227–245.

Bonner, Michelle D. 2013. "The Politics of Police Image in Chile." *Journal of Latin American Studies* 45, no. 4: 669–694.

Bonner, Michelle D. 2014a. *Policing Protest in Argentina and Chile.* Boulder, CO: Lynne Rienner.

Bonner, Michelle D. 2014b. "Never Again: Transitional Justice and Persistent Police Violence in Argentina." *International Journal of Transitional Justice* 8, no. 2 (July): 235–255.

Bonner, Michelle D. 2016. "Rethinking Debates on Media and Police Reform in Argentina." *Policing and Society* 26, no. 8: 925–943.

Bonner, Michelle D. 2018. "Holding Police Abuse to Account: The Challenge of Institutional Legitimacy, a Chilean Case Study." In Bonner et al., *Police Abuse in Contemporary Democracies*, 113–134.

Bonner, Michelle D., Guillermina Seri, Mary Rose Kubal, and Michael Kempa, eds. 2018. *Police Abuse in Contemporary Democracies.* New York: Palgrave Macmillan.

Bottoms, A. E. 1995. "The Philosophy and Politics of Punishment and Sentencing." In *The Politics of Sentencing Reform*, edited by C. Clark and R. Morgan, 17–49. Oxford: Clarendon Press.

Bresnahan, Rosalind. 2003. "The Media and the Neoliberal Transition in Chile: Democratic Promise Unfulfilled." *Latin American Perspectives* 30, no. 6: 39–68.

Bromley, Michael. 2010. "'All the World's a Stage': 24/7 News, Newspapers, and the Ages of Media." In Cushion and Lewis, *Rise of 24-Hour News Television*, 31–49.

Brown, Wendy. 2006. "American Nightmare: Neoliberalism, Neoconservativism, and De-Democratization." *Political Theory* 34, no. 6: 690–714.

Burstein, Paul. 2003. "The Impact of Public Opinion on Public Policy: A Review and an Agenda." *Political Research Quarterly* 56, no. 1: 29–40.

Caimari, Lila. 2017. *While the City Sleeps: A History of Pistoleros, Policemen, and the Crime Beat in Buenos Aires before Perón.* Oakland: University of California Press.

Calvert, Susan, and Peter Calvert. 1989. *Argentina: Political Culture and Instability.* London: Macmillan.

Calzado, M. 2015. *Inseguros: El rol de los medios y la respuesta política frente a la violencia, de Blumberg a hoy.* Buenos Aires: Aguilar.

Campbell, Liz. 2008. "Criminal Justice and Penal Populism in Ireland." *Legal Studies* 28, no. 4: 559–573.

Campbell, Margaret V. 1962. "The Chilean Press: 1823–1842." *Journal of Inter-American Studies* 4, no. 4: 545–555.

Candina, Azun. 2006. "The Institutional Identity of the Carabineros de Chile." In *Public Security and Police Reform in the Americas*, edited by John Bailey and Lucía Dammert, 75–93. Pittsburgh: University of Pittsburgh Press.

Candina Polomer, Azun. 2005. "Carabineros de Chile: Una mirada histórica a la identidad institucional." In *Seguridad y reforma policial: experiencias y desafíos*, edited by Lucía Dammert and John Bailey, 145–167. Buenos Aires: Siglo XXI.

Cane, James. 2011. *The Fourth Enemy: Journalism and Power in the Making of Peronist Argentina, 1930–1955.* University Park: Pennsylvania State University Press.

Carter, Roy E., and Orlando Sepúlveda. 1964. "Some Patterns of Mass Media Use in Santiago de Chile." *Journalism Quarterly* 41: 216–224.

Catalán, Carlos. 1988. "Mass Media and the Collapse of a Democratic Tradition in Chile." In Fox, *Media and Politics in Latin America*, 45–55.

Carroll, William K., and R. S. Ratner. 1999. "Media Strategies and Political Projects: A Comparative Study of Social Movements." *Canadian Journal of Sociology* 24, no. 1: 1–34.

Cavadino, Michael, and James Dignan. 2006. "Penal Policy and Political Economy." *Criminology and Criminal Justice* 6, no. 4: 435–456.

Centro de Estudios Legales y Sociales (CELS). 2015. *Derechos humanos en Argentina: Informe 2015.* Buenos Aires: Siglo XXI.

Centro de Estudios Públicos (CEP). 2015. "Encuesta CEP y confianza en Carabineros." PowerPoint prepared for author by Ricardo González T., coordinator, Public Opinion Area.

Centro de Estudios Públicos (CEP). 2017. *Estudio Nacional de Opinión Pública no.79* (April–May). www.cepchile.cl.

Chalmers, Douglas A. 1977. "The Politicized State in Latin America." In *Authoritarianism and Corporatism in Latin America*, edited by James M. Malloy, 23–46. Pittsburgh: University of Pittsburgh Press.

Chan, Janet. 1996. "Changing Police Culture." *British Journal of Criminology* 36, no. 1: 109–134.

Chermak, Steven, and Alexander Weiss. 2005. "Maintaining Legitimacy Using External Communication Strategies: An Analysis of Police-Media Relations." *Journal of Criminal Justice* 33: 501–512.

Chevigny, Paul. 2003. "The Populism of Fear: Politics of Crime in the Americas." *Punishment and Society* 5, no. 1: 77–96.

Chibnall, Steve. 1977. *Law-and-Order News: An Analysis of Crime Reporting in the British Press.* London: Tavistock.

Citizen Peace (Paz Ciudadana). 2015. Índice *paz ciudadana-GfK Adimark: Resultados del estudio año 2015 versión extensa.* Accessed June 15, 2016. http://www.pazciudadana.cl/wp-content/uploads/2015/12/ipc-2015-version-extensa.pdf.

Clarke, Marlea. 2018. "Supporting the 'Elite' Transition in South Africa: Police Abuse in a Violent Neoliberal Democracy." In Bonner et al., *Police Abuse in Contemporary Democracies*, 195–220.

Collier, Simon, and William F. Sater. 2004. *A History of Chile, 1808–2002.* New York: Cambridge University Press.

Comisión Ética contra la Tortura (CECT). 2012. *La Tortura es el miedo a las ideas de los otros.* Santiago: Quimantú.

Comisión Ética contra la Tortura (CECT). 2013. *En la Senda de la memoria, los derechos y la justicia.* Santiago: Quimantú.

Comisión Nacional Sobre la Desaparición de Personas (CONADEP). 1984. *Nunca* Más. Buenos Aires: Editorial Universitaria de Buenos Aires.

Comisión Provincial por la Memoria (CPM). 2013. *Informe anual 2013: 10 años.* Buenos Aires: CPM.

Comisión Provincial por la Memoria (CPM). 2015. *Informe anual 2015: El sistema de la crueldad IX, sobre el sistema de encierro y las politícas de seguridad en la provincia de Buenos Aires.* Buenos Aires: CPM.

Connolly, William E. 1995. *The Ethos of Pluralization.* Minneapolis: University of Minneapolis Press.

Cook, Timothy E. 2005. *Governing with the News: The Media as a Political Institution.* Chicago: University of Chicago Press.

Coordinadora Contra la Represión Policial e Institucional (CORREPI). 2015. "Antirepresivo 2015: Los gobiernos pasan la represión queda." Accessed April 18, 2016. correpi.lahaine.org.

Cordero, Rodrigo. 2009a. "Dígalo con números: la industria de la opinión pública en Chile." In Cordero, *La Sociedad de la opinión*, 69–92.

Cordero, Rodrigo, ed. 2009b. *La Sociedad de la opinión: Reflexiones sobre encuestas y cambio político en democracia.* Santiago: Ediciones Universidad Diego Portales.

Crofts Wiley, Stephen B. 2006. "Assembled Agency: Media and Hegemony in the Chilean Transition to Civilian Rule." *Media, Culture and Society* 28, no. 5: 671–693.

Curran, James. 1991. "Rethinking the Media as a Public Sphere." In *Communication and Citizenship: Journalism and the Public Sphere in the New Media Age*, edited by Peter Dahlgren and Colin Sparks, 27–57. New York: Routledge.

Curran, James. 2002. *Media and Power*. New York: Routledge.

Curran, James. 2005. "What Democracy Requires of the Media." In *The Press*, edited by Geneva Overholser and Kathleen Hall Jamieson, 120–140. New York: Oxford University Press.

Cushion, Stephen, and Justin Lewis. 2010a. "Introduction: What Is 24-Hour News Television." In Cushion and Lewis, *Rise of 24-Hour News Television*, 1–11.

Cushion, Stephen, and Justin Lewis, eds. 2010b. *The Rise of 24-Hour News Television: Global Perspectives*. New York: Peter Lang.

Dammert, Lucía. 2009. "¿Falsa alarma? Temor, crimen y opinión pública en Chile." In *La Sociedad cambio politico en democracia*, edited by Rodrigo Cordero, 225–250. Santiago: Ediciones Universidad Diego Portales.

Dammert, Lucía. 2012. *Fear of Crime in Latin America: Redefining State-Society Relations*. New York: Routledge.

Dammert, Lucía, and Mary Fran T. Malone. 2006. "Does It Take a Village? Policing Strategies and Fear of Crime in Latin America." *Latin American Politics and Society* 48, no. 4: 27–51.

Darley, John M. 2005. "On the Unlikely Prospects of Reducing Crime Rates by Increasing the Severity of Prison Sentences." *Journal of Law and Policy* 13, no. 1: 189–208.

Dastres, Cecilia, Cristian Spencer, Eva Muzzopappa, and Chiara Sáez. 2005. *La construcción de noticias sobre seguridad ciudadana en prensa escrita y television. ¿Posicionamiento, distorsión o comprensión?* Santiago: Centro de Estudios en Seguridad Ciudadana.

Daudelin, Jean. 2017. "*Not* Killer Methods: How to Study Latin American Violence." In *Violence in Latin America and the Caribbean: Subnational Structures, Institutions, and Clientelistic Networks*, edited by Tina Hilgers and Laura MacDonald, 39–56. New York: Cambridge University Press.

Davies, Matt. 1999. *International Political Economy and Mass Communication in Chile*. New York: St. Martin's Press.

Davis, Diane. 1999 "The Power of Distance: Re-theorizing Social Movements in Latin America." *Theory and Society* 28: 585–638.

Davis, Diane E., and Óscar Lunes Reyes. 2007. "El factor Guiliani: delincuenda, el 'cero tolerancia' en el trabajo policiaco y la transformación de la esfera pública en el centro de la ciudad de México." *Estudios Sociológicos* 25, no. 75: 639–681.

Deacon, David. 2003. "Non-governmental Organizations and the Media." In *News, Public Relations and Power*, edited by Simon Cottle, 99–115. London: Sage.

Della Porta, Donatella. 1998. "Police Knowledge and Protest Policing: Some Reflections on the Italian Case." In Della Porta and Reiter, *Policing Protest*, 228–52.

Della Porta, Donatella, and Herbert Reiter. 1998a. "Introduction: The Policing of Protests in Western Democracies." In Della Porta and Reiter, *Policing Protest*, 1–32.

Della Porta, Donatella, and Herbert Reiter, eds. 1998b. *Policing Protest: The Control of Mass Demonstrations in Western Democracies*. Minneapolis: University of Minnesota Press.

Diamond, Larry. 1999. *Developing Democracy: Toward Consolidation*. Baltimore: Johns Hopkins University Press.

Diego Portales University, Center for Human Rights. 2015. *Informe anual sobre derechos humanos en Chile 2015*. Santiago: Ediciones Univeridad Diego Portales.

Di Lodovico, Cecilia, María Helena Ripetta, Sol Amaya, Claudio Marazzita, Federico Fahsbender, and Javier Sinay. 2014. *Angeles: Mujeres jóvenes víctimas de la violencia*. Buenos Aires: Ediciones del Empedrado.

Doob, Anthony N., and Cheryl M. Webster. 2003. "Sentence Severity and Crime: Accepting the Null Hypothesis." In *Crime and Justice: A Review of Research*, edited by Michael Tonry, 143–195. Chicago: University of Chicago Press.

Domedel, Andrea, and Macarena Peña y Lillo. 2008. *El mayo de los pingüinos.* Santiago: Ediciones Radio Universidad de Chile.

Doyle, Aaron. 2003. *Arresting Images: Crime and Policing in Front of the Television Camera.* Toronto: University of Toronto Press.

Duran, Claudio. 1976. "PsychoWar of the Media in Chile under Allende." *Canadian Journal of Communication* 2, no. 3: 7–12.

Dutil, Carlos, and Ricardo Ragendorfer. 1997. *La bonaerense: historia criminal de la policía de la provincia de Buenos Aires.* Buenos Aires: Planeta.

Dzur, Albert W. 2010. "The Myth of Penal Populism: Democracy, Citizen Participation, and American Hyperincarceration." *Journal of Speculative Philosophy* 24, no. 4: 354–379.

Eaton, Kent. 2008. "Paradoxes of Police Reform: Federalism, Parties and Civil Society in Argentina's Public Security Crisis." *Latin American Research Review* 43, no. 3: 5–32.

Edelman, Murray. 1977. *Political Language: Words That Succeed and Policies That Fail.* New York: Academic Press.

Ellison, Graham. 2000. ""Reflecting All Shades of Opinion": Public Attitudinal Surveys and the Construction of Police Legitimacy." *British Journal of Criminology* 40, no. 1: 88–111.

Ellul, Jacques. 1965. *Propaganda: The Formation of Men's Attitudes.* New York: Knopf.

Encuesta nacional urbana de seguridad ciudadana (ENUSC). 2014. *Encuesta nacional urbana de seguridad ciudadana 2014: Resultados país.* Ministerio del Interior y Seguridad Pública, Government of Chile. Accessed June 15, 2016. http://www.seguridadpublica.gov.cl.

Encuesta nacional urbana de seguridad ciudadana (ENUSC). 2015. *Encuesta nacional urbana de seguridad ciudadana 2015: Resultados país.* Ministerio del Interior y Seguridad Pública, Government of Chile. Accessed June 15, 2016. http://www.seguridadpublica.gov.cl.

Entman, Robert M. 1989. *Democracy without Citizens: Media and the Decay of American Politics.* New York: Oxford University Press.

Entman, Robert, Steven Livingston, Sean Aday, and Jennie Kim. 2010. "Condemned to Repeat: The Media and the Accountability Gap in the Iraq War Media Policy." In *Public Policy and Mass Media: The Interplay of Mass Communication and Political Decision Making*, edited by K. Voltmer and S. Koch-Baumgarten, 194–213. London: Routledge.

Ericson, Richard V. 1989. "Patrolling the Facts: Secrecy and Publicity in Police Work." *British Journal of Sociology* 40, no. 2: 205–226.

Ericson, Richard V. 1991. "Mass Media, Crime, Law, and Justice: An Institutional Approach." *British Journal of Criminology* 31, no. 3: 219–249.

Fagen, Patricia. 1974. "Media in Allende's Chile." *Journal of Communication* 24, no. 1: 59–70.

Fajnzylber, Pablo, Daniel Lederman, and Norman Loayza. 1998. *Determinants of Crime Rates in Latin America and the World: An Empirical Assessment.* Washington, DC: World Bank.

Fajnzylber, Pablo, Daniel Lederman, and Norman Loayza. 2002. "What Causes Violent Crime?" *European Economic Review* 46, no. 7: 1323–1357.

Fenton, Natalie. 2010. "NGOs, New Media and the Mainstream News: 'News from Everywhere.'" In *New Media, Old News: Journalism and Democracy in the Digital Age*, edited by Natalie Fenton, 153–168. London: Sage.

Fenwick, Mark. 2013. "'Penal Populism' and Penological Change in Contemporary Japan." *Theoretical Criminology* 17, no. 2: 215–231.

Fernandez, Luis A. 2008. *Policing Dissent: Social Control and the Anti-Globalization Movement.* New Brunswick, NJ: Rutgers University Press.

Fernández Roich, Cynthia. 2017. *Media and Crime in Argentina: Punitive Discourse during the 1990s.* New York: Palgrave Macmillan.

Fishkin, James S. 1995. *The Voice of the People: Public Opinion and Democracy.* New Haven, CT: Yale University Press.

Foucault, Michel. 1991. "Governmentality." In *The Foucault Effect: Studies in Governmentality*, edited by Graham Burchell, Colin Gordon, and Peter Miller, 87–104. Chicago: University of Chicago Press.

Fox, Elizabeth. 1988. *Media and Politics in Latin America: The Struggle for Democracy.* London: Sage.

Fox, Elizabeth. 1988a. "Media Policies in Latin America: An Overview." In Fox, *Media and Politics in Latin America*, 6–35.

Fox, Elizabeth. 1988b. "Nationalism, Censorship and Transnational Control." In Fox, *Media and Politics in Latin America*, 36–44.

Fox, Elizabeth. 1997. *Latin American Broadcasting: From Tango to Telenovela.* Luton, Bedfordshire: John Libbey Media: University of Luton Press.

Fox, Elizabeth, and Silvio Waisbord. 2002. "Latin Politics, Global Media." In *Latin Politics, Global Media*, edited by Elizabeth Fox and Silvio Waisbord, 1–21. Austin: University of Texas Press.

Frühling, Hugo. 2007. "Police Legitimacy in Chile." In *Legitimacy and Criminal Justice: International Perspectives*, edited by Tom R. Tyler, 115–145. New York: Russell Sage Foundation.

Fuentes, Claudio A. 2005. *Contesting the Iron Fist: Advocacy Networks and Police Violence in Democratic Argentina and Chile.* New York: Routledge.

Gamson, William A., and David Stuart. 1992. "Media Discourse as a Symbolic Contest: The Bomb in Political Cartoons." *Sociological Forum* 7, no. 1: 55–86.

Gamson, William A., and Gadi Wolfsfeld. 1993. "Movements and Media as Interacting Systems." *Annals of the American Academy of Political and Social Sciences* 528: 114–125.

Gans, Herbert J. 2003. *Democracy and the News.* Oxford: Oxford University Press.

Garland, David. 2001. *The Culture of Control: Crime and Social Order in Contemporary Society.* Chicago: University of Chicago Press.

Garretón, Manuel Antonio. 1989. *The Chilean Political Process.* Boston: Unwin Hyman.

Geary, Roger. 1985. *Policing Industrial Disputes: 1893–1985.* Cambridge: Cambridge University Press.

Goffman, Erving. 1974. *Frame Analysis: An Essay on the Organization of Experience.* Cambridge, MA: Harvard University Press.

Goldstein, Daniel M. 2012. *Outlawed: Between Security and Rights in a Bolivian City.* Durham, NC: Duke University Press.

González, Yanilda. n.d. "The Blind Spot of Democracy: How Democratic Processes Perpetuate Authoritarian Police." Manuscript in preparation.

Green, David A. 2008. *When Children Kill Children: Penal Populism and Political Culture.* Oxford: Oxford University Press.

Guerrero, Manuel Alejandro. 2013. *La Federal: La trama policial detrás del delito,la inseguridad y el miedo.* Buenos Aires: Sudamericana.

Guerrero, Manuel Alejandro. 2014. "The 'Captured Liberal' Model of Media Systems in Latin America." In Guerrero and Márquez-Ramírez, *Media Systems and Communication Policies*, 43–65.

Guerrero, Manuel Alejandro, and Mireya Márquez-Ramírez, eds. 2014. *Media Systems and Communication Policies in Latin America.* New York: Palgrave Macmillan.

Hall, Stuart. 1980. *Drifting into a Law and Order Society.* London: Cobden Trust.

Hall, Stuart, Chas Critcher, Tony Jefferson, John Clarke, and Brian Roberts. 1978. *Policing the Crisis: Mugging, the State, and Law and Order.* London: MacMillan.

Hallin, Daniel C., and Paolo Mancini. 2004. *Comparing Media Systems: Three Models of Media and Politics.* New York: Cambridge University Press.

Hallin, Daniel C., and Stylianos Papathanassopoulos. 2002. "Political Clientelism and the Media: Southern Europe and Latin America in Comparative Perspective." *Media, Culture and Society* 24: 175–195.

Harvey, David. 2005. *A Brief History of Neoliberalism.* Oxford: Oxford University Press.

Hinton, Mercedes. 2006. *The State on the Streets: Police and Politics in Argentina and Brazil.* Boulder, CO: Lynne Rienner.

Hinton, Nicole, Daniel Montalvo, Arturo Maldonado, Mason Moseley, and Daniel Zizumbo-Colunga. 2014. "Crime and Violence across the Americas." In Zechmeister, *Political Culture of Democracy*, 3–28.

Holland, Alisha C. 2013. "Right on Crime? Conservative Party Politics and *Mano Dura* Policies in El Salvador." *Latin American Research Review* 48, no. 1: 44–67.

Holmes, Stephen. 2003. "Lineages of the Rule of Law." In *Democracy and the Rule of Law*, edited by José María Maravall and Adam Przeworkski, 19–61. New York: Cambridge University Press.

Hood, Christopher. 1995. "The 'New Public Management' in the 1980s: Variations on a Theme." *Accounting, Organizations and Society* 20 (2/3): 93–109.

Hughes, Sallie. 2003. "From Inside Out: How Institutional Entrepreneurs Transformed Mexican Journalism." *International Journal of Press/Politics* 8, no. 3: 87–117.

Hughes, Sallie. 2006. *Newsrooms in Conflict: Journalism and the Democratization of Mexico.* Pittsburgh: University of Pittsburgh Press.

Human Rights Watch (HRW). 1998. *The Limits of Tolerance: Freedom of Expression and the Public Debate in Chile.* New York.

Human Rights Watch (HRW). 2001. "Progress Stalled: Setbacks in Freedom of Expression Reform." *Report* 13 (1/b): 1–48.

Human Rights Watch (HRW). 2013. *World Report 2013: Chile, Events of 2012.* Accessed June 15, 2016. https://www.hrw.org/world-report/2013/country-chapters/chile.

Instituto Nacional de Derechos Humans (INDH). 2012. *Informe anual 2012: Situación de los derechos humanos en Chile.* Santiago.

Instituto Nacional de Derechos Humans (INDH). 2015a. *Informe anual 2014: Situación de los derechos humanos en Chile.* Accessed April 22, 2016. www.indh.cl.

Instituto Nacional de Derechos Humans (INDH). 2015b. *Informe anual 2014: Programa de derechos humanos, función policial y orden público.* Accessed April 22, 2016. www.indh.cl.

Instituto Nacional de Derechos Humans (INDH). 2015c. *Estudio de caso: Violencias y derechos humanos en la Legua.* Accessed April 22, 2016. www.indh.cl.

Inter-American Commission on Human Rights. 2011. "IACHR Expresses Concern for Violence Against Student Protests in Chile." August 6. Accessed June 15, 2016. http://www.oas.org/en/iachr/media_center/PReleases/2011/087.asp.

InterPeace. 2011. *Medios de comunicación, seguridad democrática y prevención de la violencia.* June. 1 Foro Regional Ciudad de Guatemala.

Iturralde, Manuel. 2016. "Colombian Prisons as a Core Institution of Authoritarian Liberalism." *Crime, Law, and Social Change* 65, no. 3: 137–162.

Iyengar, Shanto. 1996. "Framing Responsibility for Political Issues." *Annals of the American Academy of Political and Social Science* 546: 59–70.

Jacobs, Lawrence R., and Robert Y. Shapiro. 2000. "Issue Framing and Public Opinion on Government Spending." *American Journal of Political Science* 44: 750–767.

Jowett, Garth S., and Victoria O'Donnell. 2012. *Propaganda and Persuasion.* 5th ed. Thousand Oaks, CA: Sage.

Kelling, George L., and James Q. Wilson. 1982. "Broken Windows: The Police and Neighborhood Safety." *Atlantic Monthly* 249, no. 3 (March): 29–38.

Kingdon, John W. 2003. *Agendas, Alternatives, and Public Policies.* 2nd ed. New York: Longman.

Knudson, J. W. 1981. "The Chilean Press since Allende." *Gazette* 27: 5–20.

Konkes, Claire, and Libby Lester. 2016. "Justice, Politics and the Social Usefulness of News." *Crime, Media, Culture* 12, no. 1: 17–35.

Koopmans, Ruud. 2004. "Movements and Media: Selection Processes and Evolutionary Dynamics in the Public Sphere." *Theory and Society* 33 (3/4): 367–391.

Kratochwill, Friedrich. 2008. "Constructivism: What It Is (Not) and How It Matters." In *Approaches and Methodologies in Social Sciences: A Pluralist Perspective*, edited by Donatella Della Porta and Michael Keating, 80–98. Cambridge: Cambridge University Press.

Krohne, Walter. 2005. *Las dos caras de la libertad de expression en Chile.* Santiago: Universidad Academia de Humanismo Cristiano.

Kubal, Mary Rose. 2012. "Transnational Policy Networks and Public Security Policy in Argentina and Chile." In *Comparative Public Policy in Latin America*, edited by Jordi Díez and Susan Franceschet, 176–202. Toronto: University of Toronto.

Lacey, Nicola. 2008. *The Prisoners' Dilemma: Political Economy and Punishment in Contemporary Democracies.* Cambridge: Cambridge University Press.

Lacey, Nicola. 2010. "American Imprisonment in Comparative Perspective." *Daedalus* 139, no. 3: 102–114.

Laclau, Ernesto, 2007. *On Populist Reason.* London: Verso.

Lagos Lira, Claudia, Claudio Salinas Muñoz, and Hans Stange Marcus. 2009. "El diario de Agustín: El involucramiento de El Mercurio durante la dictadura militar Chilena (1973–1990): un estudio de casos." In *Tiempos de cambio: Polítca y comunicación en América Latina*, edited by Andrés Cañizález, 171–186. Caracas: Universidad Católica Andrés Bello.

Lakoff, George. 2002. *Moral Politics: How Liberals and Conservatives Think.* Chicago: University of Chicago Press.

Lappi-Seppälä, Tapio. 2007. "Penal Policy in Scandinavia." *Crime and Justice* 36, no. 1: 217–295.

Lasswell, Harold D. 1927. *Propaganda Technique in the World War.* New York: Knopf.

Layton, Matthew, and Mariana Rodríguez. 2014. "Citizen Security, Evaluations of the State, and Policy Preferences." In Zechmesiter, *Political Culture of Democracy*, 73–116.

Lazarfeld, Paul L., Bernard Berelson, and Hazel Gaudet. 1948. *The People's Choice: How the Voter Makes Up His Mind in a Presidential Campaign.* New York: Duell, Sloan and Pearce.

Leishman, Frank, and Paul Mason. 2003. *Policing and the Media: Facts, Fictions and Factions.* Portland, OR: Willan.

Léon-Dermota, Ken. 2003. *And Well Tied Down: Chile's Press under Democracy.* Westport, CT: Praeger.

Levitsky Steven, and Lucan Way. 2002. "The Rise of Competitive Authoritarianism." *Journal of Democracy* 13, no. 2: 51–65.

Levitsky, Steven, and Lucan A. Way. 2010. *Competitive Authoritarianism: Hybrid Regimes after the Cold War.* New York: Cambridge University Press.

Levitsky, Steven, and Daniel Ziblatt. 2018. *How Democracies Die.* New York: Crown.

Lewis, Justin. 2010. "Democratic or Disposable? 24-Hour News, Consumer Culture, and Built-in Obsolescence." In Cushion and Lewis, *Rise of 24-Hour News Television*, 81–95.

Leyton, César, and Cristián Palacios. 2014. "Introducción: Industria del Delito." In *Industria del delito: Historias de la ciencias criminológicas en Chile*, edited by Cristián Palacios and César Leyton, 7–9. Santiago: Ocho Libros and Museo Nacional de Odontología. Facultad de Odontología, Universidad de Chile.

Lineberger, Kelly P. 2011. "The United States-El Salvador Extradition Treaty: A Dated Obstacle in the Transitional War against Mara Salvatrucha (MS-13)." *Vanderbilt Journal of Transnational Law* 44: 187–216.

Linz, Juan J., and Alfred Stepan. 1996. *Problems of Democratic Transition and Consolidation: Southern Europe, South America, and Post-Communist Europe.* Baltimore: Johns Hopkins University Press.

Liotti, Jorge. 2014. "The Complex Relationship Between the Media and the Political System in Argentina: From Co-optation to Polarization." In Guerrero and Márquez-Ramírez, *Media Systems and Communication Policies*, 100–121.

Loader, Ian. 2011. "Playing with Fire? Democracy and the Emotions of Crime and Punishment." In *Emotions, Crime and Justice*, edited by Susanne Karstedf, Ian Loader, and Heather Strang, 347–361. Oxford: Hart.

MacNamara, Jim. 2014. *Journalism and PR: Unpacking "Spin," Stereotypes, and Media Myths.* New York: Peter Lang.

Maldonado, Arturo, and Mariana Rodríguez. 2014. "Safety and Security as Influences on Everyday Life." In Zechmeister, *Political Culture of Democracy*, 29–71.

Maldonado Prieto, Carlos. 1990. "Los Carabineros de Chile: Historia de una policía militarizada." *Ibero-Americana, Nordic Journal of Latin American Studies* 20, no. 3: 3–31.

Maravall, José María, and Adam Przeworski. 2003. "Introduction." In *Democracy and the Rule of Law*, edited by José María Maravall and Adam Przeworkski, 1–16. New York: Cambridge University Press.

March, James G., and Johan P. Olsen. 1995. *Democratic Governance.* New York: Free Press.

Marenin, Otwin. 1996. "Policing Change, Changing Police: Some Thematic Questions." In *Policing Change, Changing Police: International Perspectives*, edited by Otwin Marenin, 3–22. New York: Garland.

Marín, Cristóbal, and Rodrigo Cordero. 2009. "Medios masivos, opinión pública y transformaciones de la democracia." In Cordero, *La Sociedad de la opinión*, 251–279.

Mastrini, Guillermo, Martín Becerra, and Santiago Marino. 2014. "State Intervention and Market Structures: The New Overview of the Argentinian Audio-visual Sector." In Guerrero and Márquez-Ramírez, *Media Systems and Communication Policies*, 194–207.

Matravers, Amanda, and Shadd Maruna. 2005. "Contemporary Penality and Psychoanalysis." In *Managing Modernity: Politics and the Culture of Control*, edited by Matt Matravers, 118–144. London: Routledge.

Mauersberger, Christof. 2012. "To Be Prepared When the Time Has Come: Argentina's New Media Regulation and the Social Movement for Democratizing Broadcasting." *Media, Culture and Society* 34, no. 5: 588–605.

Mawby, Rob C. 2002. *Policing Images: Policing, communication and legitimacy.* Portland, OR: Willan.

Mawby, Rob C. 2010. "Chibnall Revisited: Crime Reporters, the Police and 'Law-and-Order News.'" *British Journal of Criminology* 50: 1060–1076.

McCombs, Maxwell E., and Donald L. Shaw. 1972. "The Agenda-Setting Function of Mass Media." *Public Opinion Quarterly* 36, no. 2: 176–187.

McLeod, Douglas M., and James K. Hertog. 1992. "The Manufacture of 'Public Opinion' by Reporters: Informal Cues for Public Perception of Protest Groups." *Discourse and Society* 3, no. 3: 259–275.

McNair, Brian. 2003. *An Introduction to Political Communication.* London: Taylor and Francis.

McSherry, Patrice. 1997. "Strategic Alliance: Menem and the Military Security Forces in Argentina." *Latin American Perspectives* 24, no. 6: 63–92.

Media Reform Coalition. 2014. "Media Ownership Reform: For Action." Accessed October 18, 2017. http://www.mediareform.org.uk/wp-content/uploads/2015/11/Media_Ownership_Reform-A_Case_for_Action.pdf.

Melucci, Alberto. 1985. "The Symbolic Challenge of Contemporary Movements." *Social Research* 52, no. 4: 789–816.

Melucci, Albert. 1998. "Third World or Planetary Conflicts?" In Alvarez, Dagnino, and Escobar, *Cultures of Politics*, 422–429.

Migdal, Joel S. 2001. *State in Society: Studying How States and Societies Transform and Constitute One Another.* Cambridge: Cambridge University Press.

Mill, J. S. 1906. *A System of Logic, Ratiocinative and Inductive: Being a Connected View of the Principles of Evidence and the Methods of Scientific Investigation.* London: Longmans.

Miller, Lisa. 2016. *The Myth of Mob Rule: Violent Crime and Democratic Politics.* New York: Oxford University Press.

Moloney, Kevin. 2006. *Rethinking Public Relations: PR, Propaganda and Democracy.* London: Routledge.

Moncada, Eduardo. 2016. *Cities, Business and the Politics of Urban Violence in Latin America.* Stanford, CA: Stanford University Press.

Moore, Harald F. 2010. "Immigration in Denmark and Norway: Protecting Culture or Protecting Rights?" *Scandinavian Studies* 82, no. 3: 355–364.

Mora y Araujo, Manuel. 2009. "La opinión pública en la Argentina: de la sociología académica a la profesionalización." In Cordero, *La Sociedad de la opinión*, 45–68.

Müller, Markus-Michael. 2010. "Community Policing in Latin America: Lessons From Mexico City." *European Review of Latin American and Caribbean Studies* 88: 21–37.

Müller, Markus-Michael. 2016. *The Punitive City: Privatized Policing and Protection in Neoliberal Mexico.* London: Zed Books.

Müller, Markus-Michael. 2018. "Policing as Pacification: Postcolonial Legacies, Transnational Connections, and the Militarization of Urban Security in Democratic Brazil." In Bonner et al., *Police Abuse in Contemporary Democracies*, 221–247.

Muraro, Heriberto. 1988. "Dictatorship and Transition to Democracy: Argentina 1973–86." In Fox, *Media and Politics in Latin America*, 116–124.

Nevitte, Neil. 1996. *The Decline of Deference: Canadian Value Change in Cross-National Perspective.* Toronto: University of Toronto Press.

Newburn, Tim, and Trevor Jones. 2005. "Symbolic Politics and Penal Populism: The Long Shadow of Willis Horton." *Crime, Media, Culture* 1, no. 1: 72–87.

Observatorio Ciudadano. 2008. "La violencia policial en Chile!" Documento de Trabajo no.7, 1–31.

O'Donnell, Guillermo. 1996. "Illusions about Consolidation." *Journal of Democracy* 7, no. 2: 34–51.

O'Donnell, Guillermo. 1999. "Horizontal Accountability in New Democracies." In *The Self-Restraining State: Power and Accountability in New Democracies*, edited by Andreas Schedler, Larry Diamond, and Marc F. Plattner, 29–51. Boulder, CO: Lynne Reinner.

O'Donnell, Guillermo, and Philippe C. Schmitter. 1986. *Transitions from Authoritarian Rule: Tentative Conclusions about Uncertain Democracies.* Baltimore: Johns Hopkins University Press.

O'Donnell, María. 2007. *Propaganda K: Una maquinaria de promoción con el dinero del estado.* Buenos Aires: Planeta.

Offe, Claus. 1987. "Challenging the Boundaries of Institutional Polities: Social Movements since the 1960s." In *Changing Boundaries of the Political*, edited by C. Maier, 63–106. Cambridge: Cambridge University Press.

Ostry, Jonathan D., Prakash Loungani, and Davide Furceri. 2016. "Neoliberalism: Oversold?" *Finance & Development* (IMF), 38–41.

Oxhorn, Philip D. 1995. *Organizing Civil Society: The Popular Sectors and the Struggle for Democracy in Chile.* University Park: Pennsylvania State University Press.

Oxhorn, Philip. 2011. *Sustaining Civil Society: Economic Change, Democracy, and the Social Construction of Citizenship in Latin America.* University Park: Pennsylvania State University Press.

Palacios, Cristián, and César Leyton, eds. 2014. *Industria del delito: Historias de la ciencias criminológicas en Chile.* Santiago: Ocho Libros and Museo Nacional de Odontología. Facultad de Odontología, Universidad de Chile.

Paley, Julia. 2001. *Marketing Democracy: Power and Social Movements in Post-Dictatorship Chile.* Berkeley: University of California Press.

Page, Benjamin I. 1996. "The Mass Media as Political Actors." *PS: Political Science and* Politics 29, no. 1: 20–24.

Page, Benjamin I., and Robert Y. Shapiro. 1983. "Effects of Public Opinion on Policy." *American Political Science Review* 77: 175–190.

Park, David J. 2002. "Media, Democracy, and Human Rights in Argentina." *Journal of Communication Inquiry* 26, no. 3: 237–260.

Paterson, Chris. 2010. "The Hidden Role of Television News Agencies: 'Going Live' on 24-Hour News Channels." In Cushion and Lewis, *Rise of 24-Hour News Television*, 99–112.

Patterson, Thomas E. 1998. "The Media's Limitations as an Instrument of Democracy." *International Political Science Review*19, no. 1: 55–67.

Peruzzotti, Enrique. 2013. "Populism in Democratic Times: Populism, Representative Democracy, and the Debate on Democratic Deepening." In *Latin American Populism in the Twenty-First Century*, edited by Carlos de la Torre and Cynthia J. Arnson, 61–84. Baltimore: Johns Hopkins University Press.

Peruzzotti, Enrique, and Catalina Smulovitz. 2006. "Social Accountability: An Introduction." In *Enforcing the Rule of Law: Social Accountability in the New Latin American Democracies*, edited by Enrique Peruzzotti and Catalina Smulovitz, 3–33. Pittsburgh: University of Pittsburgh Press.

Phelps, Teresa Godwin. 2004. *Shattered Voices: Language, Violence, and the Work of Truth Commissions.* Philadelphia: University of Pennsylvania Press.

Pinto, Juliet. 2008. "Muzzling the Watchdog: The Case of Disappearing Watchdog Journalism from Argentine Mainstream News." *Journalism* 9, no. 6: 750–774.

Policzer, Pablo. 2009. *The Rise and Fall of Repression in Chile.* Notre Dame, IN: University of Notre Dame.

Polumbaum, Judy. 2002. "Free Society, Repressed Media: The Chilean Paradox." *Current History* 101 (652): 66–71.

Postolski, Glenn, and Santiago Marino. 2005. "Relaciones peligrosas: Los medios y la dictadura entre el control, la censura y los negocios." In *Mucho ruido, pocas leyes: Economía y políticas de comunicación en la Argentina (1920–2004)* , edited by Guillermo Mastrini. 155–184. Buenos Aires: La Crujía.

Pratt, John. 2007. *Penal Populism.* New York: Routledge.

Putnam, Robert D. 2000. *Bowling Alone: The Collapse and Revival of American Community.* New York: Simon and Schuster.

Ramos A., Marcela, and Juan A. Guzmán de Luigi. 2000. *La guerra y la paz ciudadana.* Santiago: LOM.

Reiner, Robert. 2000. *The Politics of the Police.* Oxford: Oxford University Press.

Reiner, Robert. 2012. "What's Left? The Prospects for Social Democratic Criminology." *Crime, Media, Culture* 8, no. 2: 135–150.

Reiner, Robert, Sonia Livingstone, and Jessica Allen. 2001. "Casino Culture: Media and Crime in a Winner-Loser Society." In *Crime, Risk and Justice: The Politics of Crime Control in Liberal Democracies*, edited by Kevin Stenson and Robert R. Sullivan, 175–193. Portland, OR: Willan.

Reyes Matta, Fernando. 1986. "Mass media, polarización y cambio social: Chile durante el gobierno de Allende." In Reyes Matta, Ruiz, and Sunkel, *Investigación sobre la prensa*, 63–89.

Reyes Matta, Fernando, Carlos Ruiz, and Guillermo Sunkel, eds. 1986. *Investigación sobre la prensa en Chile (1974–1984).* Santiago: Estudios ILET.

Roberts, Julian V., Loretta J. Stalans, David Indermaur, and Mike Hough. 2003. *Penal Populism and Public Opinion: Lessons from Five Countries.* New York: Oxford University Press.

Roché, Sebastian. 2007. "Criminal Justice Policy in France: Illusions of Severity." *Crime and Justice* 36, no. 1: 471–550.

Ruckert, Arne, Laura MacDonald, and Kristina A. Proulx. 2016. "Post-Neoliberalism in Latin America: A Conceptual Review." *Third World Quarterly* 28, no. 7: 1583–1602.

Saín, Marcelo. 2008. *El Leviatán Azul: Policía y política en la Argentina.* Buenos Aires: Siglo Veintiuno.

Salazar, Gabriel. 1994. "Construcción de Estado en Chile: la historia reversa de la legitimidad." *Proposiciones* 24: 92–110. Accessed March 17, 2013. www.sitiosur.cl.

Salinas, Raquel. 1986. "La autonomia de la prensa: una illusion." In Reyes Matta, Ruiz, and Sunkel, *Investigación sobre la prensa*, 227–249.

Samet, Robert. 2013. "The Photographer's Body: Populism, Polarization, and the Uses of Victimhood in Venezuela." *American Ethnologist* 40, no. 3: 525–539.

Scheufele, Dietram A., and David Tewksbury. 2007. "Framing, Agenda Setting, and Priming: The Evolution of Three Media Effects Models." *Journal of Communication* 57, no. 1: 9–20.

Schild, Verónica. 1998. "New Subjects of Rights? Women's Movements and the Construction of Citizenship in the 'New Democracies.'" In Alvarez, Dagnino, and Escobar, *Cultures of Politics*, 93–117.

Schmitter, Philippe C., and Terry Lynn Karl. 1991. "What Democracy Is . . . And Is Not." *Journal of Democracy* 2, no. 3: 75–88.

Schneider, Cathy Lisa. 1995. *Shantytown Protest in Pinochet's Chile*. Philadelphia: Temple University Press.

Schneider, Cathy Lisa. 2014. *Police Power and Race Riots: Urban Unrest in Paris and New York*. Philadelphia: University of Pennsylvania Press.

Schumpeter, Joseph. 2003 [1943]. *Capitalism, Socialism and Democracy*. London: Routledge.

Seri, Guillermina. 2012. *Seguridad: Crime, Police Power, and Democracy in Argentina*. New York: Bloomsbury.

Seri, Guillermina, and Mary Rose Kubal. 2018. "How Policy Fields Are Born: The Rise of Democratic Security in Argentina." *Journal of Latin American Studies*. https://doi.org/10.1017/S0022216X18000354.

Seri, Guillermina, and Jinee Lokaneeta. 2018. "Police as State: Governing Citizenship Through Violence." In Bonner et al., *Police Abuse in Contemporary Democracies*, 55–80.

Sikkink, Kathryn. 1991. *Ideas and Institutions: Developmentalism in Brazil and Argentina*. Ithaca, NY: Cornell University Press.

Sinha, Maire. 2015. *Trends in Reporting Criminal Victimization to Police 1999 to 2009*. June 22. Canadian Centre for Justice Statistics. Statistics Canada. http://www.statcan.gc.ca/pub/85-002-x/2015001/article/14198-eng.pdf.

Sirvén, Pablo. 1984. *Perón y los medios de comunicación (1943–1955)*. Buenos Aires: Centro Editor de America Latina.

Sivak, Martín. 2013. *Clarín El gran diario argentino: Una historia*. Buenos Aires: Planeta.

Sommer, Eric. 2014. "How Five American Companies Control What You Think." May 14. *Global Research*. Accessed February 15, 2017. http://www.globalresearch.ca/how-five-american-companies-control-what-you-think/5382407.

Sparks, Richard. 2001. "'Bringin' It All Back Home': Populism, Media Coverage and the Dynamics of Locality and Globality in the Politics of Crime Control." In Stenson and Sullivan, *Crime, Risk and Justice*, 194–213.

Spencer Espinosa, Christian. 2005. "Análisis estadístico descriptivo de las noticias de seguridad en televisión abierta." In Dastres et al., *La construcción de noticias*, 129–178.

Squillacote, Rosa, and Leonard Feldman. 2018. "Police Abuse and Democratic Accountability: Agonistic Surveillance of the Administrative State." In Bonner et al., *Police Abuse in Contemporary Democracies*, 135–164.

Stanley, Ruth. 2010. "'Living in a Jungle': State Violence and Perceptions of Democracy in Buenos Aires." In Arias and Goldstein, *Violent Democracies*, 133–160.

Stenson, Kevin. 2001. "The New Politics of Crime Control." In Stenson and Sullivan, *Crime, Risk and Justice*, 15–28.

Stenson, Kevin, and Robert R. Sullivan, eds. 2001. *Crime, Risk and Justice: The Politics of Crime Control in Liberal Democracies*. Portland, OR: Willan.

Stern, Steven J. 2010. *Reckoning with Pinochet: The Memory Question in Democratic Chile, 1989–2006*. Durham, NC: Duke University Press.

Sunkel, Guillermo. 1986. "El Mercurio como medio de educación politico-ideologica (1969–1979)." In Reyes Matta, Ruiz, and Sunkel, *Investigación sobre la prensa*, 99–111.

Surette, Ray, and Alfred Richard. 1995. "Public Information Officers: A Descriptive Study of Crime News Gatekeepers." *Journal of Criminal Justice* 23, no. 4: 325–336.

Syvertsen, Trine. 1997. "Paradise Lost: The Privatization of Scandinavian Broadcasting." *Journal of Communication* 47, no. 1: 120–127.

Tankebe, Justice. 2010. "Public Confidence in the Police: Testing the Effects of Public Experiences of Police Corruption in Ghana." *British Journal of Criminology* 50: 296–319.

Tarrow, Sidney. 1994. *Power in Movement: Social Movements and Contentious Politics*. 1st ed. Cambridge: Cambridge University Press.

Tarrow, Sidney. 1998. *Power in Movement: Social Movements and Contentious Politics*. 2nd ed. Cambridge: Cambridge University Press.

Teichman, Judith. 2001. *The Politics of Freeing Markets in Latin America: Chile, Argentina, and Mexico*. Chapel Hill: University of North Carolina Press.

Terhorst, Philipp, Marcela Olivera, and Alexander Dwinell. 2013. "Social Movements, Left Governments, and the Limits of Water Sector Reform in Latin America's Left Turn." *Latin American Perspectives* 40, no. 4: 55–69.

Thrift , Nigel. 2004. "Intensities of Feeling Towards a Spatial Politics of Affect." *Geografiska Annaler. Series B. Human Geography* 86, no. 1: 57–78.

Tironi, E., and Sunkel, G. 2000. "The Modernization of Communications: The Media in the Transition to Democracy in Chile." In *Democracy and the Media: A Comparative Perspective*, edited by Anthony Mughan and Richard Gunther, 165–194. Cambridge: Cambridge University Press.

Tonry, Michael. 2007. "Determinants of Penal Policies." *Crime and Justice* 36, no. 1: 1–48.

Tyler, Tom R., ed. 2007. *Legitimacy and Criminal Justice: International Perspectives*. New York: Russell Sage Foundation.

Ungar, Mark. 2011. *Policing Democracy: Overcoming Obstacles to Citizen Security in Latin America*. Baltimore: Johns Hopkins University Press.

United Nations Development Programme (UNDP). 2013a. *Citizen Security with a Human Face: Evidence and Proposal for Latin America*. (Summary, Regional Human Development Report 2013–2014). New York. http://hdr.undp.org/en/content/citizen-security-human-face.

United Nations Development Programme (UNDP). 2013b. *Seguridad ciudadana con rostro humano: Diagnóstico y propuestas para América Latina*. (Regional Human Development Report 2013–2014). New York.

United Nations Development Programme (UNDP). 2015. "Human Development Report 2015." Accessed June 8, 2016. http://report.hdr.undp.org/.

United Nations Office on Drugs and Crime (UNODC). 2013. *Global Study on Homicide: Trends, Contexts, and Data*. Vienna.

Valdéa, Juan Gabriel. 1995. *Pinochet's Economists: The Chicago School in Chile.* Cambridge: Cambridge University Press.

Valech Report. 2004. *Informe de la comisión nacional sobre prisión política y tortura.* Santiago: La Nación, SA.

Vallespir, Alejandra. 2002. *La Policía que supimos conseguir.* Buenos Aires: Planeta.

Valverde, Mariana. 2006. *Law and Order: Images, Meanings, Myths.* New Brunswick, NJ: Rutgers University Press.

Wacquant, Loïc. 2004. "Penal Truth Comes to Europe: Think Tanks and the 'Washington Consensus' on Crime and Punishment." In *Crime, Truth and Justice: Official Inquiry, Discourse, Knowledge,* edited by George Gillian and John Pratt, 161–180. New York: Routledge.

Wacquant, Loïc. 2009. *Punishing the Poor: The Neoliberal Government of Social Security.* Durham, NC: Duke University Press.

Waddington, Peter A. J. 1998. "Controlling Protest in Contemporary, Historical and Comparative Perspective." In Della Porta and Reiter, *Policing Protest,* 17–140.

Waisbord, Silvio. 1998. "The Unfinished Project of Media Democratization in Argentina." In *Communicating Democracy: The Media and Political Transitions,* edited by Patrick H. O'Neil, 41–62. Boulder: Lynne Rienner.

Waisbord, Silvio. 2000. *Watchdog Journalism in South America: News, Accountability, and Democracy.* New York: Columbia University Press.

Waisbord, Silvio. 2011. "Can NGOs Change the News?" *International Journal of Communication* 5: 142–165.

Waisbord, Silvio. 2012. "Political Communication in Latin America." In *The Sage Book of Political Communication,* edited by Holli Semetko and Margaret Scamell, 437–450. London: Routledge.

Waisbord, Silvio. 2013. *Vox Populista: Medios, periodismo, democracia.* Buenos Aires: Gedisa.

Waller, Irvin. 2008. *Less Law More Order: The Truth about Reducing Crime.* Ancaster, ON: Manor House.

Walsh, James P. 2015. "Border Theatre and Security Spectacles: Surveillance, Mobility and Reality-based Television." *Crime, Media, Culture* 11, no. 2: 201–221.

Webber, Jeffery. 2010. "Bolivia's Reconstituted Neoliberalism: From Rebellion to Reform." *International Socialist Review* 73 (September–October).

Weyland, Kurt. 2003. "Neopopulism and Neoliberalism in Latin America: How Much Affinity?" *Third World Quarterly* 24, no. 6: 1095–1115.

Whitehead, Neil L. 2004a. "On the Poetics of Violence." In Whitehead, *Violence,* 55–77.

Whitehead, Neil L. 2004b. "Introduction: Cultures, Conflicts, and the Poetics of Violent Practice." In Whitehead, *Violence,* 3–24.

Whitehead, Neil L., ed. 2004c. *Violence.* Santa Fe: School of American Research Press.

Willis, Graham Denyer. 2017. "Before the Body Count: Homicide Statistics and Everyday Security in Latin America." *Journal of Latin American Studies* 49, no. 1: 29–54.

Winseck, Dwayne. 2016. "Media and Internet Concentration in Canada. Report 1984–2015." November 22. *Canadian Media Concentration Research Project.* Accessed February 15, 2017. http://www.cmcrp.org/media-and-internet-concentration-in-canada-report-1984–2015/.

Wisler, Dominique, and Marco Giugni. 1999. "Under the Spotlight: The Impact of Media Attention on Protest Policing." *Mobilization: An International Journal* 4, no. 2: 171–187.

Wolf, Sonja. 2012. "El Salvador's *Pandilleros Calmados:* The Challenges of Contesting Mano Dura through Peer Rehabilitation and Empowerment." *Bulletin of Latin American Research* 31, no. 2: 190–205.

Wolf, Sonja. 2017. *Mano Dura: The Politics of Gang Control in El Salvador.* Austin: University of Texas Press.

Wright, Sarah. 2016. "'Ah . . . the Power of Mothers': Bereaved Mothers as Victim-Heroes in Media Enacted Crusades for Justice." *Crime, Media, Culture* 12, no. 3: 327–343.

Yanow, Dvora, and Peregrine Schwartz-Shea, eds. 2014. *Interpretation and Method: Empirical Research Methods and the Interpretive Turn.* 2nd ed. Armonk, NY: M. E. Sharpe.

Zechmeister, Elizabeth J., ed. *The Political Culture of Democracy in the Americas, 2014: Democratic Governance across 10 Years of the AmericasBarometer.* Report Funded by USAID, LAPOP, AmericasBarometer, and Vanderbilt University. www.LapopSurveys.org.

INDEX